In memory of

Charles F. Cliame

EVERYWHERE WEST
THE BURLINGTON
ROUTE

Old 76 of the C&S leaves Climax, Colorado on August 25, 1943 with the last narrow-gauge train operated by the Burlington lines. The Spark arrester on the stack was a safeguard against forest fires. (Burlington Northern)

EVERYWHERE WEST THE BURLINGTON ROUTE

BY

PATRICK C. DORIN

Superior PUBLISHING COMPANY

708 SIXTH AVE. NORTH, SEATTLE, WASH.

COPYRIGHT 1976 by SUPERIOR PUBLISHING COMPANY
All Rights Reserved
Library of Congress Cataloging in Publication Data

Dorin, Patrick C.
Everywhere West

Includes index.
1. Chicago, Burlington and Quincy Railroad.
2. Railroads—The West—History—Pictorial Works.
I. Title.
HE2791.C643   1976   385′.0973   76-17317
ISBN O-87564-523-2

FIRST EDITION

Printed and Bound in the United States of America

DEDICATION
TO MY WIFE KAREN

Because of her encouragement and enthusiasm
for my work.

TABLE OF CONTENTS

INTRODUCTION

The Burlington Route operated some of the world's most beautiful and fastest trains. The silver Zephyrs were and are known the world over for their speed, comfort and dependability. The CB&Q was known equally well among shippers for its fast freight service. Through its important connections with the Great Northern, Northern Pacific, Rio Grande and Western Pacific, the "Q" operated trains to and from all the west, EVERYWHERE WEST, which became a world famous slogan.

Few railroads operated the variety of trains found on the Burlington. Coal trains took front and center in Southern Illinois. Stock trains rolled eastward from the Colorado ranches. All rail iron ore trains from the Mesabi Range ran to the Chicago and St. Louis area steel mills. Time freights covered the entire system. Some of the most famous mail trains in the USA rolled over the "Q" between Chicago and Omaha. Heavy weight passenger trains, such as the Black Hawk, had a personaility all their own and drew thousands of travelers annually. Last but not least were the Zephyrs, a fleet of streamliners that were unequaled by any other road. Few railroads could compare with the Burlington Route in terms of train services and operating efficiencies. The Road is to be commended for that, and it is the purpose of this book to tell about the train services offered on the BURLINGTON ROUTE.

A number of people have been most helpful to this author during the research and writing of this book. I would like to thank the following people for their time, assistance and encouragement, without which the book simply could not have been completed:

Mr. Albert P. Salisbury and staff of Superior Publishing Company for their encouragement and work with the layout through the final publication of the book.

My wife Karen, who spends a good deal of her time checking the manuscript, photographs and other materials for errors and other problems.

Mr. Luther Miller of RAILWAY AGE for permission to use RAILWAY AGE and RAILWAY AGE GAZETTE from 1890 to 1970 as resource materials.

Mr. Al Rung, Mr. Peter Briggs and Mr. Patrick Stafford of the Burlington Northern for their assistance.

Mr. Jim Scribbins for his photography work and assistance with the manuscript and other research.

The following people contributed a large number of photographs for use in the book: Mr. Bob Lorenz, Mr. Russ Porter, Mr. William S. Kuba, Mr. William Raia, Mr. A. Robert Johnson, Mr. Harold K. Vollrath, Mr. Al Peterson, Mr. Dick George, Mr. Tom Hoff and Mr. John H. Kuehl.

The dust jacket was provided by Russ Porter.

Mr. Sy Dykhouse for his special map work and photography.

To all of you, thank you.

Patrick C. Dorin

North Branch, Minnesota
December 1, 1975

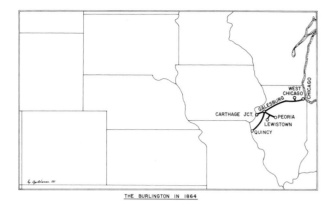

THE BURLINGTON IN 1864

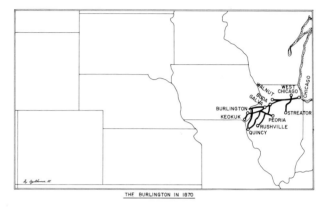

THE BURLINGTON IN 1870

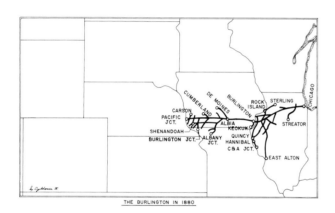

THE BURLINGTON IN 1880

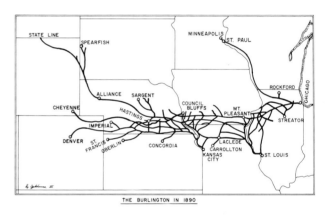

THE BURLINGTON IN 1890

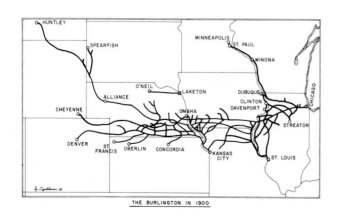

THE BURLINGTON IN 1900

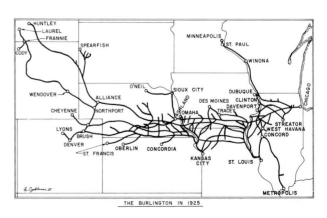

THE BURLINGTON IN 1925

Chapter 1
THE FORMATION OF THE BURLINGTON ROUTE

September 2, 1850 is a date that will long be remembered, for on that day the very first train to roll on what would become the BURLINGTON ROUTE puffed out of Batavia, Illinois at 6:30 AM. It was a most humble beginning for a railroad that eventually would command the respect and admiration of all Americans. However as modest as that first train was, it was powered by an engine that only two years before started the train service on the Galena and Chicago Union, the predecessor of the Chicago & North Western System. That little engine was the "Pioneer" and had been built by Baldwin in 1836. At first she worked on the Utica and Schenectady and later the Michigan Central before becoming Chicago's first railway locomotive in 1848. The "Pioneer" was indeed a historic locomotive before that day in September, 1850 when she was called upon to start the wheels rolling for another of the Nation's great railways.

The new railway, simply named the Aurora Branch Railroad, initially operated a 12 mile section of railroad from Aurora to Turner Junction, and had arranged for trackage rights over the G&CU from that point to Chicago. The new company's relationship with the G&CU was quite close as its leased trackage was three times the size of its own trackage. Indeed the opening day ceremonies required not only the borrowing of the Pioneer but also a coach as the Aurora Branch had not yet taken delivery of its own equipment. It was indeed a most unpretentious beginning.

The Aurora Branch Railroad was the first of 204 companies that would eventually make up a 12,000 mile railroad system in 14 states from Chicago to Colorado, and from the Gulf of Mexico to Montana. This period of expansion took nearly 70 years to complete.

The Aurora Branch Railroad was organized under a special act of the Illinois legislature on February 12, 1849. For 30 years, trackage rights over the Chicago and North Western between Turner Junction (now West Chicago) and Chicago remained in effect. Virtually the entire construction of the Aurora Branch was done on a hand-me-down basis. Second hand strap rail was purchased and used, plus the renting of the "Pioneer," one coach and some freight cars from the G&CU.

The second segment of what would become the CB&Q was the 14 mile Peoria and Oquawka from Peoria west to Edwards Siding, which was completed in 1851.

The third segment began its existence in 1851 when the people of Galesburg secured a charter for a railroad to be called the "Central Military Tract," which was to be built northeasterly to connect with any railroad leading toward Chicago. Eventually all three of these initial component railroads fell into hard financial times. A Boston entrepreneur by the name of John M. Forbes became quite interested in the three lines in the spring of 1852, and the stage was set for the eventual consolidation of the three companies.

In June of 1852 the original charter of the Aurora Branch Railroad was changed to provide for a line southwest to Mendota, Illinois, and the name was changed to the Chicago & Aurora. By December, 1853 the new construction was completed and placed into operation.

Meanwhile the Central Military Tract began construction in 1852 and completed the line between Galesburg and Mendota in 1854. This construction was completed only through the financial assistance of the interested John M. Forbes. The Peoria & Oquawka, with the same financial aid, completed its line all the way to the Mississippi River opposite Burlington, Iowa in March, 1855.

The name of the Chicago & Aurora was changed to the Chicago, Burlington & Quincy, and the Central Military Tract was consolidated into the CB&Q in 1856. The two companies thus became one railroad under the name that was to last until 1970.

The third line, the Peoria & Oquawka, which had built from Peoria to Burlington was eventually reorganized as the "Peoria & Burlington" and consolidated with the CB&Q in 1864.

Although there was virtually no construction during the Civil War, growth was rapid during the period following the war. The "Northern Cross" became the last of the railroads making up the original Burlington consolidations in Illinois. This line had been built from Quincy to Galesburg in 1856 largely with the financial aid of Mr. Forbes and other wealthy friends of New England. It was purchased by the CB&Q in June, 1864, and by the

Ever since the 1930's the words "Burlington Route" have been synonomous with the word "Zephyr." The Zephyr fleet brought much fame to the Burlington, and the reputation spread far and wide to the four corners of the earth. The result was that "BURLINGTON ROUTE" became a household word that meant speed, service, comfort and the only way to travel EVERYWHERE WEST. (Burlington Northern)

end of that year the company operated 460 miles of railroad, all in the state of Illinois.

From 1864 to 1870, the CB&Q expanded from 460 to 810 miles of line and expanded into the State of Iowa. From 1870 to 1880, the growth of the CB&Q was largely in Iowa although there was some growth in Illinois. The Burlington's extension into Iowa began on December 31, 1872 when it purchased the "Burlington & Missouri River, " which extended from Burlington, Iowa to the Missouri River with a branch from Red Oak to Hamburg. At the conclusion of the decade from 1870 to 1880, the CB&Q operated 2,100 miles of railroad in Illinois, Iowa and Missouri.

From 1880 to 1890 the growth was not confined to any one state or area, but virtually all parts of the Mid-west. Important terminals were established in St. Louis, Kansas City and St. Joseph. Denver was reached in 1881. By 1889, the CB&Q had grown until it owned over 5,600 miles of line.

The next decade was not as spectacular as the previous one. However, some very important lines came into being during the last decade of the 19th Century. The Chicago, Burlington & Northern was built in 1885 and 1886 between Oregon, Illinois to the Wisconsin-Illinois state line, and the extension to a connection with the Great Northern and the Northern Pacific was completed by 1889. With this line to St. Paul, Minnesota and other lines, the CB&Q had grown to nearly 6,300 miles by 1899.

The Burlington Route continued to grow after 1900, but significant changes were soon to take place that would set the stage for still greater changes. In 1901 the Great Northern and the Northern Pacific jointly purchased all but 2.8% of the CB&Q's stock. Although the GN and NP controlled the Burlington through stock ownership, the company was left pretty much alone in the management of its train operations and financial affairs. In 1908, for example, the CB&Q purchased the Colorado and Southern and Fort Worth and Denver Railways. This purchase, as well as the construction and purchase of other lines, brought the system mileage of the Burlington Route to 12,000 miles in 14 states by the 1920's. This was to be cut back to 11,000 after World War II. By the end of 1968, the mileage figure had dropped to 10,526 miles including the 708 mile Colorado & Southern and the 1,279 mile Forth Worth & Denver Railway.

The construction of railway lines, however, was not the only way the CB&Q expanded and grew and at the same time improved train service. For example on July 12, 1949 the ICC authorized the Burlington to establish a short cut freight route between Kansas City and St. Louis via Francis and Mexico, Missouri. The new route saved about 65 miles over the former 338 mile route via Cameron Junction, Brookfield and Palmyra, Missouri. The route, placed in operation on September 26, 1949,

The triple track speedway between Chicago and Aurora shows its stuff when there are two trains going in the same direction at the same time. This happens with as great frequency now on the Burlington Northern as it did during the Burlington Route days. The freight on the right is passing a multiple unit powered commuter train, which is ferrying power to Aurora for the Monday morning rush hour service to Chicago. (William A. Raia)

involved a rental of about 159 miles of trackage rights over the former Gulf, Mobile & Ohio Railroad, now the Illinois Central Gulf.

One of the more publicized line changes in recent decades was the Kansas City short cut. The CB&Q had originally pioneered rail service between Chicago and Kansas City, but new routes much shorter (450 miles as compared to the Q's 478 miles for freight and 490 miles for passengers) were taking business away from the Burlington. The Company had but two alternatives, either give up the business or rebuild the entire railroad with a new short cut route. In late 1949 the new route was selected and construction began. The 28 mile Carrollton branch was rebuilt. A completely new 42.5 mile segment of railroad was constructed from Cotter on the Carrollton branch to Maxwell. From Maxwell the CB&Q operated over the former Wabash Railroad tracks for 16 miles to Birmingham. Trains would then be on CB&Q rails for the final 12 miles into Kansas City. The new short cut was opened on October 28, 1952 with three speed limits: 79 miles per hour for passenger trains, 60 miles per hour for the three time freights in each direction and 50 miles per hour for all other freights. The result was the CB&Q

was able to slice 6 hours off the freight train schedules between Chicago and Kansas City, and introduced two new Vista Dome Zephyrs in each direction daily.

The Burlington Route can only be classed as one of the better railroads in North America. One measure of efficiency is the operating ratio. Between 1936 and 1969, the ratio varied from a low of 56.69 during the war year of 1943 to a high of 81.40 in 1967. Most of the time from 1936 through 1969, the ratio varied from 70 to 75 per cent. However as time goes on, the CB&Q will not be remembered for her operating ratio or other financial or traffic data. Instead she will be remembered for the Zephyrs and other world famous passenger trains, high speed freight trains and superb trackage on the main lines to Denver and the Twin Cities. She will also be remembered for the triple track speedway between Chicago and Aurora, Illinois, and for double deck stainless steel commuter trains, superb steam power, silver passenger diesels and vista domes, slumbercoaches and last but not least, the red and grey freight diesels. All of these things added up to the BURLINGTON ROUTE, and the rest of this book is devoted to the train service offered by that Railroad Company.

This style of inspection train has now totally disappeared from the American Railroad scene. The unusual coach-like compartment on the nose of the engine provided a front row seat for inspection purposes. The photo was taken at Galesburg, Illinois, in October, 1930. The locomotive was built in 1892. (Harold K. Vollrath Collection)

The only Columbia type ever built, at least in the United States, was owned and operated by the Burlington. It was built by Baldwin in 1895. The 2-4-2 included 84½ inch driving wheels, high lead truck and a six wheel tender. One of the objectives was to achieve a wide and deep firebox without resorting to a double cab or camel back arrangement. No. 590 looked like a compound but was actually a simple type. It was equipped with piston valves which were located between the two cylinders. (Harold K. Vollrath Collection)

A more modern style inspection car did not need a locomotive for part of its superstructure. These rail detector cars were operated to find hidden flaws in the rails, before they caused trouble. (William A. Raia)

The very last Burlington color scheme reflected the pending Burlington-Northern Pacific-Great Northern merger. A green and black scheme with white striping was tested on new CB&Q SD-45's, but was never adopted. This new power is shown at Electro-Motive Division's LaGrange plant on January 20, 1969. (Burlington Northern)

Chapter 2
THE STANDARD ERA
OF
PASSENGER SERVICE

Passenger service began almost immediatelly when the Aurora Branch opened in September, 1850 and service continued until the Burlington Northern merger date in March, 1970, and it continues now on certain portions of the former CB&Q with Amtrak. The "Q", however, can claim one of the finest train service records of any railroad in the entire world. Considering the population of the granger states that she served, the CB&Q operated one of the heaviest, if not the heaviest, passenger service based on a per capita population count. Her passenger train density rivaled that of the Pennsylvania and New York Central on lines out of Chicago. Yet the CB&Q did not serve the dense industrialized population centers of the type served by the PRR and NYC.

A complete history of Burlington Route passenger service would fill several volumes. The good reputation of such service was a household word even prior to the Zephyrs. The company was continuously working to up-grade the service, and this was obvious to its patrons. This chapter will concentrate primarily on the service and service improvement techniques undertaken by the CB&Q from the 1920's through to the second world war. It was during this era that the CB&Q made some of its most significant contributions to the traveling public, and to the railroad industry in general.

One of the biggest problems facing passenger service and the railroad industry in general was that of locomotive utilization during the days of steam. The Burlington began to work on this problem as early as 1911. The solution was longer engine runs, but the equipment in 1911 just was not quite ready for such operations. It took 12 more years, May, 1923 to be exact, before the CB&Q was able to assign locomotives to run through between Denver and Lincoln, Nebraska. In this case, a locomotive was able to run through or past three intermediate terminals on the 485 mile run. This became one of the longer coal-burning locomotive runs by 1925.

From 1923 to 1925 the CB&Q experimented quite extensively with the longer runs in passenger service. Part of the success of the longer runs was due to the substitution of Hulson grates for the common finger grates formerly used. With bituminous mine run coals, the CB&Q was only able to get about 200 miles or so for a run of a steam locomotive. The

problem was the excessive quantities of clinkers and ash that were accumulated during the run. The Hulson grates, on the other hand, could handle the clinkers and ash and good fires could be kept well beyond the mileage limit previously imposed on the motive power.

Results of the extension of the runs over two or more divisions had practically no bearing on the cost of repairs per mile, and real economies were secured with the more intensive use of power, savings with the elimination of intermediate engine-house expense and fuel economy. Moreover, the release of certain engines permitted the reassignment of motive power to runs where it could give more efficient performance. For example, a number of engines designed for freight service were used on passenger trains until the inauguration of the long runs enabled them to be released. According to the April 18, 1925 issue of Railway Age, the CB&Q was able to release 30 engines for other service and saved over $113,000 annually.

This type of operation was spread out over the entire system. For example, in 1925, there were six trains (Numbers 47, 48, 49, 50, 51 and 52) between Chicago and St. Paul running a total of 2,586 miles a day. Prior to the new operation these six trains utilized nine locomotives per day. With the new method, only seven locomotives were required for the six trains. The average miles per day for each locomotive increased from 276 to 369 or 93 miles.

The following tables on pages 15, 16 and 17 indicate how the long engine runs were operated on the CB&Q, both lines east and lines west.

The more efficient use of motive power enabled the CB&Q to bring about improvements in the time schedules of passenger trains. For example, by 1928 the fastest train between Chicago and St. Paul was the North Coast Limited operating on a 10 hour, 30 minute schedule as opposed to a former 11 hour, 50 minute schedule.

Improvements in motive power are only part of the answer in providing passenger service. The CB&Q did not neglect the passenger equipment as it made strides in improving the performance of its steam power. In 1928 the road placed in service five modern lounge cars with an enclosed observation sun parlor. It is also notable that the CB&Q's first

TABLE I—LONG ENGINE RUNS ON THE C. B. & Q. (LINES EAST)

Train Nos.	Present assignment				Former Assignment			
	Present terminal		Class of loco.	No. of miles	Former Terminal		Class of loco.	No. of miles
	Initial	Final			Initial	Final		
	(Chicago-Savanna-St. Paul.)							
49-51	Chicago	St. Paul	S-1-A	431	Chicago	Savanna	S-1-A	145
					Savanna	St. Paul	S-2-A	286
50-52	St. Paul	Chicago	S-2-A	431	St. Paul	Savanna	S-2-A	286
					Savanna	Chicago	S-1-A	145
47	Chicago	Minneapolis	S-1-A	442	Chicago	Savanna	S-1-A	145
					Savanna	Minneapolis	S-1-A	297
48	Minneapolis	Chicago	S-2-A	442	Minneapolis	Savanna	S-2	297
					Savanna	Chicago	S-1-A	145
	(St. Louis-Beardstown-Galesburg.)							
47-51	St. Louis	Galesburg	P-2	208	St. Louis	Beardstown	P-2	114
					Beardstown	Galesburg	K-2	94
48-52	Galesburg	St. Louis	P-2	208	Galesburg	Beardstown	K-10	94
					Beardstown	St. Louis	P-2	114
	(Galesburg-Brookfield-Kansas City.)							
55	Galesburg	Kansas City	S-2	327	Galesburg	Brookfield	S-2	204
					Brookfield	Kansas City		123
56	Kansas City	Galesburg	S-2	327	Kansas City	Brookfield		123
					Brookfield	Galesburg	S-2	204
	(Burlington-Creston-Lincoln.)							
3-5-9	Burlington	Lincoln	S-3	345	Burlington	Creston	S-3	187
					Creston	Lincoln	S-3	158
2-6-12	Lincoln	Burlington	S-3	345	Lincoln	Creston	S-3	158
					Creston	Burlington	S-3	187
25-7	Chicago	Creston	S-1	394	Chicago	Burlington		206
					Burlington	Creston	R-5	188
4-30	Creston	Chicago	S-1	394	Creston	Burlington	R-5	188
					Burlington	Chicago		206
77-79 (Frt.)	Galesburg	Creston	O-1-A	230	Galesburg	Ottumwa	O-2	117
					Ottumwa	Creston		113
70-74 (Frt.)	Creston	Galesburg	O-1-A	230	Creston	Ottumwa	O-2	113
					Ottumwa	Galesburg		117
	(St. Joseph-Brookfield-Hannibal.)							
14-16	St. Joseph	Hannibal	S-2	206	St. Joseph	Brookfield	S-2	102
					Brookfield	Hannibal	S-1	104
15-17	Hannibal	St. Joseph	S-2	206	Hannibal	Brookfield	S-1	104
					Brookfield	St. Joseph	S-2	102
	(Omaha-St. Joseph-Kansas City.)							
20-22	Omaha	Kansas City	P-5	197	Omaha	St. Joseph	P-1	133
					St. Joseph	Kansas City	S-2	64
21-23	Kansas City	Omaha	S-2	197	Kansas City	St. Joseph	S-2	64
					St. Joseph	Omaha	S-2	133
72 (Frt.)	Omaha	Kansas City	O-1-A	197	Omaha	St. Joseph	R-4	133
					St. Joseph	Kansas City	R-5	64
75 (Frt.)	Kansas City	Omaha	O-1-A	197	Kansas City	St. Joseph	R-5	64
					St. Joseph	Omaha	R-4	133

TABLE II.—SUMMARY OF SAVINGS EFFECTED BY LONG RUNS (LINES EAST.)

Passenger Service

Train Numbers	Terminals Between	Force Reductions	Fuel Savings	Total Approx. Savings Per Mo.	Engines Released For Other Service
51-52 47-48 49-50	Chicago & St. Paul	$1,950	$450	$2,400	2-Pacific Type C. B. & Q., Class S-2.
47-48-51-52	St. Louis & Galesburg	345	330	675	3-10 Wheel Type, C. B. & Q. Cl. K-10
55-56	Kansas City & Galesburg	296 (X)	165	461	1-Pacific, C. B. & Q., Class S-2
3-5-9-2-6-12	Burlington & Lincoln				4-Pacific, C. B. & Q., Class S-3
4-30	Chicago & Creston	550	495	1,045	
14-15-16-17	Hannibal & St. Joseph	...*	330	330	1-Pacific, C. B. & Q., Class S-2
20-21-22-23	Kansas City & Omaha	150	330	480	1-Pacific, C. B. & Q., Class S-2
Total		$3,291	$2,100	$5,391	12 Engines

Freight Service

72-75	Kansas City & Omaha	None	178	178	1-Prairie, Class R-5
70-74-77-79	Creston & Galesburg	None	320	320	4-Mikado, Class O-2
Total		...	$498	$498	5

Grand Total Savings (Lines East)—$5,889 per Month.
Total Engines Released (Lines East)—17 Engines.

*Payroll Saving Included in (X)

15

TABLE III.—LONG ENGINE RUNS ON THE C. B. & Q. (LINES WEST.)

Train Nos.	Present assignment — Present Terminal Initial	Final	Class of loco.	No. of miles	Former Assignment — Former Terminal Initial	Final	Class loco.	No. of miles
	(Lincoln-McCook-Denver.)							
3-5-9	Lincoln	McCook	B-1	230	Lincoln	Hastings	S-2	98
					Hastings	McCook		132
3-9	McCook	Denver	B-1	255	McCook	Akron	S-3	143
					Akron	Denver		112
6-2	Denver	Lincoln	B-1	485	Denver	Akron	S-1	112
			S-1	...	Akron	McCook		143
					McCook	Hastings	S-2	132
					Hastings	Lincoln		98
22	McCook	Lincoln	S-1	230	McCook	Hastings	S-3	132
					Hastings	Lincoln	S-1	98
	(Wymore-McCook-Denver.)							
15-17	Wymore	McCook	S-2	228	Wymore	Red Cloud	S-1	108
					Red Cloud	McCook	S-1	120
15-17	McCook	Denver	S-1-A	255	McCook	Akron	S-1	143
					Akron	Denver	S-1	112
14-16	Denver	McCook	S-1	255	Denver	Akron	S-1	112
					Akron	McCook	S-1	143
14-16	McCook	Wymore	S-1	228	McCook	Red Cloud	S-1	120
					Red Cloud	Wymore	S-2	108
	(Alliance-Sheridan.)							
41-43	Alliance	Sheridan	S-3	333	Alliance	Edgemont	S-3	111
					Edgemont	Sheridan	...	222
42-44	Sheridan	Alliance	S-3	333	Sheridan	Edgemont	S-3	222
					Edgemont	Alliance	...	111
	(Denver-Casper-Billings.)							
29	Denver	Casper	S-3	339	Denver	Cheyenne	S-3	120
					Cheyenne	Casper		119
29	Casper	Greybull	S-2	202	Casper	Greybull	S-2	202
29	Greybull	Billings	S-2	127	Greybull	Billings		127
30	Billings	Casper	S-1	329	Billings	Greybull	S-1	202
					Greybull	Casper		127
30	Casper	Denver	S-3	...	Casper	Cheyenne	S-3	...
					Cheyenne	Denver		...
	(Alliance-Seneca-Ravenna.)							
Pool† (Frt.)	Alliance	Ravenna	O-1-A	238	Alliance	Seneca	O-1-A	108
					Seneca	Ravenna		130

†There were 20 O-1-A engines in this pool running between Alliance and Seneca and Seneca and Ravenna. Since running these engines through from Alliance to Ravenna and return the pool has been reduced to 18 O-1-A engines.

TABLE IV.—SUMMARY OF SAVINGS EFFECTED BY LONG RUNS (LINES WEST.)

Passenger Service.

Train Numbers	Terminals Between	Force Reductions	Fuel Savings	Total Approx. Savings Per Mo.	Engines Released For Other Service
3-5-9-15-17 2-6-14-16-22 29-30	Lincoln & Denver, Wymore & Denver, Denver & Casper, Casper & Billings	$706	$367	$1,073	7-Pacific type, C. B. & Q., Class S-2
		120	235	355	1-Pacific type, C. B. & Q., Class S-1
41-42-43-44	Alliance & Sheridan	440	270	710	3-1 Pacific type, C. B. & Q., Cl. S-2 2 Mountain type, C. B. & Q., Cl. B-1
Total		$1,266	$872	$2,138	11 Engines

Freight Service.

Train Numbers	Terminals Between	Force Reductions	Fuel Savings	Total Approx. Savings Per Mo.	Engines Released For Other Service
Pool	Alliance & Ravenna	$1,276	$123	$1,399	2-Mikade type, C. B. & Q., Cl. O-1-A
Total		$1,276	$123	$1,399	2

Grand Total Savings (Lines West)—$3,537 per Month.
Total Engines Released (Lines West)—13 Engines.

PRINCIPAL DIMENSIONS OF BURLINGTON ENGINES USED IN LONG RUNS

	O-1-A	S-1	S-2	S-3	B-1
Wheel arrangement	2-8-2	4-6-2	4-6-2	4-6-2	4-8-2
Tractive force	52,300 lb.	37,200 lb.	37,200 lb.	42,200 lb.	52,750 lb.
Grate area	58.8 sq. ft.	54.2 sq. ft.	54.2 sq. ft.	58.7 sq. ft.	78.0 sq. ft.
Total square feet heating surface	4,145 sq. ft.	3,699 sq. ft.	3,680 sq. ft.	4,115 sq. ft.	5,629.7 sq. ft.
Weight on drivers	214,550 lb.	150,000 lb.	153,100 lb.	171,300 lb.	235,500 lb.
Weight of engine	272,300 lb.	228,000 lb.	236,100 lb.	269,200 lb.	350,000 lb.
Total weight engine and tender	467,300 lb.	376,200 lb.	396,400 lb.	432,740 lb.	555,450 lb.
Cylinders	27 in. by 30 in.	22 in. by 28 in. and 25 in. by 28 in.	22 in. by 28 in. and 25 in. by 28 in.	27 in. by 28 in.	27 in. by 30 in.

TABLE V.—INCREASE IN DAILY MILEAGE OF PASSENGER LOCOMOTIVES

Division	Train numbers	Daily train miles	No. of engines now used	No. of engines formerly used
Alliance-Sheridan	41-42-43-44	1,332	6	8
Denver-Billings	29-30	1,344	5	7
St. Louis-Galesburg	47-48-51-52	832	4	7
Nebraska District	(3-5-9-2-6-22) (15-17-14-16)	4,189	18	25
Galesburg-Kansas City	55-56	650	2	3
Hannibal-St. Joseph	14-15-16-17	824	3	4
Omaha-Kansas City	20-21-22-23	780	4	5
Chicago-St. Paul	47-48-49-50-51-52	2,586	7	9
Lincoln-Burlington	2-3-5-6-9-12	2,070	9	13
		14,607	58	81

Former average daily locomotive mileage	180
Present average daily locomotive mileage	252
Miles per day increase	72
Percentage increase	40
Locomotives released to other service	23

SOURCES FOR TABLES & MAPS FROM RAILWAY AGE:

Chapter 2—All tables and map:
Railway Age, April 18, 1925
1—p. 972
2—p. 973
3—p. 974
4—p. 975
5—p. 976
6—p. 971
7—p. 973

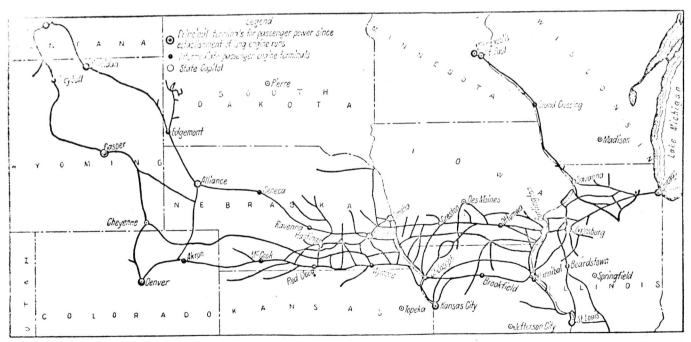

Map of the Burlington System Showing the Principal Terminals Handling Passenger Power Since Long Runs Have Been Established

The 5602 powers the Exposition Flyer, one of the fleet leaders, through Lisle, Illinois, in July, 1940. The Flyer was the first through Chicago-West Coast train operated by the Burlington, Rio Grande and Western Pacific. She was a highly popular train and led the three roads to implement the world famous "California Zephyr" after the war. (William A. Raia)

enclosed observation cars arrived in 1909 and were built of wood. The five cars that arrived in 1928 were assigned to the Black Hawk between Chicago and Minneapolis and the Nebraska Limited between Chicago and Lincoln, Nebraska. The observation room provided seating for six people. The rest of the lounge car provided seating for a total of 50 people including a special 14 seat women's lounge. The interior of the car was finished in walnut except for the buffet, which was in copper bearing steel and white enameled. They were excellent cars for their day.

To celebrate the 80th anniversary, the CB&Q installed a fleet of three new and completely modern passenger trains in 1930. The first of these was the Black Hawk, second was the Ak-Sar-Ben; successor to the Nebraska Limited and third was the Aristocrat between Chicago and Denver replacing the Colorado Limited. Two sets of trains each were required for the overnight Ak-Sar-Ben and Black Hawk, but four sets of equipment were required for the Aristocrat.

The total amount of steel standard equipment that was required to protect this new service was 45 Pullman sleepers, 8 dining cars, 8 solarium lounge cars, 8 combination smoker baggage cars and well over a dozen coaches on a reagular basis. This did not include the head-end equipment for mail, baggage and express service.

Twenty of the new Pullman cars were all section sleepers, while 14 provided drawing room and drawing room-compartment accommodations. Four salon-bedroom cars provided en suite accommodations. These cars would have been more appropriately termed sleeper lounge cars, and were operated with the club or lounge end next to the diner to provide overflow accommodations for passengers not immediately able to find seats in the dining car. A writing desk was provided in these cars as well as foursome seats for card playing, comfortable arm chairs and divans. All train sets were equipped with an enclosed observation room lounge car with the Aristocrat cars including a parlor section.

Coach passengers were treated to more luxurious accommodations than was normally available to non-Pullman passengers. The coaches were equipped with automatic temperature control, electric fans and other refinements usually associated only with Pullman cars. A feature of the four 64 passenger chair cars used on the Aristocrat trains was the Heywood-Wakefield revolving, bucket type, reclining back seats, which were available without additional extra fare charges. With a center spacing of 43 inches, the seats could be revolved independent-

The American Royal arrives in Chicago behind the 3003 with six head-end cars, two coaches, one diner and two sleepers. It is January, 1940, and the eleven car train reflects an upturn in business as the Great Depression begins to fade away. (William A. Raia)

ly under the control of a foot lever to any of five positions: all passengers facing forward; four passengers facing together; four passengers half facing each other and the windows; six passengers forming a semi-private group and all passengers facing the windows.

The trains were fleet leaders of that time. They were a credit to the CB&Q, and they provided the incentive to begin work on the newest of trains, the fabulous Zephyr fleet, to be launched in 1934.

The Burlington Route was always looking for ways to improve service, and they were not necessarily tied to the traditional ways of doing things. On April 9, 1929, the road embarked upon a program of bus substitution for local passenger trains. In effect the Burlington was working toward the development of a balanced transportation system, which in the long run they were not permitted to do because of an edict of the United States Government.

However to begin with, the CB&Q began the program by placing in service five buses covering one route between Lincoln and Omaha and two routes between Lincoln and Hastings. By 1931, a bus system covering 1,024 miles of routes had been developed. The bus fleet grew from five to 38 buses and the total investment in the highway operations totaled $392,442. The purpose of the bus operation

was the elimination of unprofitable train service. By offering bus service, the road saved money while at the same time maintaining a regular transportation system for its patrons. What is so interesting is the CB&Q grossed $305,005 on its bus operations in 1930, while at the same time the company saved $114,367 by the elimination of unprofitable, lightly traveled local trains. It is indeed unfortunate that the ICC and the U.S. Government did not permit the railroads to expand these types of services Nationwide. Perhaps, we would not be experiencing the many problems of public transportation that the USA is now (1976) going through.

The bus schedules were arranged to connect with and to supplement rail services. Long haul service was not considered after a marketing study by the CB&Q found that operating costs were greater per seat mile for the bus operations as compared to the train. This situation continues to exist in 1976. The reader should refer to the Epilogue in COACH TRAINS & TRAVEL, published by Superior Publishing Company during the summer of 1975. The chief advantage of putting on the bus service was to reduce excessive costs with unprofitable local train service. In this way, the CB&Q could reduce costs and improve the profitability of the overall passenger operations despite the fact that the bus service in of itself was not profitable.

Train No. 44, the Empire Builder, barrels through Riverside, Illinois (just 11 miles from Chicago) with an exceptionally long train during the summer of 1940—the tourist season is in full swing. 44 has just completed its overnight run from St. Paul, the last leg of its transcontinental journey from Seattle over the Great Northern. (William A. Raia)

The height of the standard era took place during the 1920's and 30's. From 1935 on standard trains and equipment began to be replaced by streamlined equipment. There were countless trains, such as the Buffalo Bill, Adventureland, General Custer, Aristocrat, Night Hawk, St. Louis Limited, Overland Express, Fast Mail, Black Hawk and many other spectacular trains. What happened to them all? Many of them were discontinued because of the Depression and the automobile. Still others were replaced by faster and more suitable trains as the CB&Q constantly strove to upgrade services on all portions of the system. The North Coast Limited and Empire Builder were replaced with streamliners. Many of the day trains and Day Expresses were replaced with one of the finest fleet of streamliners ever built and operated by one railroad — The Zephyrs. Consequently, the CB&Q built itself a reputation as being a pro-passenger railway that lasted through the 1950's and into the late, traffic losing 1960's. The standard era itself did not die out completely until after the Burlington Northern merger date. The standard dark green coaches often operated on the Black Hawk and other trains right through 1969.

Standard head-on equipment operated on a variety of trains up through 1969. Some of these cars were not retired until the loss of mail contracts and Amtrak operations precluded any further use of them.

This author remembers with delightful nostalgia riding the Western Star section in the Black Hawk (from Willmar, Minnesota to Chicago) and eating breakfast in the heavy weight dining lounge cars in the late 1950's and early 1960's. Much of the standard equipment was painted silver to match the other streamlined or Zephyr equipment, but the interiors retained the "homey" touch that can only be found on standard era equipment.

Although there are many memories of CB&Q heavy steam power pulling heavy dark green passenger trains with long strings of Pullmans, it probably can be said that the Burlington Route is remembered more often for its vast fleet of Zephyr streamliners. The year 1934 brought the Pioneer Zephyr during the height of the Standard Era (despite the Depression), which ushered in a new era, This had its origin with the unforgettable gas-electric cars.

20

In 1940, train No. 45 was an all day local between Chicago and Minneapolis. She departed Chicago around 10:20 am and arrived in Minneapolis at 9:55 pm. In contrast, No. 23, the Afternoon Zephyr departed Chicago at 4:00 pm and arrived in Minneapolis at 10:59 pm. 45 and her counterpart 52 offered head-end service, local coach service and a cafe-coach for meals. 45 is shown here at Naperville, Illinois, in July, 1940. (William A. Raia)

Burlington-Colorado & Southern trains 29 and 30 provided service between Denver and Billings, Montana. In 1950 the trains offered head-end, coach and sleeping car service between Montana and colorful Colorado. It is interesting to note that 29 and 30 never rated a name, but were the last trains to operate over the route. This photo was taken at East Bridger, Montana, in August, 1949, and the train is minus its dining car for some unknown reason. (Harold K. Vollrath Collection)

On a summer Sunday, August 31, 1947, train No. 45, the day local between Chicago and the Twin Cities, is moving away from Rochelle, Illinois, behind a Baldwin-built Hudson 3001, class S-4A. The always progressive Burlington is evident by the inclusion of two immediate pre-War streamlined coaches. The passenger cars are beneath the home signal of the C&NW's Council Bluffs line crossing and the vertical crossing gates protect the left handed rails used by the City trains and the Challengers. **Train 45,** be it remarked, is also the title of a well known traditional Bluegrass Music instrumental tune. (Jim Scribbins)

Mail trains were once a very important part of the Chicago-Omaha main line of the CB&Q, and Christmas meant an even heavier mail traffic. It is December 22, 1955, and an eastbound Christmas mail train departs Burlington, Iowa, for Chicago with a magnificent plume of smoke. (William S. Kuba)

The "Q" operated countless rail fan specials over the years, and in so doing, endeared itself to countless people and the good will generated could never be calculated in dollars and cents. Russ Porter captures on film a double header at Mendota, Illinois, in September, 1959.

Not all fan specials were long, such as the train previously shown at Mendota. This special typified the combination of the standard era and the vista dome Zephyrs during the 40's and 50's. The consist includes three rebuilt standard coaches, one standard diner, one vista dome coach and a standard green lounge car. The six car train lacked only a Pullman car to complete a rolling history of passenger transportation. (Russ Porter)

A passenger extra arrives in Savanna, Illinois, with a National Railroad Historical Society Convention train in May, 1962. The heavy weight "Omaha Club" brings up the markers end complete with drum head sign advertising the train. (Russ Porter)

For many rail fans, CB&Q Northerns, such as the 5632, were the alpha and the omega of steam. These oil burners boasted super tenders with back up lights, mars lights above the head light (both red and white) and enclosed cabs. Even while sitting still they gave the impression of being a no-nonsense locomotive. The 5632 is shown here at North La Crosse, Wisconsin, in 1959. (Russ Porter)

The interior of the engineer's side of the 5632. Many more contols than can be found on a diesel. (Russ Porter)

Long remembered will be the C&NW-CB&Q interline excursion operated in January, 1962, by the Railroad Club of Chicago and dubbed the Iron Horse 400. The yellow and green train was pulled to West Chicago by a North Western SD, then went over the Q branch to Aurora behind a pair of E-9's, at which point the piece de resistance of the trip became reality, already famous Mile 4960 was waiting to take over. (Jim Scribbins)

Near Denrock, Illinois, on a branch line, the 4960 pauses for RRCC excurtionists to detrain in anticipation of a movie run by the Iron Horse 400. (Jim Scribbins)

On the way home, CB&Q Mike 4960 peddles along with a rail fan trip across the Fox River Bridge at Sheridan, Illinois, in 1957. This particular train included double deck suburban coaches as well as the usual open door baggage car right behind the engine. (Russ Porter)

The massive size of the 5632 stands out as she sits in the sunlight beneath the U.S. Post Office at the Union Station in Chicago on a rail fan trip in 1962. (Russ Porter)

Train No. 2, the Galesburg Local, slides into Chicago on a winter morning during the early 1960's wtih two head-end cars and three coaches. Trains 15 and 2 were among the last main line locals operated by the Q. By 1965, 15 and 2 were off and an extra streamlined coach was added to the Denver Zephyr for set out or pick up at Galesburg for lhat traffic. (William A. Raia)

Trains 45 and 52, once day locals between Chicago and St. Paul, finished their days running overnight relieving the Black Hawk of burdensome head-end traffic. 45 is shown here arriving in St. Paul in the late 1950'. (A. Robert Johnson)

Train No. 7 was essentially a mail train between Chicago and Denver, but operated on a very slow local schedule for the run. This photo shows the train toward the end of its career when its consist was substantially reduced. (William S. Kuba)

The streamlined Zephyr and standard era was often brought together when the Omaha Club or some other standard lounge car brought up the marker's end of such trains. Here the Omaha Club departs Chicago on a Zephyr in 1960. (Russ Porter)

The interior of the "Omaha Club" showing the lounge furniture and large solarium windows. (Russ Porter)

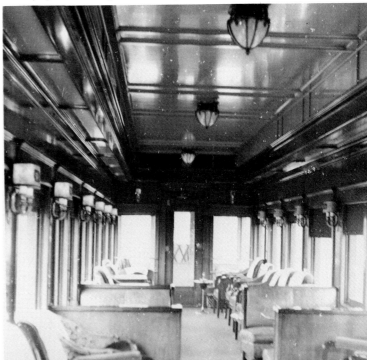

The 5632 was set aside by the "Q" for rail fan specials, and she performed admirably for the fans. Here the 5632 blasts out of the tunnel at East Dubuque, Illinois, leading a rail fan trip in 1962. (Russ Porter)

Standard steel coach No. 4431, constructed by Pullman in 1924. (Burlington Northern)

One Pullman car was named after the man who financed much of the early Burlington construction, John M. Forbes. (Burlington Northern)

Observation cars, or business cars, made a handsome ending for passenger trains. The business car "Blackhawk" was typical of the standard era with dark green color and gold lettering. (Burlington Northern)

The "Burlington" was the Q's presidents car, and was often seen coupled to Great Northern and Northern Pacific business cars just about anywhere on the Burlington Route.

PASSENGER EQUIPMENT SUMMARY

Following is a listing of passenger equipment that was owned and operated by the CB&Q, but not assigned to Zephyr and/or transcontinental streamliners, during the post World War II period. The summary is not an all time roster of CB&Q passenger equipment.

Pullman Sleeping Cars owned by the CB&Q (Post 1950)

Name	Type	Capacity
American Legion	14 Sections	28
Anaconda (FW&D)	12 Sec., 1 Drawing Room	27
Carter Lake	10 Sec., 1 DR, 1 Cmpt.	25
Castle Range (FW&D)	8 Sec., 5 Double Bedrm.	26
Clover Basin	8 Sec., 5 Double Bedrm.	26
Clover Camp	8-5	26
Clover Colors	8-5	26
Clover Veldt	8-5	26
Cornhusker	12 Sec., 1 DR	27
Cymric	12-1	27
Davenport	12-1	27
Denver Tower	8 Sec., 3 DBR, 1 DR	25
Donwell	12-1	27
El Onate	10 Sec., Obs. Lnge	20
Estes Park	12-1	27
Fontenelle	12-1	27
Happy Hollow Club	1 DR, 2 DBR, 2 Cmpt., 2 SBR-Lounge	10
Lancaster Club	1-2-2-2 Lounge	10
Lariat Range (FW&D)	10 Sec., 1 DR., 1 Cmpt.	25
Lariat Crest (C&S)	10-1-1	25
Linoma Lake	10-1-1	25
Mackenzie	12-1	27
Maneko	10 Sec., Obs. Lounge	20
Maximiliam (FW&D)	12-1	27
McKinnell	12-1	27
McKnight	12-1	27
McLeansboro	12-1	27
McNab	12-1	27
McQuesten	10 Sec., 3 DBR	26
Minneapolis	8 Sec., 3 DBR, 1 DR.	25
Missouri Tower	10 Sec., Obs. Lounge	20
Montezuma	12-1	27
Morehead	10 Sec., Lounge car	20
Mt. Lowe	10 Sec., Lounge Car	20
Mt. Lyell	12-1	27
Nachita	14 Sec.	28
New Capitol	14 Sec.	28
New Farnam	14 Sec.	28
New Omaha	10 Sec., Obs. Lounge	20
North Gate	12 Sec., 1 DR.	27
Pepin	6 Sec., 6 DBR	24
Pierre Chouteau	12-1	27
Pocomoke	6 Sec., 6 DBR	24
Poplar Branch	6-6	24
Poplar Flat	12 Sec., 2 DBR	28
Princeton University	12-2	28
Rutgers University	12 Sec., 1 DR.	27
Spanish Crest(FW&D)	12-1	27
Spanish Range (C&S)	12-1	27
Troutdale	8 Sec., 3 DBR, 1 DR.	25
Zephyr Tower		

Type	Numbers and/or Names	Length	Seating Cap'y	Built	Service
Mail & Baggage	1892, 1893	64'-3" (15' mail)			Pool
Mail & Baggage	1910 to 1949	74'-3" (30' mail)		1914-1924	Pool
Postal	2320 to 2346	64'-3" (60' mail)		1922	Pool
Box Express	8500 to 8549	52'-3"			Pool
Baggage	8600 to 8899	51'-6"			Pool
Baggage	990 to 1049	79'-2"		1950-1953	Pool
Baggage	1309	63'-3"		1914	Pool
Baggage	1401	64'-3"		1914	Pool
Baggage	1430 to 1574	74'-3"		1918-1930	Pool
Baggage	1580 to 1587	76'-9"		1916	Pool
Baggage	1593 to 1597	64'-2"		1916	Pool
Baggage	1598	83'-1"		1913	Pool
Comb Coach-Bag	3651	67'-6"	32	1928	
	3653	67'-6"	32	1927	
Comb. Coach Bag-Mail	2752	76'-11"	38 (15' mail)	1927	
Comb. Coach Bag-Dorm	3659	77'-6"	22	1928	
Coach	6110 to 6170	79'-8"	71-83	1922-1927	
Drovers Coach	5760 to 5765	82'-0"	48		
Smoker Coach	6200 to 6202	79'-8"	73		
Coach Dinette	342 to 343	80'-4"	46	1937	
Dining Car	171 to 187	83'-0"	36		
Buffet Lounge	210	83'-0"	53		
Dining Lounge	215, 216	83'-0"	54		
Cafe Coach	350 to 352	79'-8"	10 Dining 59 Coach		

All above sleepers are CB&Q unless otherwise noted. In addition, CB&Q could draw on the Pullman and/or Great Northern and Northern Pacific Pullmans for additional equipment.

Chapter 3
THE GAS-ELECTRIC
MOTOR CARS

As one could find hundreds of electric interurban cars throughout Ohio and Indiana, so could one find hundreds of gas-electric motor cars throughout the prairie states from Illinois to Colorado. In the east the electric cars sped from one hamlet to another, while west of Chicago the steam roads took it upon themselves to provide the local services that were required during the first quarter of the Twentieth Century. However as time went on, the automobile took more and more of the patronage of the local passenger train, and the steam roads sought an economical alternative to a 2-6-0 or a 4-6-0, or even a 4-4-2 coupled to a baggage car and a single coach. And that choice blossomed in the form of the gas-electric car.

The Burlington Route was very much a part of the gas-electric era. The very first car was a McGuire-Cummings rail car numbered 501, delivered in March, 1922. This was basically a bus body mounted on a truck chassis with flanged wheels. The 501 served for approximately six years in Nebraska on the old Wymore Division. In 1928 the very first gas car, actually a gas engine with a mechanical transmission instead of a gas-electric, was sold to the Rapid City, Black Hills and Western Railroad Company. However, the success of that 501 led to the purchase of a group of cars from the Edwards Railway Motor Car Company. One such car was purchased in 1922 just a short time after the arrival of the 501. This car, numbered 500, was mounted on two four wheel trucks with an overall length of 32 feet, 7 inches. The power was furnished by a 60 hp motor with the drive transmitted to the rear four wheel truck by chains. The car contained a 12 volt electric lighting system and a Westinghouse straight air system.

The passenger compartment contained seats for 39 passengers and there were folding seats in the baggage compartment for six additional people. A single toilet was placed in the forward end of the passenger compartment. The driving controls and engineer's seat were on the right hand side of the motor. The total weight of the car empty was about 19,000 pounds. The 501 was able to travel at a speed of 45 miles per hour with a fuel consumption of 10 miles per gallon. The success of the 500 led to the purchase of two more in 1925 and four more in 1926. And this was only the beginning.

In 1925, the CB&Q purchased a gas-electric car from the J. G. Brill Company. This car was 60 feet long with a seating capacity of 42 passengers with a 14 foot baggage area in the forward end. A 65 foot car was purchased, No. 552, in 1925 from the Edwards Railway Motor Company. It seated 42 passengers with a 24 foot baggage compartment, plus a 15 foot Rail Post Office section. The purchase of these cars demonstrated to the CB&Q the value of the gas-electric, and then began the systematic purchase and placing into operation a very extensive fleet of such equipment. Sixteen cars were purchased in 1927, with 31 more in 1928, and finally four cars of mail-baggage arrangement came in 1929. The fleet was made up of passenger units, passenger-baggage, passenger-RPO, passenger-mail-baggage, and full mail-baggage units. Altogether 86 of these very functional cars were purchased.

Before we get into the operating techniques, it would be wise to pause here for a moment and take a look at some unusual testing of gas-electrics that took place on the "Q".

It was in 1928, when the gas-electric was really getting down to the business of proving itself. It was widely known that electric locomotives and passenger cars could be operated in multiple units, but the gas-electric had yet to prove itself in that area. So on October 2, 1928, the CB&Q sought to demonstrate the feasibility of the multiple unit operation of such equipment. A four car train was operated from Chicago to Downers Grove and return, and consisted of two standard Burlington 46 ton, 100 passenger suburban coaches located between a Mack 270 horse power, gas electric rail car with a double power plant, and a Mack 405 hp car with a triple power plant. The two gas electric cars weighed 57 and 67 tons respectively. The train was a double powered train with the motive power units on both ends of the train. Twenty-one scheduled stops were made on the run from Chicago to Downers

Burlington gas-electric car No. 9841 is shown here at Creston, Iowa during the early 1950's when she was assigned to trains 30 and 31 between Creston and St. Joseph. The trains operated to St. Joe in the morning, while 31 departed St. Joe for Creston after 5:30 pm. The train made connections for Kansas City and Chicago at both ends of its run. (Harold K. Vollrath Collection)

Grove, while on the return trip the train ran on an express schedule with no stops. The test was not repeated nor did the Burlington set up such an operating procedure. However, the testing did prove that multiple unit operation was possible not only coupled together, but also when separated by one or more cars in between power units. The testing set the stage for such trains as the New Haven's Comet and today's Amtrak Turbos. The concept involved is exactly the same. The testing also laid additional ground work for the Zephyrs that were just around the corner.

The Burlington gas-electric operation was one of the most significant operations on steam railroads anywhere. In 1930 the CB&Q was operating 50 gas-electrics plus the seven gas-mechanical cars. The Colorado & Southern also operated two cars and the Wichita Valley operated one car.

The cars turned in a tremendous operating record of 94% availability and a reduction of 36.3% saving over steam train service. According to the February 28, 1931 issue of RAILWAY AGE, almost 60% of the motor train mileage was with trailer equipment, either one or two cars.

The gas-electric cars were assigned to lines where they would effect the greatest economics, and at the same time give adequate service. In 1930, according to RAILWAY AGE, about two-thirds of the cars had regular enginemen and one third were in pooled service. The cars were serviced with the utmost care. An example of the kind of inspection and con-

ditioning work done on the gas-electrics can be shown by a study published in the above RAILWAY AGE. Car numbers 9627 and 9628 (all gas cars on the CB&Q were renumbered with number 9 to all car numbers in 1930. For example 628 became 9628 in May, 1930) operated between Keokuk and Shenandoah, Iowa, a distance of 244 miles. They made 47 stops each way in a total time of 10 hours, 18 minutes or a running time of 8 hours, 12 minutes for a 28.8 mph average speed. The cars laid over on alternate nights at Shenandoah, and were serviced and maintained at Keokuk every other night by one mechanic. Upon arrival at Keokuk, the car was inspected by the mechanic, the gas tank was filled and the oil checked. Lubrication, the checking of electrical equipment relay contactors, examining bearings, batteries, wheels, brake equipment, flange lubricators, etc., required attention on a daily basis. The car heating plant in winter was also given attention and a new fire made after each trip. The car was cleaned inside and out by a coach cleaner. Other details such as the valve-tappet adjustment, cleaning magnetos, spark plugs, etc., received attention on a once a week basis. Other important inspection and conditioning work was done twice a month, once a month and sometimes on a mileage basis. In order to make sure that none of the work was overlooked, a compact card (form 1659) was carried in the cab. This card showed just what the detailed requirements were, and provided spaces for the signature of the maintainer and for the date each

Train No. 110, using gas-electric 9816, departs Burlington en route to Quincy via Carthage in August, 1952. (William S. Kuba)

operation and/or inspection was performed. A new card was furnished each month.

The cars were refinished by painting on the average of about every two years. The front ends of the cars were painted red and yellow to attract the attention of motorists at road crossings, and so that the cars could be seen at greater distances by trackmen.

There were very few delays to the gas-electrics due to failures. The CB&Q kept a close watch on failures. When one would occur, the fact was recorded and a report by wire was dispatched to the general office where arrangements were made for an investigation. At the end of each month, the failures were tabulated, analyzed and a mimeographed form was sent out to all interested with a view to prevent future failures of that type. However, failures were few and far between as might be expected with the 94% availability. During the year 1930, only 21 failures were experienced throughout the entire year with 57 cars, which ran a mileage of 3,341,004, or in other words, 160,000 miles per failure.

Part of the success of the motor cars or gas-electrics was due to the fact that enginemen and crews were instructed by district motor car supervisors who spent their entire time in the field, and were familiar with the condition of every car as well as the qualifications of individual men. Engineers were provided with three bulletins covering the general construction and operation of the equipment, and were required to familiarize themselves with the details. To assist in this instruction work, the three bulletins were combined into a pocket size booklet for all personnel connected with the operation and running of the gas-electric motor cars. Individual instruction of enginemen and motor-cars was found to give the best operating results. The supervisors were also required to make periodical surprise checks to determine if the men were on the alert. The district supervisors also kept a monthly statement of individual car performance, quantities of gasoline, lubricants and other supplies used. If any of the cost figures appeared excessive, the cause was determined and remedied as soon as possible. The ability of the crew was also reflected in the performance of the car. There were numerous other factors included in the success of the gas-electric cars. For example, the CB&Q did not overload the motor cars (handle extra trailers of excessive weight), operate at excessive speeds (over 35 mph on branch lines and 50 mph on main lines), and a determined effort to provide adequate lubrication at all times. The result of this good care insured that many of the gas-electrics would remain in operation right through the 1950s. At least one of the cars, the mail baggage motor No. 9767, was repainted in the Zephyr color scheme. This particular car had the distinction of pulling the "Silver Pendulum" between St. Joseph and Brookfield, Missouri, as connection for the Kansas City Zephyr. The 9767 lasted until 1961 when motor failure side tracked the beautiful car after 31 years of successful service. The car had been re-powered with a diesel engine. Still other cars even saw switching, way freight and mixed train service before retirement. There seemed to be no limit to the variety of service the gas-electrics were placed.

The doodlebug era lasted from 1923 to the early 1960s for almost 40 years of railroad operating history. The bulk of the era commenced from about 1927 and was virtually over with by 1957. Thirty years may seem like a lot to some, but it is only a drop in the bucket when compared to entire spectrum of railroad history. Only the US and Canada enjoyed this type of equipment with its bouncey, skip-right-along, air horn atmosphere. Historians, Geographers, rail fans and other interested people did not seem to notice the doodlebug until they were

Car No. 9841 offered coach, mail and baggage facilities and once served throughout the Illinois-Iowa area of the CB&Q. Few train rides could compare wtih a galloping doodlebug. (William S. Kuba)

fast disappearing from the rails. Consequently, few photographs were taken of them throughout the country. After all, they replaced the beautiful but costly 4-4-0s and other delightful steam power.

One thing that is interesting to speculate on is why the CB&Q did not invest in Rail Diesel Cars, when they so heavily invested in gas-electric motor cars for service over almost the entire system. It is even still further interesting that the gas-electrics sired the first Zephyr, No. 9900 (even numbered in the 9000s as were all the other motors), which was built by the Budd Company, the same company that constructed the immortal RDCs. Which are, by the way, still seeing service and some cars have seen service continuously now for over 25 years. However, by the time the RDC made its debut the handwriting was already on the wall for both branch line and local passenger service. The automobile cut deeply into those markets from 1946 on, and the CB&Q recognized that investments for those markets would not be a paying proposition. And this is why the CB&Q invested so heavily into one of the finest fleets of streamliners ever put together by one railroad—THE ZEPHYRS.

Passenger service in the Southern Illinois coal country was held down by gas-electrics such as the 9844 shown here at Beardstown, Illinois. The doodlebug service added a romantic touch to this heavy coal traffic rail line, which never was graced by the likes of a Zephyr. (William S. Kuba)

Not all doodlebugs were combination baggage, mail coach cars. The 9773, for example, was a full baggage and mail car with a 30 foot rail post office section. The car was powerful enough to pull one or two trailer coaches. When this photo was taken in September, 1948, the 9773 was assigned to trains 133 and 134 between Aurora and Streator, Illinois. The train operated to Streator in the morning, and back to Aurora in the late afternoon. (Harold K. Vollrath Collection)

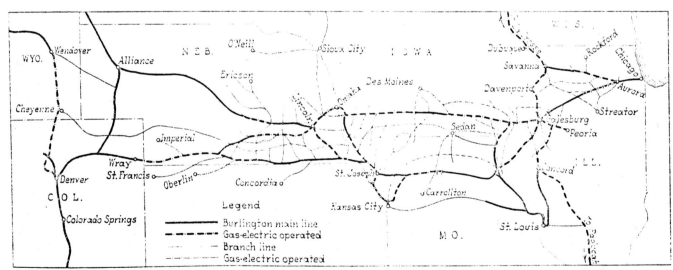

Map Showing Wide Distribution of Gas-Electric Rail Car Operation on the Burlington Lines

—map Railway Age, p. 439, Feb. 28, 1931;
Table Railway Age, p. 441, Feb. 28, 1931

Assignment of Passenger Motor Cars on C. B. & Q., Lines East and West

Car no.	Present assignment		*Car length	Railway post office	Baggage-express	Passengers Smoker	General	Built by	In service
9500	Emergency-Atchison, Kan.		32 ft. 7 in.	None	7 ft. 10 in.	None	42	Edwards	1- 2-23
9502	Emergency-Hannibal, Mo.		43 ft. 0 in.	None	17 ft. 2 in.	None	41	Edwards	12- 3-24
9503	Litchfield-Concord, Ill.		43 ft. 0 in.	None	17 ft. 2 in.	None	40	Edwards	2-27-25
9505	Armour-Atchison, Kan.		43 ft. 2 in.	None	19 ft. 7 in.	10	27	Edwards	3-15-26
9506	Hannibal-Quincy, Ill.		43 ft. 2 in.	None	24 ft. 5 in.	10	17	Edwards	3-26-26
9507	Shop train—W. Burlington, Iowa....		43 ft. 2 in.	None	26 ft. 10 in.	None	22	Edwards	6- 3-26
9508	Unassigned, Havelock, Neb........		43 ft. 2 in.	None	26 ft. 10 in.	10	12	Edwards	5- 3-26

Gas-Electric Cars

Car no.	Present assignment		*Car length	Railway post office	Baggage-express	Smoker	General	Built by	In service
9509	Rochelle-Rockford, Ill.	X-C	60 ft. 0 in.	None	14 ft. 6 in.	None	42	Brill	1-11-27
M 9450	Beardstown-Davenport, Iowa	B-W	65 ft. 0 in.	None	None	25	52	Pullman	8-10-28
M 9525	Red Cloud-Wray-McCook, Neb.......	B-G	65 ft. 0 in.	None	24 ft. 10 in.	15	24	Pullman	8- 1-28
9528	McCook-Imperial-Red Cloud, Neb...	B-G	65 ft. 0 in.	None	24 ft. 10 in.	15	24	Pullman	8- 9-28
M 9527	Savanna-N. LaCrosse, Wis.	B-G	65 ft. 0 in.	None	39 ft. 8 in.	None	32	Pullman	8-23-28
9529	Burlington-Washington, Iowa	B-G	65 ft. 0 in.	None	39 ft. 8 in.	10	19	Pullman	12-13-28
9526	Earlville-Barstow, Ill.	X-B-G	65 ft. 0 in.	None	36 ft. 0 in.	None	22	Pullman	8-20-28
M 9530*	Lincoln-Table Rock, Neb.	D-G	65 ft. 7 in.	None	27 ft. 8 in.	12	27	H.K.P. Co.	6- 9-26
9625	Burlington-Carrollton, Mo.	B-W	65 ft. 0 in.	15 ft. 0 in.	None	16	37	Pullman	8-15-28
9626	Burlington-Carrollton, Mo.	B-W	65 ft. 0 in.	15 ft. 0 in.	None	16	37	Pullman	8-16-28
9627	Keokuk-Shenandoah, Iowa	B-W	65 ft. 0 in.	15 ft. 0 in.	None	16	37	Pullman	10-26-28
9628	Keokuk-Shenandah, Iowa	B-W	65 ft. 0 in.	15 ft. 0 in.	None	16	37	Pullman	8-15-28
9629	Lincoln-Columbus, Neb.	B-G	65 ft. 0 in.	15 ft. 0 in.	None	16	37	Pullman	8-16-28
9813	Ft. Madison-Ottumwa, Iowa	B-G	65 ft. 0 in.	15 ft. 0 in.	21 ft. 5 in.	None	22	Pullman	12-22-28
9812	Villisca-Bigelow-Napier, Mo........	B-G	65 ft. 0 in.	15 ft. 0 in.	24 ft. 3 in.	17	None	St. L. C.	10- 1-27
9811	Hastings-Stromsburg, Neb.	B-G	65 ft. 0 in.	15 ft. 0 in.	27 ft. 2 in.	17	None	St. L. C.	9-30-27
9734	Chariton-St. Joseph, Mo.	A-G	65 ft. 0 in.	15 ft. 0 in.	33 ft. 3 in.	None	None	Pullman	2-27-29
9735	Villisca-St. Joseph, Mo.	X-A-G	65 ft. 0 in.	15 ft. 0 in.	33 ft. 3 in.	None	None	Pullman	3-14-29
9725	Aurora-Streator, Ill.	B-G	65 ft. 0 in.	15 ft. 0 in.	39 ft. 1 in.	None	None	St. L. C.	5- 3-27
9726	Buda-Rushville, Ill.	B-G	65 ft. 0 in.	15 ft. 0 in.	39 ft. 1 in.	None	None	St. L. C.	5- 3-27
9727	Creston-St. Joseph, Mo.	B-G	65 ft. 0 in.	15 ft. 0 in.	39 ft. 1 in.	None	None	St. L. C.	9-23-27
9728	Galesburg-Burlington	B-G	65 ft. 0 in.	15 ft. 0 in.	39 ft. 1 in.	None	None	St. L. C.	9-22-27
M 9729	Ravenna-Aurora, Ill.	B-G	65 ft. 0 in.	15 ft. 0 in.	39 ft. 1 in.	None	None	Pullman	8-24-28
9730	St. Joseph-Creston, Iowa	B-W	65 ft. 0 in.	15 ft. 0 in.	39 ft. 1 in.	None	None	Pullman	8-24-28
9731	Emergency, Lines east	B-G	65 ft. 0 in.	15 ft. 0 in.	39 ft. 1 in.	None	None	Pullman	9-11-28
9732	DesMoines-Cainsville, Mo.	B-G	65 ft. 0 in.	15 ft. 0 in.	39 ft. 1 in.	None	None	Pullman	12-26-28
9733	DesMoines-Creston, Iowa	B-G	65 ft. 0 in.	15 ft. 0 in.	39 ft. 1 in.	None	None	Pullman	12-26-28
M 9569	Brookfield-Kansas City, Mo........	X-E-G	75 ft. 0 in.	None	25 ft. 0 in.	18	37	Pullman	10-27-28
M 9566	Creston-Omaha, Neb.	B-G	75 ft. 0 in.	None	26 ft. 1 in.	15	42	St. L. C.	10-24-27
M 9567	St. Joseph-Kansas City, Mo.	B-G	75 ft. 0 in.	None	26 ft. 1 in.	15	42	St. L. C.	10-21-27
M 9568	Lincoln-Kearney, Neb.	B-G	75 ft. 0 in.	None	29 ft. 0 in.	10	39	St. L. C.	10-14-27
M 9570	Aurora-Rochelle-Oregon, Ill.	X-A-G	75 ft. 0 in.	None	29 ft. 0 in.	10	29	Pullman	11-15-28
9571	Cody-Frannie, Wyo.	B-G	75 ft. 0 in.	None	40 ft. 8 in.	10	19	Pullman	12-19-28
9665	Quincy-Kansas City, Mo.	A-G	75 ft. 0 in.	15 ft. 0 in.	None	16	44	Pullman	10-27-28
9666	Quincy-Kansas City, Mo.	A-G	75 ft. 0 in.	15 ft. 0 in.	None	16	44	Pullman	11-15-28
M 9835	Omaha-Schuyler, Neb.	B-G	75 ft. 0 in.	15 ft. 0 in.	22 ft. 7 in.	10	27	St. L. C.	5- 7-27
9836	Centerville-Carrollton, Mo.	B-G	75 ft. 0 in.	15 ft. 0 in.	22 ft. 7 in.	10	27	St. L. C.	5- 6-27
M 9843	Beardstown-Metropolis, Ill.	X-B-G	75 ft. 0 in.	15 ft. 0 in.	22 ft. 7 in.	10	27	Pullman	7-27-28
M 9845	Beardstown-Metropolis, Ill.	B-W	75 ft. 0 in.	15 ft. 0 in.	22 ft. 7 in.	10	27	Pullman	7-27-28
9837	Burlington-Oskaloosa, Iowa	B-G	75 ft. 0 in.	15 ft. 0 in.	25 ft. 6 in.	10	22	St. L. C.	10-28-27
M 9841	Burlington-Quincy, Ill.	B-G	75 ft. 0 in.	15 ft. 0 in.	25 ft. 6 in.	None	32	Pullman	8-14-28
9838	Streator-Denrock, Ill.	B-G	75 ft. 0 in.	15 ft. 0 in.	28 ft. 5 in.	10	14	St. L. C.	10-27-27
9839	Republican-Oberlin, Kan.	B-G	75 ft. 0 in.	15 ft. 0 in.	28 ft. 5 in.	10	14	St. L. C.	10-26-27
9840	Palmer-Burwell, Neb.	B-G	75 ft. 0 in.	15 ft. 0 in.	28 ft. 5 in.	10	14	St. L. C.	11- 3-27
9842	Aurora-Clinton, Ill.	X-B-G	75 ft. 0 in.	15 ft. 0 in.	28 ft. 5 in.	10	14	Pullman	8- 1-28
9844	Emergency, Lines east	B-W	75 ft. 0 in.	15 ft. 0 in.	28 ft. 5 in.	None	27	Pullman	7-26-28
9846	Creston-Cumberland, Iowa	B-G	75 ft. 0 in.	15 ft. 0 in.	28 ft. 5 in.	10	14	Pullman	8- 2-28
9847	Nebraska City-Holdrege, Neb.	B-G	75 ft. 0 in.	15 ft. 0 in.	28 ft. 5 in.	10	14	Pullman	8- 2-28
9848	Nebraska City-Holdrege, Neb.	B-G	75 ft. 0 in.	15 ft. 0 in.	28 ft. 5 in.	10	14	Pullman	8- 3-28
M 9849	Burlington-Quincy, Ill.	B-G	75 ft. 0 in.	15 ft. 0 in.	28 ft. 5 in.	10	14	Pullman	12-13-28
9565	Red Cloud-Aurora, Neb.	B-G	75 ft. 0 in.	None	26 ft. 1 in.	13	42	St. L. C.	5-16-27
M 9765	Peoria-DesMoines, Iowa	A-G	75 ft. 0 in.	15 ft. 0 in.	43 ft. 3 in.	None	None	Pullman	2-27-29
M 9766	Peoria-DesMoines, Iowa	A-G	75 ft. 0 in.	15 ft. 0 in.	43 ft. 3 in.	None	None	Pullman	2-27-29
M 9767	Lincoln-Sioux City-O'Neill, Neb. ...	A-G	75 ft. 0 in.	15 ft. 0 in.	43 ft. 3 in.	None	None	Pullman	11- 3-30
M 9768	Lincoln-Sioux City-O'Neill, Neb. ...	A-G	75 ft. 0 in.	15 ft. 0 in.	43 ft. 3 in.	None	None	Pullman	11- 4-30
M 9769	Peoria-Quincy, Ill.	A-G	75 ft. 0 in.	15 ft. 0 in.	43 ft. 3 in.	None	None	Pullman	10-29-30
M 9770	Wymore-Omaha, Neb.	A-W	75 ft. 0 in.	15 ft. 0 in.	43 ft. 3 in.	None	None	Pullman	10-28-30
C. & S. 401	Cheyenne-Wendover, Wyo.	A-G	75 ft. 0 in.	15 ft. 0 in.	22 ft. 7 in.	27	None	Pullman	28
C. & S. 402	Fort Collins-Denver, Colo.	A-G	75 ft. 0 in.	None	50 ft. 2 in.	None	None	Pullman	29
W. V. 20	Stamford-Wichita Falls, Tex.	A-G	75 ft. 0 in.	15 ft. 0 in.	14 ft. 0 in.	None	None	Pullman	30

A—8 cylinder, Model 148 Electro-Motive power plant—400 hp.
B—6 cylinder, Model 120 Electro-Motive power plant—275 hp.
C—6 cylinder, Brill-Westinghouse power plant—250 hp.
D—6 cylinder, Model 106 Electro-Motive power plant—225 hp.
E—Mack Dual power plant, Model AQ—120 hp. each.
W—Westinghouse electrical equipment.
G—General Electric electrical equipment.
X—Double-end control.
M—Main line operation.
*—Converted into gas-electric at Havelock shops and placed in service November 1929.

Chapter 4
THE WAY OF THE ZEPHYRS

The Original Zephyr

The largest fleet of "named" streamliners in the United States was the Burlington Routes' famed Zephyrs. The highly successful trains competed with the equally famous Eagles, Chiefs, Hiawathas and 400's on almost every route. The Zephyr fleet covered every major line of the CB&Q except to and from Montana. The trains can lay claim to being world famous and people form other parts of the USA often traveled to "Zephyr" land just to ride the shovel nose speedsters. No where else in the world could one find and/or ride such a fine fleet.

The Zephyrs had their origins with the loss of passenger traffic. Ralph Budd reported in early 1934 that only 20% as much local rail traffic was performed in 1933 as in 1920, and that despite the drop in rail traffic, the total passenger miles for all forms of transportation had actually increased. It was this condition that led the Burlington to collaborate with the Edward G. Budd Manufacturing Company and General Motors in the development of a high speed streamliner that would reduce costs and attract passengers back to the rails.

The train, powered by a General Motors diesel, rolled out of the Budd Company's plant in the spring of 1934. The train consisted of three car bodies mounted on four trucks. She carried seats for 72 passengers in the second and third cars, while the first car contained the motor, a 30 foot mail compartment and a baggage section. The motor was a 600 horsepower Winton diesel electric power plant designed for speeds of approximately 110 miles per hour

The passenger accommodations were divided among three sections. At the rear of the second car (combination type) was a 16 foot smoking compartment with 20 seats. At the front of the third car was a compartment for 40 passengers, and at the rear was a solarium lounge with 12 chairs. Side doors and steps were provided for passengers in the two rear cars. In the second car, the entrance was between the smoking compartment and the buffet adjoining the baggage compartment. In the rear car, the entrance was at the rear of the main passenger compartment.

The interior decorations were all finished in the pastel shades used on the smooth wall surfaces without striping. The only ornamentation consisted of the polished stainless steel bands above the windows and along the ceilings at the open side of each lighting duct and the stainless steel window sills. The smoking compartment had walls finished in pastel rose with golden rose window drapes. The seats were upholstered in leather medium brown in color. The floor was covered with Linotile with a dark mottled surface neutral in tone. The lavatory and buffet floors were covered with linoleum to harmonize with the Linotile.

The walls of the main passenger compartment were finished in a warm gray with a hint of green. The seats were upholstered with Chase Velmo low-pile mohair. The color was gray-green with a gold background, the pile woven to form a striped pattern. The silk window drapes in this section were covered with a plain taupe Chase Seamloc carpet. The lounge walls were finished in gray, in this case with a suggestion of purple-blue. The furnishings consisted of lounge chairs and tables. The frames were scratchbrushed aluminum and the upholstery was a purpleblue with gold background. The window drapes were gold and the carpet a plan platinum-gray Chase Seamloc. The ceilings were finished in a light cream. The outside surfaces of the window shades had an aluminum finish to match the unpainted stainless steel exterior of the train. All lighting was indirect with the lights being concealed in longitudinal ducts below the ceiling along each side of the car. The exterior of the conduit was blended into the surface of the ceiling by smooth flowing curves.

The seats in the smoking and coach sections were built on alumnium frames, with the backs being adjustable to a semi-reclining position. They were built with an 18 inch clear space underneath for the stowing of hand baggage. Facilities for holding overcoats and hats were provided by a metal rod and spring clip fastened to the backs of each of the paired chairs.

The buffet was equipped to supply grill service and to serve ice cream and both hot and cold drinks. Food and beverage service could be provided at either the counter or at the seats in the coach sections. Removable trays, which could be bracketed between the seats, served as dining tables.

The Burlington Route became more famous because of the Zephyrs than for any other reason. It is interesting to note that the streamliners almost were named for a kind of beer, when the last word in the dictionary, "zythum," was nominated to describe the last word in trains in 1934. However, Ralph Budd happened to be reading Chaucer's Canterbury Tales and came across the word "zephyrous." It appealed to him and the pioneer streamliner was christened in the name of the gentle west wind, which began a tradition that continues today with Amtrak Zephyrs. (Burlington Northern)

The Pioneer Zephyr originally consisted of three units, and was the prelude to bigger and greater Zephyrs. (Burlington Northern)

This little 3 car Zephyr, numbered 9900, was eventually named the Pioneer Zephyr. After a nine week tour of eastern and western states, the Zephyr ran a spectacular 13 hours, 5 minute sprint from Denver to Chicago on May 26, 1934 to signal the re-opening of the Century of Progress in Chicago. The train spent but one day at the Fair, and then traveled west for additional tours including a stint for a movie (the Zephyr is renamed the Silver Streak) and to open the Dotsero Cutoff in Colorado for the Denver & Rio Grande Western Railroad. Altogether over 2 million people viewed the Zephyr in over 200 cities throughout the USA.

On November 11, 1934, the Zephyr went into service between Lincoln and Omaha, Nebraska and Kansas City, Missouri. There was an immediate increase in business. During the first 30 days of operation, the schedule was maintained except for four days westbound into Lincoln due to slight delays caused by meets with other trains, and on one occasion when the Zephyr was struck by a truck. Between Omaha and Lincoln patronage increased 111% as compared with the traffic on steam trains in October, 1934. Southbound out of Omaha and Council Bluffs, the train carried an average of 49 passengers per trip as compared with 26 on steam trains on October, an increase of 88%. Southbound into Kansas City, the average passenger count was 60 compared to 35 the previous month. Northbound out of Kansas City averaged 57 per trip compared to

31, while the average count into Council Bluffs and Omaha was 49 per trip compared to 21 during October. The latter was an increase of 135%. Not only was there an increase in the number of passengers carried, but the distance traveled increased too. The number of passengers carried one mile averaged 29 on the Zephyr with a previous figure of 25 on steam trains.

Several times during the first two months of operation the number of seats were inadequate. For example, on November 28, 99 passengers were on board at one time. Often a steam train had to supplement the Zephyr service, and from December 7, 1934 through the Christmas-New Years Holidays, a steam train ran daily supplementing the Zephyr's limited capacity.

As passengers presented their tickets to the conductor during the first few weeks, the conductor would ask, "Are you riding this train because it is the Zephyr or would you be making the trip at this particular time if this were an ordinary steam train instead of the Zephyr?" (P. 837, Railway Age, Vol. 95, No. 25, December, 1934) During the 25 day period November 16 to December 10, 1934, 58% of the passengers replied that they would have used a steam train, 17% would have used some other train except for the Zephyr, 13% would have used an automobile, bus or airplane and 12% would not have been making the trip at all and were merely riding the Zephyr out of curiosity.

Coach seating on the Pioneer Zephyr was among the best that could be found on any type of coach during the mid-1930's. (Burlington Northern)

As 1934 turned to 1935, the Zephyr began to do its stuff for which it was intended. The average cost per mile was 4.22 cents per mile as compared to 5.08 cents for steam for general maintenance. The overall total costs were 34.21 cents per mile for the Zephyr as compared to 63.75 cents for steam. The fuel costs were 28% of the steam costs. The objective of lowering costs and at the same time attracting passengers was being accomplished.

The original schedule saw the Zephyr depart Lincoln at 7:30 AM each morning making the 55 mile run to Omaha in 55 minutes arriving at Omaha at 8:25 AM. The steam train that was replaced had departed Lincoln at 6:55 AM and arrived in Omaha at 8:10. The Zephyr laid over at Omaha for 35 minutes and departed Omaha for Kansas City at 9:00 AM, arriving there at 1:00 PM, taking 240 minutes for the 195 mile run, including among others, a station stop of six minutes at St. Joseph, Missouri. The schedule shaved 80 minutes off the former steam schedule. Returning the Zephyr departed Kansas City at 2:30 PM and arrived at Omaha at 6:30. She departed Omaha 30 minutes later arriving at Lincoln at 7:55 PM.

The original Zephyr's route between Lincoln and Kansas City was (and is) 84% tangent or straight track with a maximum curvature of three degrees. Of the 250 miles of line over which the Pioneer Zephyr operated, 105.1 miles were double track in 1935. Between Kansas City and Omaha the line lies in the Missouri River Valley and there are few grades. Between Omaha and Lincoln there are a number of short grades of 1.25% in both directions.

The Pioneer Zephyr led a varied and wide spread career, and one might say it is still in service in a historical sort of way. Because of the increase in traffic, a fourth car was added in 1935 which increased the capacity of articulated train from 72 to 112. In 1938, the Pioneer was assigned to the St. Louis-Kansas City run as the Ozark State Zephyr. Four years later she operated between Lincoln and McCook, Nebraska. In 1949 she ran on the Colorado & Southern Railway between Denver and Cheyenne, but lasted only about 1 year for she returned to the lines east and operated between Galesburg and Quincy from 1950 to 1953. In that year she was re-assigned as a connection to Kansas City Zephyr between Brookfield and St. Joseph. Her final assignment came in 1957 between St. Joseph and Lincoln. In 1960 she was donated to the Museum of Science and Industry in Chicago, where one can visit and board the streamliner and dream of her famous exploits over the rails. To this writer, it is a bit sad that she cannot run on historical tours, such as many steam locomotives older than the Pioneer and not nearly as famous are still doing in 1975. However, one must be satisfied that the train did not go to the scrap line as this particular train is highly significant in the history of railroading.

Tables could be set up in the four seat sections for serving meals. This photo shows a table setting for two on the Pioneer. (Burlington Northern)

The buffet grill was equipped to serve hot and cold meals as well as beverages of one's choice. (Burlington Northern)

The interior of the Pioneer observation room contained seats facing inward, which was not the most conducive for looking out the windows to view the passing scenery. The window drapes were placed in such a way as to create the illusion that the entire room had a complete wrap around glass window. (Burlington Northern)

This photo shows the Pioneer Zephyr after the fourth car had been added. The train is zipping along at high speed along the Missouri River, just north of St. Joseph, Missouri in 1935. (Burlington Northern)

The First Twin Zephyrs

It could be said that there was no other territory so hotly contested as the Chicago-Minneapolis runs of the Burlington, Milwaukee Road and Chicago & North Western. Nowhere else in the USA did the rail traveler have such a variety of top-notch trains to choose from as he did between the Twin Cities and Windy City. The Pioneer Zephyr started a trend, and the CB&Q placed into service a pair of streamliners, numbered 9901 and 9902 and named the Twin Zephyrs, on April 21, 1935—just a few short months after the first Zephyr went into service.

The Twins began a daily one way trip operation running the 431 miles between Chicago and St. Paul in 390 minutes of 6½ hours. The original schedule called for one departure from Chicago at 2:00 PM, arriving at St. Paul at 8:30 PM and Minneapolis at 9:00 PM. Southbound the Twin departed Minneapolis at 12:01 PM and St. Paul at 12:30 PM arriving in Chicago at 7:00 PM. The original schedule paused for crew changes at Savanna, Illinois and North LaCrosse, Wisconsin, at an average speed of 66.3 miles per hour and a top speed of 90 miles per hour. The average occupancy was over 97% during those first few weeks, and the CB&Q took a second look at the operation. The result was that on June 2, 1935, the trains went into a double daily operation with each Twin making a round trip, or 882 miles per day per train. The Twins were also netting over 73¢ per mile for their owners. However

before we get too far ahead of ourselves on the Twins' operations, let's take a look at some of the events before they went into service, and also the type of trains that they were.

The first three car Zephyr Twin (9901) came out of the erecting shops in early 1935. On March 23rd, the 9901 carried 88 passengers from the Budd Company plant in Philadelphia for a trip over the Seaboard Air Line to points in Florida visiting such places as Washington, D.C., Fredericksburg, Virginia; Richmond, Raleigh, N. C., Columbia, S. C., Savannah, Ga., Jacksonville, Fla., Ocala, Winter Haven, Sepbring, West Palm Beach, Miami, Tampa, St. Petersburg and Sarasota. This trip was completed on April 2 at which time a total of 136,237 people had passed through the train at the several stops made for public inspection. The next step was test runs on the CB&Q.

On April 6th, the 9901 set a record by covering the 431 miles between Chicago and St. Paul in 5 hours, 33 minutes for an average speed of 77.7 miles per hour. The trial run was to test the train and track before beginning service. The train left Chicago at 8:10 AM and arrived in St. Paul at 1:43 PM. The top speed was 104 miles per hour with a fuel performance of 2.6 miles per gallon. The train immediately turned and returned to Chicago, arriving there at 8:12 PM, just 12 hours and 2 minutes after its original departure. Between April 8th and the 14th,

The original Twin Cities Zephyrs of 1935 pose together in the Chicago Union Station. What dynamic looking trains. They appear to be running at high speed even standing still deep in the Union Station. The trains were together for the pre-revenue service celebrations. (Burlington Northern)

the 9901 toured several cities on the CB&Q arriving back in Aurora, Illinois, on the 14th to be reunited with its Twin. The next publicity event was a masterpiece of public relations.

Forty-four sets of human twins participated in the reunion of the two trains at Aurora on April 14th. These twins were selected by the Burlington from territory along its lines and ranged in age from 3 to 73 years. These twins boarded 9902 at Chicago at 10:55 AM on April 14th and arrived at Aurora at the same time the 9901 was arriving from Kansas City. After reunion ceremonies, one of each pair of twins was assigned to each of the trains and the two trains traveled abreast of each other on the three track line from Aurora to Chicago.

The christening of the Twin Zephyrs took place at Chicago on April 15th, when Marion and Frances Beeler, twin sisters, each simultaneously broke a bottle of champagne on each train. Following the ceremonies, the trains started on a non-stop run to the Twin Cities carrying 120 members of the Chicago Association of Commerce. Both trains departed Chicago at 7:30 AM and arrived in St. Paul at 1:15 PM and 1:36 PM. Upon arrival there was a luncheon at the Minnesota Club. At 4:00 PM the group boarded the trains for the return trip to Chicago arriving there at 10:09 PM. Again, the Twins demonstrated the capability of traveling the entire distance from Chicago to Minneapolis and return in the same day, and the stage was set for the

eventual "Twin" service daily. On April 16th the trains were exhibited at the Union Station in Chicago. On the following day, both trains were placed in revenue service to carry excursionists from Chicago to Aurora and transported 1,144 people. On April 18 both trains were exhibited at the Great Northern station in Minneapolis and on the next day at the Union Stateion in St. Paul. On April 20, train 9902 returned to Chicago and on April 21st, both trains began their daily runs in regular service, a service that was to last until Amtrak day on May 1, 1971.

Except for floor plans and various other details, the Twin Zephyrs were replicas of the Zephyr 9900. The three car trains had a capacity of 88 passengers as compared to 72 with the first train. The first car of each train contained the engine room and a 28 foot baggage compartment. The second car contained a kitchen, a lunch counter and seating for 40 passengers. The third car contained 24 coach seats and 24 parlor car seats. Throughout the train large storage closets were provided for hand baggage, packages and service equipment in addition to the usual baggage racks over the seats.

Interior decorations were carried out with the same luxuriousness as on the original Zephyr. The color scheme was plain but distinctive pastel shades of green, blue and grey, blending harmoniously with the drapery, upholstery and carpets and relieved only by continuous bands of stainless steel moldings

42

At 100 miles per hour, passengers could enjoy lunch at their seats in the new Twin Zephyrs. Tables could be set up in the coach section, as with the Pioneer, for the passengers use. The streamlined interior of the original Twins included baggage racks, indirect lighting, drapes, carpeting and comfortable upholstered seats.(Burlington Northern)

above and below the windows. Reflected light from tubular ducts in the ceiling provided diffused illumination of suitable intensity at eye level.

The kitchen facilities on the Twins was much more extensive than on the first Zephyr. The new kitchen and pantry was designed to provide continuous buffet or dinner service for a 10 hour period. The pantry contained two ice boxes, a crushed ice compartment with cooling coils for a drinking fountain above and cold compartment for ice cream, cream and milk. The kitchen was equipped with a range, steam tables, warming closet, coal bin, a large refrigerator, ice boxes for fish and crushed ice, an emergency sink with table top and a cabinet provided with the latest four unit coffee urn designed for railroad safety service. A cutting board and serving table were provided at the door between the pantry and the kitchen. An air curtain at this opening protected the pantry from the heat, odors and gases which originated in the kitchen. Overhead storage and linen lockers were provided in all three compartments. The kitchen annex was located beyond the car connection in the baggage-locomotive car. This area contained the storage lockers and garbage cans.

Communication was provided between each seat in the train and the pantry-kitchen by an annunciator. The pantry could provide counter service for four passengers at one time, while 16 passengers could be served in the dinette (across the vestibule

from the pantry) on the removable Formica tables. Individual trays could be attached to all reclining seats in the coach compartments and to the arms of lounge (parlor) chairs in the observation section. Where opposed seats occurred at the bulkheads in the 24 passenger compartment, removable section tables could be set up if desired.

The twice daily service of 9901 and 9902 departed Chicago and Minneapolis at 8:00 AM and arrived at their final terminals at 3:00 PM. The afternoon Zephyrs departed at 4:00 PM and arrived at their final terminals 10:59 PM, one minute faster than the morning trains.

The original Twin Zephyrs were later replaced by 7 car trains on December 18, 1936. These trains will be covered later in this chapter. 9901 went into service as the Sam Houston Zephyr between Fort Worth and Houston on the Fort Worth & Denver Railway. Unfortunately, the train was destroyed by fire in December, 1944. Train 9902 went into service as the Ozark State Zephyr in 1936 but was re-assigned to the Texas Rocket in 1938. The war interrupted much progress on the CB&Q, and the 9902 was assigned to a train simply called "Zephyr 9902" between Chicago and Ottumwa, Iowa, in 1945. Two years later the train was re-scheduled to operate between Chicago and Hannibal, Missouri. She continued in this service until discontinued in 1954. This ended the careers of the original Twin Zephyrs, 9901 and 9902, that began in 1935.

The Mark Twain Zephyr poses for the Burlington photographer at the West Quincy depot on January 4, 1955. (Burlington Northern)

The Mark Twain Zephyr

It was Columbus Day in 1935 when the fourth Zephyr was delivered to the CB&Q. On that day, the Mark Twain Zephyr arrived in Chicago and began a series of exhibition runs during the next few days. On October 25th, the 9903 was formally christened at Hannibal, Missouri with appropriate ceremonies. She began service between St. Louis, Missouri and Burlington, Iowa on October 28th.

Before going into service, the 9903 was operated in a series of test runs just as the 9900, 9901 and 9902 had been before it. It had been an exciting year since the 9900 hit the rails. Speed was the key note, and the 9903 zipped along at 122 miles per hour for a distance of three miles between McCook, Nebraska and Oxford. The test run was made over a new right-of-way which had replaced a considerable stretch of track washed away by floods of the Republican River in May of 1935. The new track was built to the highest possible standards and was capable of carrying trains at speeds up to 150 miles per hour.

The Mark Twain Zephyr was a four car train, but for the speed tests the baggage car was removed from the train. The Electro-Motive 600 horsepower diesel electric power plant was furnishing power for a three car train weighing about 240,000 pounds. The record speed was made on a stretch of straight track eastbound on a downgrade varying between .10 and .30 per cent. The following chart shows the speed of the test run:

—Speed Record of Mark Twain—Railway
   Age, p. 564, Nov. 2, 1935

Speed Record of the "Mark Twain" between McCook, Nebr., and Oxford

	Time, central standard	Miles from previous station	Average speed, miles per hour
Left McCook, Nebr.	1:07:30 p.m.		
Passed Red Willow	1:13:05 p.m.	6.39	68.7
Passed Indianola	1:16:34 p.m.	4.34	76.9
Passed Bartley	1:21:14 p.m.	5.92	76.1
Passed Cambridge	1:27:07 p.m.	7.81	79.7
Passed Holbrook	1:34:07 p.m.	8.31	71.3
Passed Arapahoe	1:38:22 p.m.	5.68	80.2
Passed Edison	1:42:24 p.m.	6.78	100.1
Arrived Oxford	1:46:30 p.m.	7.8	114.0*

44

*Maximum speed attained for a distance of three miles between Edison and Oxford, 122 m.p.h.

The four car train rolled on five trucks, was approximately 280 feet long and weighed about 287,000 pounds when supplied with fuel, water and sand ready for operation. The seating capacity was 92 passengers.

The combination power car contained a 30 foot convertible railway post office and a 15 foot compartment for storage mail. The second car was a 64 foot baggage car. The third car included a kitchen compartment for dining car service, a 16 passenger dinette section and a 20 passenger coach section with men's and women's lavatories. The fourth car contained a 40 passenger coach compartment, toilet accommodations for men and women, luggage and equipment locker space and a 16 passenger lounge compartment. Overhead racks extended throughout all the coach sections. The interior decor was similar to the Twin Zephyrs.

The Mark Twain Zephyr operated on the St. Louis-Burlington run for its entire career, with a few exceptions. The Mark Twain Zephyr was discontinued in the mid-1950's, although a train schedule without a name continued to operate until 1958. The 9903 was eventually retired and is now on display in the town park at Mount Pleasant, Iowa.

The Zephyrs in Early 1936

The CB&Q did not simply put the trains into operation and let them operate themselves. They continuously evaluated their performance, while the rest of the railroad industry watched and often considered the entire investment a waste. An analysis published by Ralph Budd in April, 1936 in Railway Age magazine revealed high performance all the way across the board.

For example, the Twin City Zephyrs ran from 90 to 95 miles per hour, with the average speed for the 431 Chicago-St. Paul segment being 66.3 miles per hour including six stops.

The Lincoln-Omaha-Kansas City run averaged 50 to 60 miles per hour with the highest speed being 80 mph. The Mark Twain Zephyr ran with a top speed of 80 miles per hour with an average of 40 miles per hour because of 60 stops on its 442 mile round trip. All Zephyr runs were making their schedules over 94% of the time, and their availability for service averaged 97%.

The CB&Q was also conscious of the accident potential with the high speeds, and many were concerned that there would not be adequate front end protection for the enginemen. However, it is interesting to note that the shovel nose lower section and the rounded, sloping contour above tended to lift obstacles and throw them into the clear. No damage was done to the Zephyrs in any of the highway crossing accidents beyong scratching and denting, with the exception of a gasoline truck accident in December, 1944 which destroyed the 9901 by fire. The Zephyrs also proved to be excellent snow plows.

Patronage exceeded expectations and the fixed consist of the Zephyrs presented a problem. For

The Mark Twain Zephyr also included an observation room with the chairs facing inward, and a serving table at the extreme end of the car. (Burlington Northern)

example, in July and August, 1935, over 5000 passengers could not be accommodated on the Zephyrs. Therefore this type of data influenced the CB&Q to expand the Zephyr fleet, and to build bigger trains. The cost of Zephyr operations amounted to 31¢ per train mile as compared to 69¢ per train mile for steam trains with a similar capacity and speed. The safety factors of the Zephyrs matched or exceeded that of steam trains.

Overall the experience pointed to the future expansion of the Zephyr fleet and the decisions were made in late 1935 and early 1936 to expand the fleet substantially. One of these decisions was the operation of the Advance Denver Zephyrs.

The Denver Zephyrs were on order, but the CB&Q had several reasons for beginning the new service sooner than originally anticipated. So on May 31, 1936, the Mark Twain Zephyr and Pioneer Zephyr were transferred from their runs (previously described) and placed in a 16 hour daily operation between Chicago and Denver. The move was designed to capitalize on summer business and to protect the Chicago-Denver mail contract. The time table provided for a 5:30 PM departure from Chicago with arrival in Denver at 8:30 AM the next morning, 1034 miles at an average speed of 64.63 miles per hour. Departure from Denver was at 4:00 PM with a 9:00 AM arrival in Chicago. Features of the trains included free pillow service, economy meals, reserved seats at no extra cost and a hostess.

The schedules of the Zephyrs were protected by steam trains. The Lincoln-Kansas City run remained on the same schedule, while 15 minutes were added to the Mark Twain's daily round trip between St. Louis and Burlington.

Business on the Advance Denver Zephyrs was 100% of capacity with 70 to 75% being through travel. The trains operated consistently on time, and attracted many people to track side to see the trains speed through. As many as 200 people came to see

The finest of all the pre-vista dome Zephyrs was the 1936 Denver Zephyr. The ultra-modern beauty offered coach, parlor and sleeping car accommodations all on the same train, and one of the fastest rides in the country on one of the longest runs for an overnight—every night—trip. (Burlington Northern)

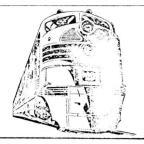

the Zephyrs each day at such stations as Burlington and Galesburg. And one can be sure that these were not all rail-fans. The operation of the Advance Denver Zephyr set the stage for the largest and most luxurious Zephyrs to ride the rails yet, the Denver Zephyrs.

The First Denver Zephyr

The first Zephyr to carry sleeping cars were delivered to the CB&Q in October, 1936 for service on a fast overnight run between Chicago and Denver. Appropriately named, the Denver Zephyrs, trains 9906 and 9907, were placed in service on November 7, 1936 on a 16 hour schedule between Lake Michigan and the Colorado Rockies. Each train consisted of two diesel units, a baggage-mail car with auxiliary power, baggage-dormitory lounge, 2 coaches, diner, 3 twelve section sleepers, 1 six bedroom, three compartment, one drawing room sleeper and an observation parlor car. Six of these cars were used in a test run from Chicago to Denver on October 23rd with a new record of 12 hours, 12 minutes and 27 seconds. To this writer's knowledge, this record still stands.

Each train, as originally constructed, provided 102 coach seats and 93 sleeping car berths, 10 parlor car seats. In addition, there were 104 lounge and dining car seats with 31 additional seats in the men's and women's dressing rooms. Crew quarters were provided ahead of the cocktail lounge with bunks for 12 people. Behind the locomotive, each train consisted of six independent cars, some of which were single body units while others were two and three car or unit articulated vehicles. The first car was a single unit with the auxiliary power unit which supplied 220 volt, 60 cycle, three phase current for operation of lights, bar refrigeration and air-conditioning

equipment. Back of the power unit compartment was a 30 foot railway post office and a 24 foot baggage unit. The second car was an independent unit with a 23 foot baggage space and dormitory for the dining car crew including a shower room and lockers. The same car included a quarter circle bar, cocktail lounge and cocktail lounge annex. The bar had a mahogany top and was faced in mulberry. Back of it was a peach colored etched edge-lighted mirror with metal trim. The refrigerators were faced with stainless steel in harmony with the balance of the metal trim of the bar. The lounge proper was furnished with six fixed tables, two fixed curved sofas and 10 movable small chairs, the sofas and chairs being upholstered in dark tan leather. The cocktail annex was separated from the lounge by an ornamental aluminum grille and contained accommodations for 16 passengers at tables between transverse leather upholstered seats. Lighting was furnished by indirect lights mounted in a pair of overhead ducts. The interior walls were painted mulberry below the belt rail to match the face of the bar and were covered with quartered oak paneling between the belt rail and the upper window rail. The area above the upper window rail and ceiling was painted buff. Venetian blinds at the windows were painted green on the inside and silver on the outside. The floor was covered with a light brown linoleum.

The third body was a semi-articulated coach seating 64 passengers with a vestibule at the forward end. The seats were of the rotating type with three position reclining backs and removable center arm rests. They were upholstered in a cheerful bluish green striped plush and were provided with ash trays built into the back accessible to the person behind. Provision was made for setting tables

The Denver Zephyr was the biggest of the articulated streamliners placed in service by the Burlington. The eastbound DZ is shown here prior to departure from Denver in July, 1943. (Harold K. Vollrath Collection)

The observation car on the DZ was the finest of any placed in service by 1936. The soft chair seating and the eye catching upholstery invited passengers to ride the DZ again and again. (Burlington Northern)

The head-end lounge car on the DZ offered snacks, light meals and one's favorite beverage between Chicago and Denver. The car was similar in many respects to the lead car on the second Twin Cities Zephyrs. (Burlington Northern)

between pairs of seats. Drapes were light olive green, roller curtains were sea green and the carpeting was taupe. At the forward end of the car just behind the vestibule were the ladies'·and men's rooms and at the rear were two luggage lockers. Lower walls at the ends of the car and the pier panels were gray-green while the upper walls and ceiling were cream.

The fourth body unit was a fully articulated coach seating 38 passengers. The seats were upholstered in henna with a two tone striped pattern. The drapes were a golden tan with the lower walls rust, the upper walls and ceiling flesh color and the floor carpeted in mahogany. Between the forward end of the car and the entrance doors were two men's rooms, one a lavatory room and the other a toilet room. At the rear of the car was a luxuriously furnished ladies' lounge and annex. The lounge contained leather upholstered chairs and sofa, dressing tables, mirrors, wall clock, dental fountain and three blue porcelain wash stands.

The fifth unit was a semi-articulated 40 passenger diner with a 23 foot kitchen. Back of the kitchen were fruit refrigerators on the one side and a pair of lockers on the other, one for bread, glassware, etc., and the other for equipment. At the rear of the car was the steward's compartment, in which the linen locker, steward's locker, a bottle refrigerator, a buffet and the steward's desk were located. The desk was furnished with a telephone with which he could communicate with the bar at the forward end of the train as well as the buffet in the rear car. The chairs had comfortable leather upholstery with four seats at each table.

The sixth and seventh units were an articulated pair of section sleepers, each of which contained 12 sections with a men's room at the forward end and a ladies' room at the rear end. The seats in one of the cars was upholstered in a dark brown with a light tan figure design. The lower and end walls were in greenish gray-blue and the section partitions and ceiling were drab. Section curtains were brown as was the carpet. The roller curtains on the windows were chocolate. In the other car, the walls and ends were in dark brown and the ceiling and section partitions a bluish tint. The seat were upholstered in blue with tan stripes and the section curtains were in Copenhagen blue. The roller curtains were chocolate and the carpet brown. The berths were 1½ inches longer and slightly wider than those on conventional trains of the period. There were also four "tall men" berths which measured 6 feet, 8 inches long. Wide windows offered an unobstructed view to the passengers. At each lower berth seat adjacent was placed a small mirror. An air conditioning outlet was placed at the foot of each lower berth and was exposed only when the berth was made up. The air conditioning outlet for the upper berth was placed at the side of the overhead duct. These outlets were furnished with a shutter control.

The eighth and ninth body units constituted another two unit articulated car, the forward one being a 12 section sleeper and the other containing 1 drawing room, 3 compartments and 6 bedrooms. The section sleeper was decorated with walls of dark green-blue, and the ceiling and section partitions in robin's egg blue. Seats were upholstered in taupe with a dark brown checkered plaid. Section curtains were Copenhagen blue, the carpet brown and the window roller curtains chocolate.

In the room car, each room had an individual decorative treatment in which Flexwood was used freely with carefully selected upholstery and drapes. Each room had a small illuminated clock and was fitted for a portable radio which could be obtained from the porter. Another feature was an electric outlet for electric razors, curling irons and other electric appliances. There were similar outlets and clocks in all sleeper and coach wash rooms.

The tenth unit was a single car, a combination parlor and observation lounge car with a buffet placed mid-length. The front section contained 10 revolving parlor chairs upholstered in fawn. The lower walls were coconut brown, the upper walls were sand with an oyster white ceiling. The draperies were brilliant rose with white stripes and the roller curtains were fawn. At the end of the car adjoining the parlor section there was a toilet at either side. Behind the parlor section was an ebony writing desk with stainless steel legs and trim, and two card sections of four seats each. The lounge area contained 16 single seats and three 2 seat sofas upholstered in various colors and patterns. The walls and draperies were the same as in the parlor section. The buffet was mahogany with the top being stainless steel and glass. All body units including the motive power were named.

The motive power was made up of two diesel units, one an 1800 hp unit with the second being a 1200 hp unit plus the train heating boilers.

The Denver Zephyrs (9906 and 9907) were very popular trains. An additional sleeping car with 4 bedrooms, 1 compartment, 4 chambrettes and 4 roomettes was added to each train in 1939. The chambrettes and roomettes were new single occupancy rooms at that time. The chambrette was bigger than a roomette, and later became known as a single duplex room. They were the first cars on the Burlington to contain such accommodations, and at the same time not include the open sections.

The Denver Zephyrs continued to operate on the high speed schedule until October, 1956 when the second Denver Zephyrs went into service. At that time, the first Denver Zephyrs went to the Colorado & Southern Railway and Fort Worth & Denver Railway for Texas Zephyr service. The trains served in that capacity until 1967 when the TZ was discontinued.

As mentioned previously, the Denver Zephyrs were delivered to the CB&Q in November, 1936. The excitement of the super coach-sleeper streamliners did not even have a chance to die down when the Budd Company delivered in December, 1936, the second Twin Cities Zephyrs, which were bigger and better than the first Twins.

The diner and three coaches between the E-5's and the power-RPO-baggage car on train 1, indicate the Denver Zephyr has a tour group aboard as it departs from the Windy City on an August, 1949 Sunday afternoon. The stainless steel E units were a Burlington exclusive. (Jim Scribbins)

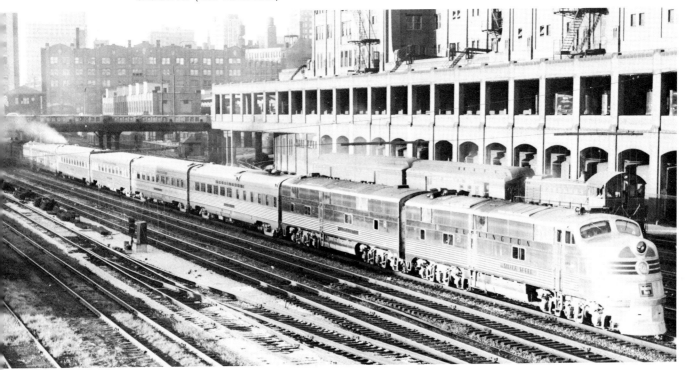

Table 5

No. 7	No. 3 Ak-Sar-Ben Note 2	No. 15 Fast Mail	*No. 1 Denver Zephyr	No. 17 California Zephyr •	No. 11 Nebraska Zephyr Note 2	No. 19 Colora-doan Note 1	Mls.	Central Standard Time	*No. 10 Denver Zephyr •	No. 18 California Zephyr •	No. 12 Nebraska Zephyr Note 2	No. 6 Colora-doan	No. 14	No. 30 Ak-Sar-Ben Note 2
AM	PM	PM	PM	PM	PM	AM			AM	PM	PM	PM	AM	AM
12.15	10.00	7.50	5.00	3 30	12 45	11.30	0	Lv Chicago Ar	9.05	1 30	8 45	9 30	7.00	8.00
1.11	10.48			h 4.06	h 1.21		38	Lv Aurora Ar	j	z12 44	g 7 57	8 35	6.10	7.11
	7.45	7.45	↓3.10	↓3.10	↓10.29	↓10.20		⊙ Lv Peoria Ar	↓12.40	↓9 25	↓9 25		7.15	7.15
4.45	1.00	10.35	7.09	5 59	3 05	2 00	162	Lv Galesburg Ar	6.46	10.53	5 55	5 30	3.35	5.00
6.25	1.50	11.32	7.51	6 35	3 55	2 47	206	Lv Burlington Lv	6.03	10.07	5 10	4.15	2.30	4.10
8.30	3.06	1.24	8.56	7 46	5 15	4 00	280	Ar Ottumwa Lv	4.53	8.55	3 55	2.05	12.43	2 50
12.05	5.20	4.35	10.44	9 45	7 13	6 24	393	Ar Creston Lv	3.05	6.58	2 03	11.40	9.30	12.35
2.58	b 7.15		v12.08			f 8 28	492	Ar Council Bluffs Lv			12 29			10.46
3 40	8.00	7.45	12.30	9 15	9 05	9 05	496	Ar Omaha Lv	1.15	5.00	12 15	9 25	6.30	10.30
4 30	8.30,	8.30	12.40	11 59	9 25	10.20	496	Lv Omaha Ar	1.10	4.55	11 59	8.55	5.45	10.05
5.40	9 55	9 55	1.45	1.04	10 30	11.20	551	Ar Lincoln Lv	12.11	3.55	11 00	7.45	4.30	9.00
6.00			1.52	1.19		12.03	648	Ar Hastings Lv	12.04	2.09		7.10	3.50	
8 30			3.23	2.49		1.52	779	Ar McCook (CT) Lv	10 41	12.14		5.20	1 00	
12.35			5.32	4.49		5.00	779	Lv McCook (MT) Lv	8 38	11.09		2.05		
11.55			4 35	3.55		4.15	956	Ar Ft. Morgan Lv	7.35			12.45	8.22	
4.35			7.13						a 5 07					
6 30			8.30	8.20		8.10	1034	Ar Denver Lv	4.00	7.15		8.45	6.50	
AM	AM	AM	AM	AM	PM	AM		Mountain Standard Time	PM	AM		PM	PM	PM

EQUIPMENT
(Regularly Assigned Cars Are Air-Conditioned)

CHICAGO-DENVER
THE DENVER ZEPHYR

Radio reception in Parlor Lounge, Diner, and Chair Car. Individual Radios in most rooms. Valet Service, Shower Bath, Buffet.

WESTBOUND—No. 1

	Car
Burlington Parlor Lounge	
Chicago to Denver	A
Standard Sleeping Cars	
Chicago to Denver	
1 D.R., 1 Compt., 4 D.B.R., 4 Chambrettes, 4 Roomettes	1
1 D.R., 3 Compt., 6 D.B.R.	2
12 Sections	3
12 Sections	4
12 Sections	5

Dining Car—Chicago to Denver
Cocktail Lounge—Chicago to Denver (For all passengers)
Reclining-Revolving Chair Coach
Chicago to Denver—3 cars 10-11-12 (Seats Reserved)

EASTBOUND—No. 10

	Car
Burlington Parlor Lounge	
Denver to Chicago	A
Standard Sleeping Cars	
Denver to Chicago	
1 D.R., 1 Compt., 4 D.B.R., 4 Chambrettes, 4 Roomettes	1
1 D.R., 3 Compt., 6 D.B.R.	2
12 Sections	3
12 Sections	4
12 Sections	5

Dining Car—Denver to Chicago
Cocktail Lounge—Denver to Chicago (For all passengers)
Reclining-Revolving Chair Coach
Denver to Chicago—3 cars 10-11-12 (Seats Reserved)

■ALL SPACE on the Denver Zephyrs — both COACH and PULLMAN—is RESERVED and SPECIFICALLY assigned in advance, reservations for trips under 300 miles not being made prior to date of departure. Coach seat reservation must be claimed at train gate at Chicago by 4.55 p.m. or at Denver by 3.55 p.m. Checked baggage is carried only for through movement between Chicago and Denver and not to or from intermediate points. No extra fare on any Burlington train.

CHICAGO-SAN FRANCISCO
CALIFORNIA ZEPHYR

WESTBOUND No. 17

	Car
Vista-Dome Observation-Lounge	
Chicago to San Francisco	
3 D.B.R., 1 D.R.	CZ-10
Standard Sleeping Cars	
Chicago to San Francisco	
16 Sections	CZ-12
10 Rmette., 6 D.B.R.	CZ-14-15
New York to San Francisco	
10 Rmette., 6 D.B.R. (Note 3)	CZ-11
Vista-Dome Buffet-Lounge	
Lounge for all passengers;	
Dome for sleeping car passengers	
Chicago to San Francisco	
Dining Car	
For all Meals	
Vista-Dome Chair Coaches	
Chicago to San Francisco	CZ-20-21-22

EASTBOUND No. 18

	Car
Vista-Dome Observation-Lounge	
San Francisco to Chicago	
3 D.B.R., 1 D.R.	CZ-10
Standard Sleeping Cars	
San Francisco to Chicago	
16 Sections	CZ-12
10 Rmette., 6 D.B.R.	CZ-14-15
San Francisco to New York	
10 Rmette., 6 D.B.R. (Note 3)	CZ-11
Vista-Dome Buffet-Lounge	
Lounge for all passengers;	
Dome for sleeping car passengers	
San Francisco to Chicago	
Dining Car	
For all Meals	
Vista-Dome Chair Coaches	
San Francisco to Chicago	CZ-20-21-22

●ALL SPACE on the California Zephyrs—both COACH and PULLMAN—is RESERVED and SPECIFICALLY assigned in advance, reservations for trips under 400 miles not being made prior to date of departure. Coach seat reservations westbound from Chicago must be claimed at train gate by 3.25 p.m. Dome seats are not reserved. Checked baggage is carried only for through movement between Chicago and Denver and not to or from intermediate points. Banana messenger, caretaker and circus tickets not honored. No extra fare on any Burlington train.

CHICAGO-DENVER
COLORADOAN

WESTBOUND No. 19

	Car
Burlington Dining-Parlor Car	
Chicago to Omaha	P-191
Sleeping Car	
Omaha to Denver	
12 Sec., D.R.	190
Chair Coach	
Chicago to Denver	

EASTBOUND—No. 6

	Car
Burlington Dining-Parlor Lounge	
Lincoln-Omaha to Chicago	P-6
Sleeping Car	
Denver to Omaha	
12 Sec., D.R.	60
Chair Coach	
Denver-Chicago	

WESTBOUND No. 7
Coach
Chicago to Denver

EASTBOUND No. 14
Coach
Denver to Chicago

CHICAGO-OMAHA-LINCOLN
NEBRASKA ZEPHYR

WESTBOUND—No. 11

	Car
Burlington Parlor Lounge	
Chicago to Omaha-Lincoln	
30 Seats and D.R.	P-11
Dining Car—For all meals	
Cocktail Lounge—Chicago to Omaha (For all passengers)	
Reclining Chair Coaches	
Chicago to Omaha-Lincoln	

EASTBOUND—No. 12

	Car
Burlington Parlor Lounge	
Lincoln-Omaha to Chicago	P-12
Dining Car—For all meals	
Cocktail Lounge—Omaha to Chicago (For all passengers)	
Reclining Chair Coaches	
Lincoln-Omaha to Chicago	

AK-SAR-BEN

WESTBOUND—No. 3

	Car
Lounge Sleeping Car	
Chicago to Lincoln	311
Sleeping Cars	
Chicago to Omaha-Lincoln	
1 D.R., 2 Compt.	311
2 S.B.R., 2 D.B.R.	312
14 Sections	314
10 Sec., 2 D.B.R., 1 Compt.	315
12 Sections, 1 D.R.	329
Chicago to Quincy	
(May be occupied at Quincy until 8.00 a.m.)	
Dining Car—For Breakfast	
Chair Coach—Chicago to Omaha-Lincoln	

EASTBOUND—No. 30

	Car
Lounge Sleeping Car	
Lincoln-Omaha to Chicago	301
(Lounge Seats Assigned)	
Sleeping Cars	
Lincoln and Omaha to Chicago	
1 D.R., 2 Compt.	301
2 S.B.R., 2 D.B.R.	301
14 Sections	302
10 Sec., 2 D.B.R., 1 Compt.	303
12 Rmet., 2 S.B.R., 3 D.B.R.	304
Dining Car—For Breakfast	
Chair Coach	
Lincoln and Omaha to Chicago	

FAST MAIL

WESTBOUND—No. 15
Chair Coach
Chicago to Omaha-Lincoln

EASTBOUND—No. 14
Coach
Lincoln-Omaha to Chicago

Note 1:—Checked baggage handled on No. 19 at Chicago and at Burlington and intermediate stops to Omaha and beyond.

Note 2:—No train baggageman. Checked baggage is carried only for through movement between Chicago-Omaha and points beyond, not to or from intermediate points.

Note 3:—New York-San Francisco sleeping car operates between New York and Chicago via New York Central one day and Pennsylvania the next.

REFERENCE NOTES:
‖ Meal stop. ⊙ Connection
♦ Burlington Trailways Bus leaves from and arrives at Union Bus Depot. C. B. & Q. rail tickets honored on these buses.
a Stops to receive revenue passengers for Lincoln or east when notified at Denver.
b Stops to let off revenue sleeping car passengers from Chicago.
f Flag stop.
g Stops to let off revenue passengers.
h Stops to receive revenue passengers for Omaha or beyond.
j Stops to let off revenue passengers from Denver.
v Stops to let off revenue passengers from Chicago.
z Stops to let off revenue passengers from west of Denver.

Time from 12.01 midnight to 12.00 noon is shown by LIGHT faced figures and time from 12.01 noon to 12.00 midnight by HEAVY faced figures.

The second Twin Cities Zephyrs were made up of seven cars plus the locomotive unit. These trains remained in service on the Twin Cities run until replaced by the vista dome Zephyrs after World War II, whereupon they were transferred to the Nebraska Zephyr run. The Twin Cities Zephyr is shown here at Westmont, Illinois on April 9, 1945. (Burlington Northern)

The Second Twin Zephyrs

The new Twin Zephyrs (9904 and 9905) were christened at 6:30 PM on December 17, when Governor Petersen of Minnesota in his office at the capitol in St. Paul closed a switch and set up a radio "tone beam," which co-incidentally released two suspended bottles of champagne, one in the Union Station at St. Paul and the other in the Great Northern station in Minneapolis.

The christening of the seven car Zephyrs, in which two pairs of sisters, one pair from Minneapolis and the other from St. Paul participated, marked the completion of a week of transportation activities in the Twin Cities. Prior to the christening celebration, on December 15th, a delegation of more than 100 industrial leaders from St. Paul and Minneapolis traveled non-stop to Chicago and return. This train left Minneapolis at 6:30 AM, St. Paul at 7:00 AM and upon arrival in Chicago were guests of the Chicago Association of Commerce at a luncheon at the Union League club. This journey to Chicago came as a courtesy visit in acknowledgement of the journey on the first Twin Zephyrs, to the Twin Cities in April, 1935 by a Chicago delegation. The reader should note the short time between the implementation of the first Twins in service and the beginning of the second Twins between Chicago and the Twin Cities.

The two new trains went into revenue service on December 18, 1936. Each of the trains consisted of an 1800 hp diesel electric locomotive and six fully articulated stainless steel passenger units built by the Budd Company. The two new trains replaced the former 3 car sets, which went into service as the Sam Houston Zephyr and the Ozark State Zephyr.

Each train consisted of a combination power-baggage-cocktail-lounge unit, two coach units, dining car, parlor car, and parlor observation car. There were 120 coach seats, 50 parlor car seats, 10 seats in the observation room and 32 dining room seats. There were an additional 32 seats in the cocktail lounge and anex of the first body unit.

The first unit was over 76 feet long and contained the train power and heating plants, a small baggage compartment and the cocktail lounge with bar. The baggage room also contained a storage area for a combination radio-phonograph, a storage locker for ice, beer and liquor and an equipment locker.

The remained of the car was devoted to the cocktail lounge and cocktail lounge annex, with an arrangement essentially the same as the Denver Zephyrs. The quarter circle bar in the forward left-hand corner had a genuine mahogany top and a painted front face to match the rust colored wainscoating of the car. Lounge accommodations consisted of two semi-circular sofas and ten tubular stainless steel frame movable chairs. The tables were black Formica tops mounted on aluminum pedestals.

Behind the cocktail lounge and separated from it by an ornamental aluminum grille was the cocktail lounge annex which included four facing pairs of double seats with a table. The seat upholstery in this car was Eagle-Ottawa handbuffed genuine leather, colonial-grain tan color. The flooring was evergreen linoleum. The wainscoting and the bar front were painted rust and the ceiling was painted in varying shades of peach with the lighter shades at the top and the more intense directly over the windows. The side walls, between the belt rail and the upper window rail, were finished in gray Harewood. The window sills were finished in black hardwood, the venetian blinds were painted with a greenish-gray color with rust colored tapes and operating cords. The window drapes were tan in color. All the metal trim in the car was of uniform tone and presented a

The second Twin Cities Zephyrs offered elegant dining in a spcaious dining car, which was a vast improvement over previous meal arrangements on the first TC Zephyrs. (Burlington Northern)

pleasing contrast against the painted and wood surfaces.

The first car was lit from overhead ducts, which furnished indirect lighting from concealed lamps, and by column lights in vertical fixtures on the pier panels and rear partitions which furnish diffused direct light. The bar proper was illuminated by concealed lights in an overhead cove.

The second car was a 64 foot coach and contained 60 seats. The seats contained ash trays and provision was also made for mounting tables between the facing pairs of seats at the forward end of the car. These tables were similar, though somewhat narrower, than those used in the cocktail annex of the first car. The seats were upholstered in a bluish-green striped pattern plush, with draperies in light olive green. The roller curtains were sea green and the carpet taupe. The wainstocting and the pier panels were painted a gray-green color while the upper walls and ceiling were shaded cream.

The third car was also a 60 seat coach and was essentially the same except that it was turned end for end. The seats were upholstered in henna with a two-tone striped pattern. The draperies were a golden tan. The lower walls were a rust color, the upper walls and ceiling a flesh color with the floor being covered with a mahogany carpet.

The fourth car was a dining car with the kitchen at the forward end. The kitchen was 23 feet long and similar to the Denver Zephyr kitchen. The dining room provided tables for 32 passengers at 8 tables. The chairs were of wood construction upholstered in colored leather. The color treatment varied in the dining cars of the two trains. In one car—Vulcan—the walls were blue-gray and the ceiling a light blue gray. The curtains were pearl gray. The other diner—Ceres—favored red and brown for its base colors. The lower walls were light chocolate with a shaded light gray-green color used on the upper walls and ceiling. The curtains were red, window sills black hardwood and the Venetian blinds were terra cotta on the inside and silver on the outside. The floor was covered with henna rust carpet and bordered in peach. The chairs were black matte finish upholstered with red morrocco leather.

The kitchen range was coal fired and contained a charcoal grill. A steam table was placed adjacent to

Success of the Twin Cities and Denver Zephyrs prompted the Q to streamline two 4-6-4's for either second section operation or to pinch hit during the rare diesel failures. No. 4000, Aeolus, was the first streamlining in 1937 and is refered to as the world's first stainless steel steam locomotive; and "Big Alice the Goon." (Bob Lorenz)

The Twin Cities Zephyr and "Aeolus" thunder down the main line side by side by West Hinsdale, Illinois. (Burlington Northern)

the range. There were refrigerators for ice cream, milk, meat, poultry and general provisions. There were sinks and large work tables. The rear of the diner was fitted with a steward's desk, a linen locker, a steward's locker and a bottle refrigerator. A telephone system provided communication between the steward's desk and the bar at the head-end, and the porter at the rear of the fifth car.

The fifth car was a parlor car with nineteen parlor car chairs. These were upholstered in a fawn colored material. The lower walls were painted in coconut brown, the upper walls in sand, and the ceiling finished in oyster white. The rear of the car contained a drawing room with two transverse seats and a longitudinal sofa upholstered with striped plush.

The sixth car was over 75 feet long and accommodated 24 rotating parlor car seats, six occasional chairs in the observation lounge and a card playing section with a table and a pair of double transverse seats. Upholstery was in fawn and brown.

The twin daily service in both directions was extremely popular, and the schedules were never

more than 7 hours between Chicago and Minneapolis, and were as fast as 6½ hours for the run. The popularity taxed the seating capacity so much that by the fall of 1938, the CB&Q added a diner-coach to each train. They were added just ahead of the dining car so that patrons in the dinette portion of the car could be served from the adjacent full length diner. This increased the diner capacity of the train from 32 to 48. The coach portion accommodated 40 passengers, thereby increasing the coach seating from 120 to 160. However, this was not enough. Parlor car business was not enough for two parlor cars, so in 1942 the 19 parlor car seats in the fifth car were replaced with 42 coach seats, increasing coach capacity to 202. The trains performed outstanding service, and when they were replaced by the third set of Twin Zephyrs in 1947, they went into service as the Nebraska Zephyrs between Chicago and Lincoln. The dining cars were converted to cafeteria cars in 1966, and they continued in service until February, 1968. The second Twin Zephyrs had contributed an outstanding service record for Burlington passengers.

The General Pershing Zephyr was the first non-articulated Zephyr and is shown here with its original consist. (Burlington Northern)

The General Pershing Zephyr

The ninth Zephyr to grace the Burlington Route rails made a radical departure from previous designs. This train was not articulated. The CB&Q experienced many problems with the inability to change the consist of the articulated trains to accommodate different passenger loads. The very popularity of the trains almost had a tendency to kill them when too many people were left standing on the platforms because of no room on board. Therefore General Pershing equipment was bult as individual units.

The locomotive was a combination 1000 hp unit with a baggage compartment at the rear of the car body. The same shovel nose graced the front end, which by April, 1939 (the time of delivery for the 9908) had become a Burlington trade mark. Indeed the nose graced the time tables for years before "E" units gradually replaced them on the very famous "Everywhere West" red passenger folders.

The three car train provided facilities for daylight runs with complete dining and lounge service and with coach seats for 122 passengers. The first coach contained seats for 70 passengers with a women's lounge at the front end and two men's toilets on opposite sides of the aisle at the rear. The second coach was slightly shorter and provided seats for 52 passengers with full men's and women's lounges, one at each end. Each coach had one vestibule at one end only.

The third car was the diner lounge observation car. the front contained a kitchen and pantry in a 13 foot length. The dining room was 19 feet long and served 24 passengers at 6 tables. The parlor lounge was 31 feet long and provided loose chairs for 22 passengers. The dining and parlor lounge areas were separated by the entrance vestibule. The color schemes were built around mountain brown in the first coach, nut pine in the second coach and flesh tinted light drab in the last car. The interior decor was kept simple, with just one color except for mahogany carpeting and draperies of sand color with horizontal tufted stripes of brown. The overall general scheme was suggestive of the tones of an autumn landscape.

The train entered service on April 30, 1939, between Kansas City and St. Louis. It operated trains Numbers 32 and 33 making a daily round trip of 558 miles. It originally departed Kansas City at 9:00 AM and arrived at St. Louis at 2:00 PM, leaving St. Louis at 3:00 PM and arriving back in KC at 8:00 PM. The running time of five hours covered a distance of 279 miles, including five regular stops and three conditional stops at an average speed of 55.8 miles per hour. The train seldom operated faster than 90 miles per hour, and was not considered the speedster its older sisters were. The train operated on the original route intended until 1942, when the war changed many operating assignments of passenger power and rolling stock. The train also operated a daily round trip between Lincoln and Kansas City later in 1939.

The last car of the GPZ was an observation parlor dining car, which provided a very cozy atmosphere for parlor car passengers. (Burlington Northern)

The dining room provided seating for 18 passengers, and it could be said that the last car of the General Pershing Zephyr was one of the most versatile cars found in the Zephyr fleet. (Burlington Northern)

The Silver Streak Zephyr with a heavy load, pauses at Dubuque, Iowa carrying green flags indicating a following section in March, 1940. (H. K. Vollrath Collection)

NORTHBOUND—READ DOWN | | | | | | | | SOUTHBOUND—READ UP

43 Daily	41 Daily	23 Daily	21 Daily	27 Daily	Mls.	Table No. 9	Mls.	20 Daily	26 Daily	22 Daily	44 Daily	42 Daily	
PM	AM	PM	PM	AM				PM	PM	AM	AM	PM	
f 6.30	9.00	k11 58	4.00	9.00	0	Lv...Kansas City, Mo., 3, 5 ...Ar	250	1.20	9.25	6.55	6.55	5.45	
	9.19	f		9.19	12	Missouri River Parkville	238			6 22	6.22	f 5.19	
		f			19	Waldron	231			f 6 12	f 6.12	f 5.10	
		f			23	Platte River Farley	227				f 6.04	f 6.04	f 5.05
		f			27	East Leavenworth	223					5.00	
7 12	9.44	f	4 38	9 44	29	Lv Beverly, Mo. Lv	221	12 36		b 5.55	b 5.55	4.55	
f7 35	f10.05		f 5 15	f10.05	35	Ar Leavenworth, Kan. Lv	227	f12 15				f 4 20	
f6 45	f 9 25		f 4 20	9 25	35	Lv Leavenworth, Kan. Ar	227	f12 55				f 5 15	
	9.49	f		9.49	33	Weston	217			5 50	5.50	4.45	
		f			39	Iatan	211					f 4 37	
7.35	10.07	f	4 55	10.07	46	Ar Armour Lv	204	12.16		5.32	5.32	4 30	
f7 55	f10.23		f 5 09	f10.23	50	Ar Atchison, Kan. Lv	210	f11 56		f 5 15	f 5.15	f 4 10	
f7.15	f 9 45		f 4 10	9 45	50	Lv Atchison, Kan. Ar	210	f12 30		f 5 50	f 5.50	f 5 09	
7.35	10.07		4 55	10.07	46	Lv Armour Ar	204	12.16		5.32	5.32	4 30	
		f			48	Rushville	202					f 4 18	
	10.22	f		10.22	53	Halls	197					f 4 12	
					61	South St. Joseph	189					4 03	
8 05	10.35	1.35	5 21	10.35	64	Ar St. Joseph Lv	186	11 53	7.50	4 55	4.55	3 50	
8 17	11.00	2.00	5.29	10.50	64	Lv 3, 6, 12 Ar	186	11.45	7.35	4.20	4.35	3 35	
		2.16			73	Amazonia, 44	177					3 17	
	f11.18	f 2.23			77	Nodaway	173			f 3.55			
	f11.26	f 2.32			84	Nodaway River Forbes	166			f 3.45		f 3 09	
	11.37	2.45			92	Forest City	158			f 3.30		2.59	
	11.45	2.57		e11 20	98	Ar Napier, 6 Lv	152			f 3.15		2.50	
		2.57		f11 27	98	Ar	152			f 3.15			
		3.03		11.36	102	Bigelow, 41, 42	148			3.03			
		3.15		11 47	110	Craig, 41	140		6.35	f 2.47			
		a 3.24		11 59	115	Corning, 41	135	10.48		f 2.39			
				f12.05	120	Nishnabotna	130			f 2.33			
		3.40	6.30	12.15	125	Langdon	125	10.35	6.15	f 2.27			
				f12 20	129	Phelps	121			f 2.19			
		a 3.56		12.31	134	Watson, Mo.	116			f 2.12			
		4.10	6.53	12 47	142	Nishnabotna River Hamburg, Ia., 51	108	10.14	5.50	2.00			
		4.30	c 7.01	1.00	150	Ar Payne, Ia. Lv	100	10.02	5.32	1.43			
				†1 20	156	Ar Nebraska City, Neb. Lv	106	f 9 49	5.05				
				†12.40	156	Nebraska City Ar	106	f10.20	5.55				
		4.30		1.00	150	Lv Payne, Ia. Ar	100	10.02	5.32	1 43			
				1.10	156	Percival	94			f 1.31			
		5.00		1.19	161	McPaul	89			f 1.24			
				1.26	166	Bartlett	84			f 1.19			
		5 30		1 40	175	Ar Pacific Junction, 1 Lv	75		4.56	1.07			
		5 55	7 48	2.13	191	Ar Council Bluffs, 1 Lv	59	9.14	4.33	12.25			
		6.10	8.10	2 30	192	Ar Council Bluffs Transfer, Ia., 1 Lv	58	9.10	4.27	12.20			
					195	Missouri River Ar Omaha, Neb., 1 Lv	55	9.00	4.15	m11 45			
		7.00	8 20	2.45	195	Lv Ar	55	8.25					
11 35	4.15	8.30	8.35	4.30	195		55						
		9 55	9 35	5 40	250	Ar Lincoln, 1, 12 Lv	0	7.30		p12 15	11 45		

Operates via Table Rock—See Table No. 12

Operates via Wymore and Beatrice—See Table Nos. 6 and 52.

Silver Streak Zephyr

WESTBOUND—READ DOWN

Omaha-Ashland-Lincoln

Mls.	Table No. 10	1 Daily	3 Daily	7 Daily	21 Daily	11 Daily	19 Daily	17 Daily			
		AM	AM	PM	PM	PM	PM	PM			
0	Omaha, 1, 9 Lv	12.40	8 30	4 30	8 35	9 25	10.20	11.59			
4	South Omaha		8 38								
8	Ralston		f 8 43								
15	Chalco		f 8 52								
21	Gretna		f 9 02								
	Platte River										
31	Ashland, 56, 57		9.20	5.09		n					
38	Greenwood		f 9 29								
43	Waverly		f 9 37								
50	Havelock		h 9 46								
55	Lincoln, 12, 52, 53, 54, 55 Ar	1.45	9.55	5.40	9 35	10 30	11 20	1.04			
		AM	AM	PM	PM	PM	PM	AM			

Denver Zephyr (Note 1) · Silver Streak Zephyr · Nebraska Zephyr · Coloradoan · California Zephyr (Note 2)

EASTBOUND—READ DOWN

Lincoln-Ashland-Omaha

Mls.	Table No. 11	20 Daily	6 Daily	12 Daily	14 Daily	30 Daily	10 Daily	18 Daily			
		AM	AM	AM	PM	PM	AM	AM			
0	Lincoln, 1, 9, 12, 52, 53, 54, 55 Lv	7.30	7.45	11.00	4 30	9 00	12.11	3.55			
4	Havelock										
12	Waverly				4 43						
17	Greenwood				4 48						
24	Ashland, 1, 56, 57				4 56						
	Platte River										
34	Gretna				f 5 10						
40	Chalco				f 5 17						
47	Ralston				f 5 26						
	South Omaha										
55	Omaha, 1, 9 Ar	8 25	8 55	11 59	5 45	10 05	1.10	4 55			

Silver Streak Zephyr · Coloradoan · Nebraska Zephyr · Ak-Sar-Ben · Denver Zephyr (Note 1) · California Zephyr (Note 2)

REFERENCE NOTES

† —Daily except Sunday. ♀—Motor Train.

‖—Meal stop.

♀—Burlington Trailways Bus.

—Train-Auto Service available at this point.

a—Stops to let off revenue passengers from Kansas City or St. Joseph or receive for Council Bluffs or Omaha.

b—Stops to let off revenue passengers from Lincoln or beyond.

c—Stops to let off revenue passengers from Kansas City and beyond.

e—Stops to receive revenue passengers for Council Bluffs or beyond.

f—Flag stop.

h—Stops only to let off revenue passengers.

j—Stops only to receive revenue passengers.

k—Sleepers ready at 10:00 p.m; may be occupied at Omaha until 8:00 a.m.

m—Sleepers ready at 9:30 p.m.

n—Stops to let off revenue passengers from east of Omaha.

p—Sleeper ready at 10:00 p.m.

Note 1—All space on the Denver Zephyrs—both COACH and PULLMAN—is RESERVED and SPECIFICALLY assigned in advance, reservations for trips under 300 miles not being made prior to date of departure. Checked baggage is carried only for through movement between Chicago and Denver and not to or from intermediate points. No extra fare on any Burlington train.

Note 2—ALL SPACE on the California Zephyr—both COACH and PULLMAN is RESERVED and SPECIFICALLY assigned in advance, reservations for trips under 400 miles not being made prior to date of departure. Dome seats are not reserved. Checked baggage is carried only for through movement between Chicago and Denver or beyond and not to or from intermediate points. Banana messenger, caretaker, and circus tickets not honored. No extra fare on any Burlington train.

The Silver Streak Zephyr was the second non-articulated Zephyr streamliner. The train with its original consist is shown here in this Burlington Route publicity photo. (Burlington Northern)

The Silver Streak Zephyr

The last Zephyr to be built intact as a train for a particular service was the Silver Streak Zephyr No. 9909. This train consisted of a 2000 HP diesel electric unit, 1 baggage car, 1 baggage-RPO car, two 52 seat chair cars and 1 dining parlor observation car. With the exception of the last car, these were delivered in March, 1940 for the Kansas City-Omaha-Lincoln run. A run which was not discontinued until 1959. However, the train itself did not remain together for very long. The coaches eventually found their way all over the system in both Zephyr and non-Zephyr trains. The locomotive and part of the train were re-assigned to the Sam Houston Zephyr after the 9901 had been destroyed.

Zephyrs 9908 and 9909 represented the first step toward even finer, longer and heavier Zephyrs—that would have to wait for their development after World War II. However, before we get too far ahead of ourselves, let's take a look at Zephyr operations just prior to that tragic war.

The Zephyrs in 1940

The CB&Q had been purchasing a number of streamlined coaches for service on several trains. And the Zephyrs were setting records. For example, on June 16th, 1940, the CB&Q operated 17 stainless steel cars and a 4000 hp diesel electric locomotive to carry 500 Kiwanians from Chicago to Minneapolis

for their International convention in that city. This was the longest stainless steel train ever operated. The train was operated as a second section of the Morning Twin Cities Zephyr, and covered the 437 miles in seven hours. Ten of the cars had been just delivered to the Q in June. Further the CB&Q was deep in the process of exchanging power and cars from one train to another, and the original consist of the fixed Zephyrs was frequently changed, and the trains were not always operating on their original assignments. In other words, the streamliners were no longer experiments on the Burlington but had become a regular part of the passenger train operation, and their runs and consist were based on operating efficiency and passenger demand.

For example, after the Mark Twain Zephyr served in Advance Denver Zephyr service, it operated as a second section for the Denver Zephyr between Chicago and Burlington handling local traffic. One of the original Twin Zephyrs operated for awhile as the Texas Rocket, yes, that's right, the Texas Rocket. It operated along with the Sam Houston Zephyr between Houston and Dallas-Fort Worth. The first Ak-Sar-Ben Zephyr was placed into service on an eastbound run only between Lincoln and Chicago on December 11, 1940.

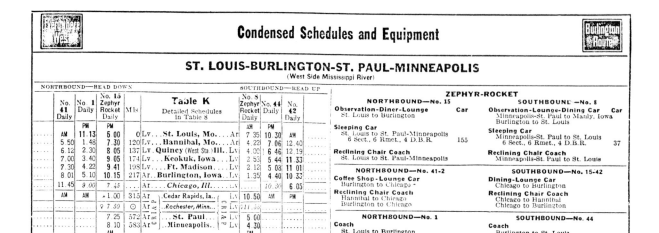

Condensed Schedules and Equipment — Burlington Route

ST. LOUIS-BURLINGTON-ST. PAUL-MINNEAPOLIS
(West Side Mississippi River)

No. 41 Daily	No. 1 Daily	No. 15 Zephyr Rocket Daily	Mls	Table K — Detailed Schedules In Table 8	No. 8 Zephyr Rocket Daily	No. 44 Daily	No. 42 Daily
NORTHBOUND—READ DOWN					SOUTHBOUND—READ UP		
PM	PM				AM	PM	
AM 11.13	5 00		0	Lv...St. Louis, Mo....Ar	7 35	10 30	AM
5 50	1.48	7.30	120	Lv...Hannibal, Mo....Ar	4 22	7 06	12.40
6.12	2.30	8 05	137	Lv..Quincy (West Sta.)Ill..Lv	4 00	6 46	12.19
7.00	3.40	9 05	174	Lv...Keokuk, Iowa...Lv	2 53	5 44	11.33
7.30	4.22	9.41	198	Lv...Ft. Madison....Lv	2 12	5 08	11 01
8 01	5.10	10.15	217	Ar..Burlington, Iowa..Lv	1.35	4 40	10 33
11.45	9.00	7 45		Ar..Chicago, Ill.....Lv		10.30	6 05
AM	AM	▶1.00	315	Ar Cedar Rapids, Ia.... Lv	10.50	AM	PM
		9 7 30		Ar Rochester, Minn... Lv	711 35		
		7 25	572	Ar St. Paul... Lv	5 00		
		8.10 AM	583	Ar ..Minneapolis.. Lv	4 30 PM		

ZEPHYR-ROCKET

NORTHBOUND—No. 15		SOUTHBOUND—No. 8	
Observation-Diner-Lounge St. Louis to Burlington	Car	Observation-Lounge-Dining Car Minneapolis-St. Paul to Manly, Iowa Burlington to St. Louis	Car
Sleeping Car St. Louis to St. Paul-Minneapolis 6 Sect., 6 Rmet., 4 D.B.R.	155	Sleeping Car Minneapolis-St. Paul to St. Louis 6 Sect., 6 Rmet., 4 D.B.R.	37
Reclining Chair Coach St. Louis to St. Paul-Minneapolis		Reclining Chair Coach Minneapolis-St. Paul to St. Louis	

NORTHBOUND—No. 41-2	SOUTHBOUND—No. 15-42
Coffee Shop-Lounge Car Burlington to Chicago	Dining-Lounge Car Chicago to Burlington
Reclining Chair Coach Hannibal to Chicago Burlington to Chicago	Reclining Chair Coach Chicago to Hannibal Chicago to Burlington

NORTHBOUND—No. 1	SOUTHBOUND—No. 44
Coach St. Louis to Burlington	Coach Burlington to St. Louis

Altogether the CB&Q operated the following Zephyr streamliners in 1940:

Pioneer Zephyr	Lincoln-Omaha and Kansas City
Sam Houston Zephyr	Fort Worth-Dallas and Houston
Texas Rocket	Fort Worth-Dallas and Houston
Denver Zephyrs	Chicago-Denver
Twin Zephyrs	Chicago-Twin Cities
Mark Twin Zephyr	St. Louis-Burlington
General Pershing Zephyr	St. Louis-Kansas City
Silver Streak Zephyr	Lincoln-Omaha and Kansas City
Texas Zephyr	Denver and Fort Worth-Dallas (C&S and FW&D)
Ak-Sar-Ben Zephyr	Lincoln to Chicago (Dec. 11, 1940)

Despite the size of the fleet in 1940, a new train would be added early in 1941, which would add a new chapter to Zephyr operations—The Zephyr-Rocket.

The Zephyr-Rocket

The Zephyr-Rocket represents joint co-operation between two railroad companies in the operation of a passenger train, which began service on January 7, 1941, between St. Louis and the Twin Cities. The Burlington and the Rock Island teamed up to put on an overnight train over the shortest route. The train was appropriately named after the Zephurs and the Rockets, the streamliner fleet of both railroads.

The Zephyr-Rocket was christened by the Minneapolis Civic and Commerce Association and the St. Paul Association of Commerce along with the Kiwanis Club of Minneapolis. The christening was done by Miss Mary Lou McDonnell, queen of the St. Paul Winter Carnival and was accompanied by the Winter Carnival King, Joseph L. Shiely. At St. Louis the St. Louis Association of Commerce co-operated and the new service was accepted by the mayor of that city. Officers of both railroads participated. The northbound train was christened by Miss Gladys McRee, the St. Louis Veiled Prophet Queen.

The new trains provided service between Minneapolis and Burlington, Iowa, over the Rock Island, a distance of 365.6 miles, and over the Burlington between Burlington and St. Louis, a distance of 221 miles. The trains departed the Twin Cities around 5:00 PM with an 8:00 AM arrival in St. Louis, and the same type of schedule was followed northbound. The train was discontinued in 1967.

Equipment for the Zephyr-Rocket was provided by both companies. The original consist included one locomotive from each road that operated through to each terminal. Next there was a baggage car and a mail and baggage car. Each road supplied a pair of head-end cars. Each road supplied one streamlined coach. Two sleeping cars were assigned to each train and bringing up the rear were Rock Island dining parlor observation cars on both sets of equipment. The Zephyr Rocket represented what a joint effort could do, and the train offered the only through service between Minneapolis, St. Paul and St. Louis. Since the train's discontinuance, it is difficult to travel between the Missouri and Minnesota cities.

The Zephyr-Rocket was the last new train on the CB&Q, although the Texas Zephyr had also gone into service in 1940 between Denver and Dallas. However, that was a C&S train, which will be covered in the chapter on CB&Q subsidiaries. It is interesting to note, however, that the Zephyr-Rocket and the Texas Zephyr were the only two Zephyrs assigned standard heavy weight sleeping cars as part of their original consist.

Meanwhile, the rest of the Zephyr fleet was getting streamlined coaches from the pool when traffic requirements dictated a different consist than the fixed articulated consist of many of the Zephyrs. However, after the war, the best was yet to come—the Vista Domes.

The "pattern" dome coaches, rebuilt from flat-top cars presented unique interiors since their floors were not depressed beneath the domes, and the rest rooms remained at the end of the car. Because of limited head room, an unusual seating arrangement was effected beneath the dome with aisles on each side of the car, two pairs of seats facing forward in the center, and other seats back to back non-reclining and facing the sides of the coach. None the less, a most splendid innovation in rail travel derived from these two coaches. See page 19, The Domeliners, for further information on these cars. (Jim Scribbins)

The regular seating portion of the "pattern" dome 4714, Silver Dome, illustrating the use of two aisles to pass beneath the dome. (Jim Scribbins)

The First Streamlined Vista Dome Car

The CB&Q reconstructed a flat top coach in 1945 into the first streamlined Vista-Dome coach, and renamed it the "Silver Dome." This first car was equipped with a flat glass enclosed dome with seats for 24 passengers. The entire car was air conditioned to ensure a comfortable temperature and ample ventilation in summer and winter. Lighting was also arranged so that at night all lights in the dome except those illuminating the floor could be extinguished. This permitted the passengers to see the right of way ahead illuminated by the locomotive's headlight, and the entire countryside bathed in moonlight.

The reconstruction of the car required changes on the main floor. The main passenger compartment contained 18 reclining seats in the conventional arrangement. Beneath the dome were 16 seats. Four of these could be used to form a card playing section and 12 were placed back-to-back along the center of the car, facing outward toward the windows. The two rows were separated by a glass partition. A short stairway led up to the dome.

A large, daintily appointed women's lounge and spacious men's room were located at opposite ends of the car.

The seats and carpets for the floors including the hallways were in peach color. The window drapes in the main passenger section were blue. The lower walls under the dome were a red tile and the upper walls a pale yellow on metal. The dome was finished in grey and green with a maroon carpet. The stair

carpeting was peach. All trim throughout the car was done in stainless steel.

The car was test run on the Twin Cities Zephyr and on other runs as far away as Texas. The reaction of nearly all passengers was most positive, and the decisions were made to build a fleet of Zephyr Domeliners, a construction period that would begin in 1946-47 and last through 1956, and Zephyr dome cars continue to operate over Burlington Northern routes in Amtrak trains in 1976.

The Nebraska Zephyr

Although the third Twin Cities Zephyr and the California Zephyr stole the spotlight from 1947 on, the first post-war Zephyr was the Nebraska Zephyr. This new Zephyr began operation between Chicago, Omaha and Lincoln on November 16, 1947, with the equipment from the second Twin Cities Zephyrs. The 9904 and 9905 remained in that service from 1947 through their retirement in 1968. Altogether, the second Twins served the CB&Q for nearly 32 years, which demonstrates the fine workmanship of the Budd Company, the fine maintenance program operated by the Burlington, and the popularity of the trains themselves.

Few changes were made in the trains after they went into Nebraska Zephyr service. The cocktail lounge in cars 960 and 961 (Venus and Apollo respectively) was replaced with a 42 seat coach compartment in mid-1963. Three years later the dining cars were converted to cafeteria cars with vending machines during the spring of 1966.

The equipment continued to operate for less than two more years.

The original schedule called for departure from Chicago at 12:45 PM with a 9:15 PM arrival in Omaha and 10:30 PM into Lincoln. Eastbound the train departed Lincoln at 11:00 AM and Omaha at 12:15 PM with an 8:45 PM arrival into Chicago.

The NZ was discontinued between Omaha and Lincoln in 1970, and was completely discontinued in 1971.

The Third Twin Zephyrs

The most dramatic and most functional Twin Zephyrs of all were the domeliners introduced in December, 1947, although several of the cars went into service a few weeks ahead of that time. The official date for the new trains was December 19th, and they were indeed excellent creations of the passenger train art. The vista dome Twin Zephyrs were among the finest intermediate distance passenger trains ever constructed and operated, and were for a good many years the world's fastest trains over various sections of track between Aurora and St. Paul.

As originally constructed, the trains consisted of two diesel electric units, one buffet lounge baggage car, four dome coaches, one diner and one dome parlor observation car. They operated in the usual double daily operation between Chicago and Minneapolis and St. Paul, as had been customary for over 10 years by the end of 1947. Following introductory functions, which included excursions between Chicago and Aurora and a style show on wheels held by the Junior League of Chicago, the trains went into service on December 19, 1947.

The operating procedures of the Twin Zephyrs was one of precision railroading from the morning departure from either terminal to the late evening arrival at Chicago or Minneapolis. Each set of equipment made one round trip per day between Chicago and the Twin Cities. What this meant was that everyone had to be on their toes during the turning operation at Chicago and Minneapolis. The turning of the Morning Zephyr into the Afternoon Zephyr at Minneapolis has to be one of the fastest, if not the fastest turn around of a long distance train in the

USA. The complete process, during the 1950s and early '60s had to be completed in 30 minutes or less. (The Chicago turning had 90 minutes to complete the job including a half hour through a car washer.)

According to the May 19, 1952 issue of RAILWAY AGE, these fast turns enabled each set of Zephyrs to cover 974 miles in a day at an average speed of 66 miles per hour including station and terminal time from 8:00 a.m. to 10:45 p.m. This means that the gross earnings per train were double what they could be if four separate sets of equipment were used to operate the service. Let's take a look now at the Minneapolis turn.

The Morning Zephyr, train No. 21, crossed the stone arch bridge at 3:29 p.m. Arrival in the Great Northern depot was just a few moments away and passengers were ready to detrain.

3:35 p.m. As passengers departed, coach cleaners began the task of sweeping and cleaning. Electricians went through the train checking electrical equipment and making adjustments.

3:40 p.m. The dining car chef weighed in the remaining food supplies for the commissary report. At the same time, the train arrived in the coach yard where crews began inspections, watered the entire train as well as refueled the locomotives.

3:42 p.m. The steward, chef and headwaiter completed commissary reports for the Morning Zephyr and began the preparations for the Afternoon Zephyr meals.

3:50 p.m. The train completes the last leg of the trip around the wye and as the "Afternoon Zephyr" pulls into the station. Nine minutes later, the train is loaded and ready to depart. The conductor checks with the Station Master for last minute stragglers, and gives the highball at 4:00 p.m. The Afternoon Zephyr is en route to Chicago for a 10:45 p.m. arrival time.

Three New Zephyrs in 1953

The year 1953 was a big year for the introduction of new Zephyrs. During that year the Ak-Sar-Ben Zephyr, the American Royal Zephyr and the Kansas City Zephyr went into service. Actually, the Ak-Sar-Ben Zephyr was the second such Zephyr so named, with the first one going into service between Lincoln and Chicago, eastbound only. The train was a day schedule and ran only until 1947 when it was replaced by the Nebraska Zephyr. However the new Zephyrs in 1953 were superb trains in all respects, and part of the new service had to do with the new high speed *Kansas City Short-Cut*.

The Kansas City route was one of the biggest news items in *American Railroading,* and the Burlington added to the excitement of the time by announcing that they would double through passenger service between Chicago and Kansas City, and would do it with new domeliner Zephyrs. It caught the public's eye and everybody sat up and took notice.

February 1, 1953 was the big day when the two new Zephyrs, Kansas City and American Royal,

The Nebraska Zephyr is shown here near Galesburg, Ill., in August, 1948, long before the combination with either the Coloradoan or the Kansas City Zephyr. The articulated train was to carry on in the grand Zephyr tradition for many years, and who could know that August afternoon that in 1976 neither the train nor the equipment would be running. Alas, even the name "Burlington Route" will have been changed. (William A. Raia)

The Nebraska Zephyr, train No. 11, scoots by Lisle, Illinois on July 27, 1951 at a cool 80 miles per hour. (George-Paterson Collection)

When the Twin Cities Zephyrs were transferred to the Nebraska Zephyr, the new name was proudly displayed on the letter boards. The car "Apollo" was the auxiliary power unit-cocktail lounge car operated on the head-end. (Sy Dykhouse)

Neptune was a 60 seat chair car. (Sy Dykhouse)

Mars was the second 60 seat chair car. (Sy Dykhouse)

Vulcan was a 32 seat dining car. (Sy Dykhouse)

went into service offering superb travel to not only Kansas City and Chicago, but also to St. Joseph. Up to this point the only through train was the 13 hour overnight American Royal, a diesel powered train with standard coaches and sleepers. The new Kansas City Zephyr made the day trip in 8 hours, while the new overnight American Royal Zephyr was scheduled for 9 hours, 55 minutes to Kansas City and 10 hours, 45 minutes to St. Joseph.

However there was more to the service. The Kansas City Zephyr was provided with new connecting service to and from St. Joseph with the Pioneer Zephyr and the Mark Twain Zephyr.

The CB&Q left no stone unturned in announcing the new Zephyr services. A most carefully planned campaign of advertising and publicity heralded the debut in newspapers, magazines, on billboards, radio and TV programs, and in ticket offices and station windows up and down the line.

Furthermore the effort was not limited to just simply announcing the new Zephyrs. The public was invited to inspect the new equipment and ride it on special, low cost 90 minute excursion runs. A special train made up of equipment for both day and night service went into exhibition and excursion service on January 23rd in Chicago. On that day the train was on display for public inspection in the Union Station. On the following day the special made five excursion runs to Aurora plus a longer trip to Earlville. On January 25th, the special carried a group of sellers and ticket agents from Kansas City over the new Short Cut to Brookfield and return. Public exhibition and excursions operated to Hannibal, Missouri, were provided at Quincy, Illinois on January 26th.

The Kansas City Chamber of Commerce got into the act on January 27th with a public affairs luncheon to honor Burlington President Harry C. Murphy. The affair was followed by still another trip over the new line. Subsequent exhibitions were held at Atchison, Kansas, and Leavenworth, which were not on the route of the new Zephyrs but were close enough to St. Joseph and Kansas City to be important sources of revenue. January 28th found the train on exhibition at Macon, Mo., and Brookfield and operating public excursions out of Brookfield

Jupiter was a 24 seat parlor observation car. All cars in this set belonged to the "Train of the Gods." (Sy Dykhouse)

Train No. 11 was combined with the old "Coloradoan" between Chicago and Lincoln, Nebraska. The result was an exceptionally long train of head-end cars with the articulated streamlined equipment bringing up the rear. The Coloradoan had been a head-end traffic train between Chicago and Denver. Eventually the traffic disappeared leaving only the remains of the combined Kansas City Zephyr and the Nebraska Zephyr. Train No. 11 is shown here near Zearing, Illinois. (William A. Raia)

and Chillicothe. The day was completed with a two hour exhibition at Chillicothe.

On January 29th, a 5½ hours exhibition at St. Joseph was followed by three excursions to East Leavenworth (on another route of the CB&Q) while January 30 was devoted to a 12 hour exhibition in Kansas City Union Station. Think of how the Santa Fe must have felt for this would be the first time that they would have any serious passenger competition between Chicago and Kansas City.

Christening ceremonies opened the final day of activities at Kansas City. Participants included the Queen of American Royal, the Miss Judith Anderson of Liberty, Missouri, and her court in the presence of a crowd of spectators as well as radio and TV audiences of Kansas City's WDAF. Several mayors and other city and town officials were on hand for the festivities. Included in the special party to watch the champagne bottles broken first on the observation car of the Kansas City Zephyr and then on the diesel locomotive of the American Royal Zephyr were N. C. Dezendorf, vice president of General Motors and general manager of Electric-Motive Division; Fitzwilliam Sargent, vice president of the Budd Company and Burlington President H. C. Murphy. The entire affair reminded one of the christening that took place in 1934 when Electro-Motive and the Bodd Company had completed the Pioneer Zephyr. After the ceremonies, five public excursions to East Leavenworth wound up the festiv-

ities just in time to arrange the equipment for scheduled service starting the next morning. After the trains went into service, a follow up ad campaign was undertaken. It could not be said that the new Zephyrs to Kansas City were unknown to the public for travel between Chicago and Kansas City-St. Joseph.

The equipment ordered for the Kansas City and American Royal Zephyrs was part of a larger order for cars going into service on the Ak-Sar-Ben Zephyr, California Zephyr (covered in Chapter 5) and the Black Hawk, a train that never had the distinction of becoming a Zephyr. In fact, altogether a total 34 cars were ordered, all from the Budd Company. The Budd Company, by the way, built nearly every car that the CB&O operated in the Zephyr streamliners and domeliners. The 31 new Burlington cars were assigned as follows: 17 to the new Chicago-Kansas City service including four vista dome cars; 6 cars for the Chicago-Minneapolis service on the Black Hawk; 5 cars including one vista dome car for the Ak-Sar-Ben Zephyr, which replaced the Ak-Sar-Ben between Chicago and Omaha-Lincoln in February, 1953; and 3 cars for the California Zephyr. Three additional cars were also built for the Western Pacific and the Rio Grande for service on the CZ.

The equipment for the Kansas City Zephyr train sets included 2 coaches with seats for 50 passengers each, 1 vista dome coach buffet lounge car, 1 dining car and 1 vista dome parlor observation car. The

63

No. 47-53 ●The Black Hawk	●No. 53 Oriental Limited	●No. 51 North Coast Limited	No. 45	●No. 23 Afternoon Zephyr	●No. 49 Empire Builder	●No. 21 Morning Zephyr	Miles	Table F Central Time	●No. 44 Empire Builder	●No. 22 Morning Zephyr	●No. 24 Afternoon Zephyr	No. 52	●No. 50 North Coast Limited	●No. 54 Oriental Limited	No. 48-54 The Black Hawk
PM	PM	PM	PM	PM	PM	AM			PM	AM	PM	AM	AM	AM	AM
11.15	11.15	11 00	9 00	4 00	1.00	8.45	0	Lv....Chicago......Ar	2.00	2 40	10 45	9 30	7.45	8.15	8.15
12.03	12.03	11 48	9 47	b 4 34	e 1 36	b 9.19	38	Lv....Aurora......Ar	·g 1.18	v 2.02	v 10.07	8.40	6.54	7.20	7.20
2.31	2.31	2.04	1.23	6 07	3.17	10.52	145	Lv....Savanna.....Lv	11.32	12.29	8.34	‖ 5.15	4 30	5.00	5.00
3.30	3.30	d3.20	2.20	6 30	3 40	11.15	186	Lv....Dubuque.....Lv	10.35	11.15	7 35	3.20		3.40	3.40
4.21	4.21	d3.50	4 18	7 23		12.08	239	Ar.Prairie du Chien.Lv	....	11.02	7.05	1.23	k 2.18	2.38	2.38
5.21	5.21	4 52	5.48	8 07	5 21	12.52	297	Ar....La Crosse....Lv	9.17	10 20	6 23	11 35	1.21	1.44	1 44
6.15	6.15	....	7 00	8 50	6 05	1.30	327	Ar....Winona......Lv	....	9 38	5 38	10.00	12.20		
8.15	8.15	8 00	9 40	10 15	7 45	3.00	427	Ar....St. Paul.....Lv	7.15	8.25	4 30	7.15	10.45	11.15	11.15
c8.50	9.35	9 25	10.20	10 45	8.40	3 30	437	Ar...Minneapolis...Lv	6.35	8.00	4.00	6.30	9.35	10.05	n10.30
AM	AM	AM	AM	PM	PM	PM			AM	AM	PM	PM	PM	PM	PM

THE VISTA DOME TWIN ZEPHYRS
Radio Reception in Coaches
Diner, Parlor and Club Cars and Drawing Room
Checked baggage is carried only for through movement between Chicago and
St. Paul-Minneapolis and not to or from intermediate points.

NORTHBOUND—Nos. 21 and 23
Burlington Vista-Dome Parlor Car
Chicago to Minneapolis
27 Parlor seats and D.R. P-21, P-23
Burlington Parlor Car
28 Seats and D.R. P-211, P-231
Dining Car
Chicago to Minneapolis
Vista-Dome Reclining Chair Coaches
Chicago to Minneapolis
Club-Lounge Car
Buffet and Refreshment Service

SOUTHBOUND—Nos. 22 and 24
Burlington Vista-Dome Parlor Car
Minneapolis to Chicago
27 Parlor seats and D.R. P-22, P-24
Burlington Parlor Car
Minneapolis to Chicago
28 Seats and D.R. P-221, P-241
Dining Car Minneapolis to Chicago
Vista-Dome Reclining Chair Coaches
Minneapolis to Chicago
Club-Lounge Car
Buffet and Refreshment Service

NORTHBOUND—No. 47-53
Dining-Lounge Car (Buffet Service)
La Crosse to St. Paul-Minneapolis
Sleeping Cars (Ready at 10.00 p.m.) Car
Chicago to St. Paul-Minneapolis
8 Sections, 5 Double Bedrooms 472
8 Sec., 5 D.B.R. 473
Reclining Chair Coaches
Chicago to St. Paul-Minneapolis

No. 49—EMPIRE BUILDER—No. 44
No. 51—NORTH COAST LIMITED—No. 50
No. 53—ORIENTAL LIMITED—No. 54
For Equipment see page 5

THE BLACK HAWK
SOUTHBOUND—No. 48-54
Dining-Lounge Car (Buffet Service)
Minneapolis-St. Paul to La Crosse
Sleeping Cars Car
Minneapolis-St. Paul to Chicago
8 Section, 5 Double Bedrooms 482
St. Paul to Chicago
8 Sec., 5 D.B.R. 483
(Sleeping cars ready 9.30 p.m.)
Dining Car A C—For breakfast
Reclining Chair Coaches
Minneapolis-St. Paul to Chicago

Nos. 45 and 52—Coaches

train was also generally assigned one mail and baggage car, either a streamlined car or a standard RPO-Baggage painted with shadow lines to imitate fluted siding.

The equipment for the American Royal Zephyr included two cars with 6 sections, 6 roomettes and four double bedrooms, 1 car with 10 roomettes and 6 double bedrooms, one dome coach buffet lounge car and 2 50 passenger coaches. The reader will note that the coaches and the vista dome coach buffet lounge car were making one round trip per day between Chicago and Kansas City.

Decorations were chosen for attractive and restful effects. Various shades of soft colors such as nut pine, rust, beige, brown, green, blue and various combinations of rose, gray and tan were employed in all of the passenger cars. Two color combinations were employed in the coaches. In one the walls were originally cocoanut brown below and cocoa beige above with a cafe au lait ceiling. The carpet was green; the upholstery, turquoise and the draperies in a green, brown and yellow patterned material. In the other combination, the walls were nut pine in two shades. The carpet was originally henna and brown; the upholstery, rust and the drapes patterned in a green and rose.

The parlor sections of the dome parlor cars were done in a rose tan with ceilings of delicate tones of beige. Carpets were rose and the chairs upholstered variously in sandalwood, loganberry and brown. Drapes were lemon color.

These same wall colors were also used in the bedrooms of the sleeping cars. The upholstery in the bedrooms was a combination of gray taupe at the top and down the center of the backs of the seats and in the center of the cushions, with a rose gray at the sides of the backs and cushions. Roomettes had walls and ceilings or orchid gray and upholstery of roseclay. The sleeping cars were carpeted throughout in green.

Three upholstery colors were used in the vista domes. In the buffet lounge coach, the seats were originally in alpine rust and the carpet henna and brown. In the parlor observation the seats were turquoise and the carpeting rose. The CZ dome observation sleeper was upholstered in sandalwood and rose carpeting.

Each of the 50 passenger coaches included a dressing room at each end. Two toilet rooms opened off the men's dressing, which contained a three seat sofa. The women's dressing room contained a dressing table and cosmetic shelf the full length of one side.

In the coach section the windows were a fantastic 76½ inches wide and the seats were spaced 47 inches between centers. All seating was rotating, reclining with leg and foot rests, plus built in ash trays and a special spring-clip ticket holder which included the seat number. The backs and cushions of the seats were foam rubber. General illumination was furnished by seven fluorescent fixtures over the center aisle. Incandescent reading lights over each seat in the underside of the baggage racks were controlled by each passenger. These were among the finest Zephyr coaches ever built.

The 71 passenger vista dome buffet lounge car was an unusual combination of facilities. Entering the car from the non-vestibule end, the aisle passed between a men's room on one side and lockers on the other to the coffee shop. Here were seats for 17 in two built in banquette sections and built-in sofa seats along the sides of the car.

From the inner end of the coffee shop, a stairway led to the dome with 24 reversible seats. Beneath the dome was a small lounge for six. This was separated from the passageway by clear glass panels on either side of the entrance and with large mirrors mounted on the transverse wells. Adjoining the lounge was a buffet section from which snacks and beverages were prepared and served.

Beyond the buffet section the passageway led up to a 24 passenger coach section. At the inner end of this section was a dormitory with a toilet, folding lavatory and a single tier of three bunks for crew members. Between the coach section and the vestibule were a conductor's space and a women's washroom.

The dome parlor car contained one section in the front for seven passengers. In the area beneath the dome were the men's and women's toilets as well as a drawing room for five passengers. The rear section contained 20 individual movable chairs. The dome provided the customary 24 seats. The rear of the car was not curved but flat with observation windows on both sides of the end door. The door was provided with a diaphragm for mid-train operation.

The dining cars, two for the Kansas City Zephyr and one for the Ak-Sar-Ben Zephyr contained seats for 48 passengers in the main dining room. The room was divided into three sections. At each end were a pair of banquette sections seating four. These were separated from the main dining room by clear glass panels on each side of the aisle. Each panel was decorated with an etched vine pattern. The ceiling over the banquette sections was dropped below that in the main section. An outstanding decorative feature of the diner was a horseshoe shaped bar facing the dining room at the kitchen bulkhead. The outer face was covered with a large carved and painted lineoleum mural and the entire wall behind it was a mirror on which was etched an elaborate pattern in antique gold. Antique silver repoussees decorated each end of the main dining section above the center aisle.

One 10-6 sleeper and two 6-6-4 sleepers were assigned to the American Royal Zephyr between Chicago, Kansas City and St. Joseph. The Black Hawk, meanwhile, received one 6-6-4 and two 10-6 cars for each train set. (The six 6 double bedroom, 5 compartment cars were assigned to the California Zephyr only.) Two 10-6 cars (one for each train set) and one 16 section sleeper were assigned to the Ak-Sar-Ben Zephyr as well as the dome observation lounge, 3 bedroom and 1 drawing room sleeper. The reader will note that odd number of cars were assigned to the Ak-Sar-Ben Zephyr. This came about because cars were pooled between the California Zephyr and the Ak-Sar-Ben Zephyr. Equipment into Chicago on the Ak-Sar-Ben Zephyr would go out west on the California Zephyr that afternoon, while equipment from the inbound CZ would go to the Ak-Sar-Ben. All cars operating on the CZ and ASBZ were lettered "California Zephyr."

The Ak-Sar-Ben and American Royal operated separately until declining patronage brought about their combination between Chicago and Galesburg in 1961. The St. Joseph connection for the American Royal Zephyr was discontinued in 1962, but the main line Zephyrs continued to operate in fine fashion until the Ak-Sar-Ben Zephyr was discontinued in 1970.

The Kansas City Zephyr, meanwhile, had been combined with the Nebraska Zephyr between Chicago and Galesburg in 1962. The articulated equipment, somehow, did not seem to fit in being coupled to a Zephyr domeliner. However, the KCZ was discontinued in 1968.

Although this photo has been widely used, the author is using it here because it typifies the Twin Cities Zephyrs' finest hour. The "Vista Dome Twin Cities Zephyrs" were and are among the finest intermediate distance trains ever operated in North America. The consist shown here was typical, but it often expanded to as much as 14 cars. The first dome in the train was the original dome built by the CB&Q in their own shops to test passenger reaction to the concept. The photo sums up the Vista Dome Zephyrs with the Mississippi River on one side and the hight bluffs on the other. It is an area where nature truly smiles for 300 miles. (Burlington Northern . . . .

The last Zephyr of this group to be discontinued was the American Royal Zephyr. She did not give up the run until the Amtrak era began service Nationwide.

Although the 1953 Zephyr trains were fine intermediate distance trains, and operating with the finest sleepers ever operated over CB&Q trackage on two of the trains, the operations and experiences and knowledge gained set the stage for the design and purchase of the finest overnight-everynight train ever operated by the "Q"—The 1956 edition of the "Denver Zephyr."

The Vista Dome Denver Zephyr

What must rank as one of the finest overnight trains ever built and operated by a U.S. railroad is the Vista Dome Denver Zephyr. What other train can the reader think of that offered vista domes (three of them), leg rest coaches, slumber-coaches, roomettes, bedrooms, compartments, parlor car seating, day service drawing room, dining car, observation lounge and coffee shop service. Only the vista dome North Coast Limited and California Zephyr could equal the DZ, and these were trains also operated by the Burlington .

The new second edition Denver Zephyrs went into service late in October, 1956, with not only overnight Chicago-Denver service, but through service to Colorado Springs via the Denver & Rio Grande Western Railroad. Each of the new Zephyr train sets contained revenue space for approximately 325 passengers with a train make-up of 12 passenger cars not including head-end equipment, and not counting seats in dining and lounge facilities.

Originally each train contained two slumber-coaches which could accommodate 80 passengers or nearly one fourth of the Zephyr's full passenger load.

These unique cars offered single or double rooms for coach fare plus $7.50 or $13.50 respectively. The single rooms were arranged in a duplex roomette type of arrangement whereas the double rooms were all on the main floor level.

Aside from the slumbercoaches and the vista dome coffee shop cars, all of the new equipment was built almost identical to the dining cars, sleepers and coaches previously described. The dome coffee shop cars were known as the "Chuck Wagon" and this designation and the brand "DZ" was used in the decorative scheme of the cars. The cars carried carved plaques and murals depicting range country life, and copper trim was used extensively. The area under the dome was occupied by an eight seat lunch counter and booth for four, and the standard level over the "A" end was a 19 seat coffee shop.

The section at the "B" end was a dormitory which could accommodate 16 crew members. The dome of the car duplicated the arrangement of the other domes built for the CB&Q with 24 revolving, non-reclining seats.

The Denver Zephyr operated with its original consist (with some variation in the slower spring and late fall seasons) from October, 1956 through the late 1960's. Only then did traffic fall substantially, and only then did the CB&Q reduce the size of the train. Although only one slumbercoach operated during the non-summer months, the DZ continued to operate until after merger date, and was selected by Amtrak. Today, however, the train has been replaced by the San Francisco Zephyr running over the same route as the Denver Zephyr on a somewhat slower schedule.

The Vista Dome Denver Zephyr was the last of the Zephyrs. It began operation a little more than 22 years after the Pioneer Zephyr began service in 1934.

Business is so good that an extra flat-top coach has been cut into the normal seven consist of the Afternoon Twin Zephyr, train 23, as it races through LaGrange on its no-nonsense dash to the Twin Cities, behind a shovel nose-E5 combination. The vista dome Twins were superb examples of what a day-time train should be, with all coaches and the parlor having glass roofs, and a baggage-bar as the head-end car and a full diner separating the classes. It is August, 1949. (Jim Scribbins)

The Budd-built dome was and is the finest for viewing the scenery. The shortness enabled everyone in the dome to truly view the world up, down and all around. (Budd Company)

An eastbound Twin Zephyr zips past the Bay City, Wisconsin depot with a five car section of campers on the head-end returning from Minnesota to the Chicago area. The train is 53 miles from Minneapolis on the North La Crosse and St. Croix Subdivision of the Chicago and Aurora Division during the summer of 1958. (Russ Porter)

It represented the CB&Q' faith in the passenger train when most other railroads already had their backs to the wall with declining patronage due to the automobile and government subsidized air and bus service. The CB&Q was able to continue its fine Zephyr service until the mid-1960's when the interstate highway system neared completion, and when the post office announced the withdrawal of Rail Post Office cars, and the nearly total loss of all mail contracts.

The result was that the Zephyr suffered along with the rest of the CB&Q passenger fleet. In 1967, there were eight Zephyrs still in service as follows:

California Zephyr

Denver Zephyr
Nebraska Zephyr
Ak-Sar-Ben Zephyr
Kansas City Zephyr
American Royal Zephyr
Afternoon Twin Zephyr
Morning Twin Zephyr

By 1968 the fleet was reduced by one with the loss of the Kansas City Zephyr. This remained more or less intact until 1970 when only the Denver Zephyr remained in the timetable still performing the basic overnight service that became the tradition with Zephyr service since 1936. In 1970, the Burlington was no longer the "Way of the Zephyrs."

This photo typifies the close cooperation between the Burlington and the Great Northern. This photo of a Zephyr passing Highlands, Illinois (16.3 miles west of Chicago) demonstrates the use of Great Northern equipment when the need for extra equipment arose. (William A. Raia)

A nine car Twin Zephyr barrels along the Mississippi River at Alma, Wisconsin in June, 1967. The high speed train is powered by three E units and includes three head-end cars, two dome coaches, one flat top coach, one diner, one more dome coach and finally a flat top parlor car carrying the markers. (Bob Lorenz)

As the new Twin Zephyrs went into service, the Burlington assigned one of its early articulated Zephyrs to a Hannibal-Chicago round trip. The trains were simply named Zephyr 9902, after their power unit and were occasionally referred to as the Baby Zephyr. Train 5 departed Chicago shortly ahead of the suburban rush and ran on the center track to Aurora. A pleasant surprise on an August, 1949 afternoon was S-4a 4004 with two Budd coaches, one of them the "pattern" dome normally used on the Twin Zephyrs, and a conventional diner parlor car. (Jim Scribbins)

AMERICAN ROYAL

WESTBOUND—No. 55		EASTBOUND—No. 56	
Sleeping Cars	**Car**	**Sleeping Cars**	**Car**
Chicago to Kansas City		Kansas City to Chicago	
8 Sec., 1 D.R., 3 D.B.R.	551	8 Sec., 1 D.R., 3 D.B.R.	561
Chicago to St. Joseph		St. Joseph to Chicago	
12 Sections, 2 D.B.R.	555	12 Sections, 2 D.B.R.	566
Dining Car—For Dinner		**Dining Car**—For Breakfast	
Chair Coach		**Chair Coach**	
Chicago to Kansas City and St. Joseph		St. Joseph and Kansas City to Chicago	

WESTBOUND—No. 3		EASTBOUND—No. 4-30	
Sleeping Car	**Car**	**Sleeping Car**	**Car**
Chicago to Quincy—12 Sec., D.R.	329	Quincy to Chicago—12 Sec., D.R.	429
(Occupancy until 8.00 a.m.)		**Dining Car**—For Breakfast	
Chair Coach—Chicago to Galesburg		**Chair Coach**—Galesburg to Chicago	
Coach—Galesburg to Kansas City		**Coach**—Kansas City to Galesburg	
Cameron Jct. to St. Joseph		St. Joseph to Cameron Jct.	

ZEPHYR 9902

WESTBOUND—No. 5-42		EASTBOUND—No. 41-2	
Burlington Parlor Car	**Car**	**Burlington Parlor Car**	**Car**
Chicago to Hannibal	P-99	Hannibal to Chicago	P-40
Chair Coach—Chicago to Hannibal		**Chair Coach**—Hannibal to Chicago	
Dinette Service		**Dinette Service**	

Kansas City Zephyr, train 35, emerges from beneath Chicago's Post Office. It is October, 1962 and equipment knowledgeable persons will recognize that only the dome coach could have been from its original consist in 1953. (Jim Scribbins)

It is October, 1962, and train 35 is making one of its last runs as an independent Kansas City Zephyr. Before the month was over, the KCZ was consolidated with the articulated Nebraska Zephyr between Chicago and Galesburg, a practice that had been followed once before in the 1950's. (Jim Scribbins)

The KCZ whips around the Naperville curve with a consist of one RPO-baggage, one flat top coach, one dome coach, one dining car, one dome parlor car and one more coach carrying the markers. (Russ Porter)

Silver Patio was built for the American Royal Zephyr and Kansas City Zephyr service, and provided coach, buffet and lounge car service.

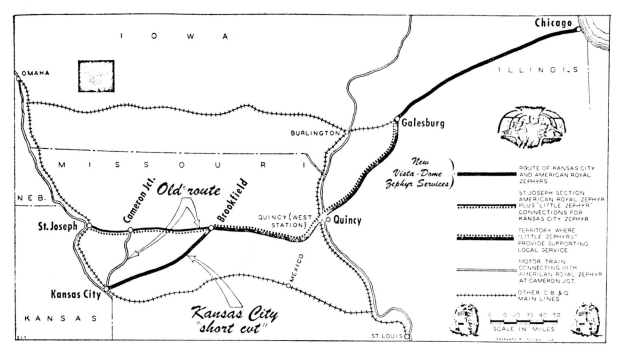

Map of Kansas City short cut: Railway Age,
p. 71, Feb. 9, 1953

Here's How the New Schedules: Railway
Age, p. 72, Feb. 9, 1953

HERE'S HOW THE NEW SCHEDULES . . .

	Westbound					Eastbound		
New Route Miles from Chicago	#55 American Royal Zephyr	#35 Kansas City Zephyr	Daily			#36 Kansas City Zephyr	#56 American Royal Zephyr	New Route Miles from K.C.
0	10:00 p.m.	12:30 p.m.	Lv	Chicago	Ar	8:00 p.m.	7:55 a.m.	466
162	12:40 a.m.	3:03 p.m.	Lv	Galesburg	Ar	5:42 a.m.	5:10 a.m.	304
262	3:10 a.m.	5:10 p.m.	Lv	Quincy (West Station)	Lv	3:45 p.m.	2:55 a.m.	204
466	7:55 a.m.	8:45 p.m.	Ar	Kansas City	Lv	12:01 p.m.	10:00 p.m.	0
468	8:45 a.m.	*9:55 p.m.	Ar	St. Joseph	Lv	*11:00 a.m.	8:30 p.m.	. . .

*Connecting Zephyr service between Brookfield and St. Joseph

. . . COMPARE WITH THE OLD

	Westbound			Eastbound	
Old Route Miles from Chicago	#55	Daily The American Royal		#56	Old Route Miles from K.C.
0	6:30 p.m.	Lv Chicago	Ar	8:25 a.m.	490
162	10:30 p.m.	Lv Galesburg	Lv	4:55 a.m.	328
262	12:40 a.m.	Lv Quincy	Lv	2:45 a.m.	228
490	7:33 a.m.	Ar Kansas City	Lv	8:00 p.m.	0
468	7:10 a.m.	Ar St. Joseph	Lv	8:15 p.m.	. . .

AND HERE'S THE NEW EQUIPMENT LINEUP . . .

For the "Kansas City Zephyrs"

Chicago-Kansas City
Reclining Seat Coaches
Vista-Dome Buffet-Lounge (For all passengers)
Dining Car
Vista-Dome Parlor-Observation
Chicago-St. Joseph
Connecting Service at Brookfield, Mo., with "Pioneer" and "Mark Twain Zephyrs"

For the "American Royal Zephyrs"

Chicago-Kansas City
Reclining Seat Coaches (Equipped with leg and foot rests)
Vista-Dome Buffet-Lounge (Serving evening refreshments and breakfast)
10 Roomette-6 Double Bedroom Sleeping Car
6 Section-6 Roomette-4 Double Bedroom Sleeping Car
Chicago-St. Joseph
Reclining Seat Coaches (Equipped with leg and foot rests)
6 Section-6 Roomette-4 Double Bedroom Sleeping Car

Train 10, the Denver Zephyr, rounds the last curve going into Chicago with Silver Veranda bringing up the rear in 1960. The Vista Dome Denver Zephyr was but four years old when this photo was taken, and was the last completely new train constructed for the Burlington Route. (Russ Porter)

An interior of a 1956 Denver Zephyr coach equipped with leg rest seats, drapes, carpeting and individual reading lamps. The DZ coaches were the ultimate in coach equipment design operated by the CB&Q. (Burlington Northern)

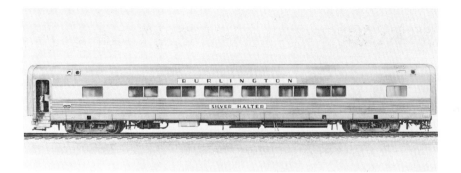

Silver Halter was a flat top, leg rest equipped coach built and operated on the Denver Zephyr in 1956. (Burlington Northern)

Diesel-Powered · Stainless Steel
NO EXTRA FARE

● You will find new travel thrills—new convenience and comfort—aboard these sleek, streamlined trains. Varied accomodations including delightful parlor cars for daytime travel . . . luxurious sleeping cars for overnight trips . . . spacious, fully-carpeted coaches with comfortable reclining seats for either day or night . . . friendly dining cars, serving delicious Burlington meals.

Burlington passengers enjoy fine service between Chicago and the Pacific Northwest, too—the Empire Builder, the North Coast Limited and the Oriental Limited.

THE *Vista-Dome* *Zephyrs* **put the SEE in Scenery**

THE CALIFORNIA ZEPHYRS
Through the Colorado Rockies and Feather River Canyon—the Scenic Way across America

THE TWIN ZEPHYRS
Over the famous Mississippi River Scenic Line—"where Nature Smiles 300 Miles"

THE *Zephyr* FLEET

TWIN ZEPHYRS
featuring *Vista-Dome* cars—
Chicago-St. Paul Minneapolis

DENVER ZEPHYR
Chicago-Omaha-Lincoln-Denver

CALIFORNIA ZEPHYR
featuring *Vista-Dome* cars—Chicago-Omaha-Denver-Salt Lake City-San Francisco (in cooperation with the Rio Grande and Western Pacific)

NEBRASKA ZEPHYR
Chicago-Omaha-Lincoln

ZEPHYR 9902
Chicago-Burlington-Quincy-Hannibal

ZEPHYR ROCKET
St. Louis-St. Paul-Minneapolis

MARK TWAIN ZEPHYR
St. Louis-Hannibal-Burlington

SILVER STREAK ZEPHYR
Kansas City-St. Joseph-Omaha-Lincoln

TEXAS ZEPHYR
Denver-Fort Worth-Dallas

SAM HOUSTON ZEPHYR
Houston-Dallas-Fort Worth

Condensed Schedules and Equipment of the Denver Zephyr

VISTA-DOME DENVER ZEPHYR
CHICAGO—OMAHA—DENVER—COLORADO SPRINGS

Table D
(Detailed Schedule in Table 1)

Mls.	WESTBOUND		1 Daily	Mls.	EASTBOUND		10 Daily
	Burlington Route		PM		*Rio Grande R.R.*		PM
*0	**Chicago, Ill.** (C.T.)	Lv	5.00	0	**Colorado Springs, Colo.** (M.T.)	Lv	▲ 1.08
162	Galesburg, Ill.	Lv	7.17	75	Denver	Ar	3.00
206	Burlington, Iowa	Lv	7.59		*Burlington Route*		
280	Ottumwa	Lv	9.06	75	Denver	Lv	4.00
393	Creston	Lv	10.52	153	Fort Morgan	Lv	5.07
443	Red Oak	Lv	11.36	187	Akron, Colo. (M.T.)	Lv	5.39
492	Council Bluffs, Ia.	Lv	x 12.22	330	McCook, Nebr. (C.T.)	Lv	8.38
496	**Omaha, Nebr.**	Ar	12.45	383	Oxford	Lv	9.24
		Lv	12.55	407	Holdrege	Lv	9.49
551	Lincoln	Ar	2.00	429	Minden	Lv	d10.08
		Lv	2.07	461	Hastings	Lv	10.41
648	Hastings	Ar	3.35	558	Lincoln	Ar	12.04
680	Minden	Ar	c 4.04			Lv	12.11
702	Holdrege	Ar	4.24	613	**Omaha, Nebr.**	Ar	1.08
779	McCook, Nebr. (C.T.)	Ar	5.37			Lv	1.15
922	Akron, Colo. (M.T.)	Ar	6.43	716	Creston, Iowa	Ar	3.01
956	Fort Morgan	Ar	7.14	829	Ottumwa	Ar	4.44
1034	**Denver**	Ar	8.30	903	Burlington, Iowa	Ar	5.55
	Rio Grande R.R.			947	Galesburg, Ill.	Ar	6.38
1034	**Denver**	Lv	9.00	1071	Aurora	Ar	a 8.21
1109	**Colorado Springs**	Ar	▲10.40 AM	1109	**Chicago**	Ar	9.00 AM

EQUIPMENT

WESTBOUND, No. 1	Car	EASTBOUND, No. 10	Car
Vista-Dome Parlor Observation-Lounge		**Vista-Dome Parlor Observation-Lounge**	
Chicago to Denver		Denver to Chicago	
"The Colorado Room," lounge.		"The Colorado Room," lounge.	
11 parlor seats, 1 parlor drawing room	A	11 parlor seats, 1 parlor drawing room	A
Sleeping Cars		**Sleeping Cars**	
Chicago to Denver		Denver to Chicago	
10 roomettes, 6 double bedrooms	DZ-1	10 roomettes, 6 double bedrooms	DZ-1
10 roomettes, 6 double bedrooms	DZ-2	10 roomettes, 6 double bedrooms	DZ-2
6 double bedrooms, 5 compartments	DZ-3	6 double bedrooms, 5 compartments	DZ-3
Chicago to Colorado Springs		Colorado Springs to Chicago	
10 roomettes, 6 double bedrooms	DZ-4	10 roomettes, 6 double bedrooms	DZ-4
Dining Car		**Dining Car**	
Chicago to Denver		Denver to Chicago	
Vista-Dome Chuck Wagon		**Vista-Dome Chuck Wagon**	
Chicago to Denver and Colorado Springs		Colorado Springs and Denver to Chicago	
Lunch Counter-Coffee Shop-Lounge		Lunch Counter-Coffee Shop-Lounge	
●*Slumbercoach*		●*Slumbercoach*	
Chicago to Colorado Springs		Colorado Springs to Chicago	
24 single rooms, 8 double rooms	CS-7	24 single rooms, 8 double rooms	CS-7
Chicago to Denver		Denver to Chicago	
24 single rooms, 8 double rooms	CS-8	24 single rooms, 8 double rooms	CS-8
Vista-Dome Reclining-Seat Coach		**Vista-Dome Reclining-Seat Coach**	
Chicago to Denver		Denver to Chicago	
46 seats, leg rests	DZ-11	46 seats, leg rests	DZ-11
Reclining-Seat Coaches		**Reclining-Seat Coaches**	
Chicago to Colorado Springs		Colorado Springs to Chicago	
50 seats, leg rests	DZ-10	50 seats, leg rests	DZ-10
Chicago to Denver		Denver to Chicago	
50 seats, leg rests	DZ-12	50 seats, leg rests	DZ-12

ALL SPACE on the Denver Zephyrs is RESERVED and specifically assigned in advance. Coach seat reservations must be claimed at train gate at Chicago by 4.55 p.m., Denver by 3.55 p.m. No charge for coach seat reservations. Checked baggage is carried only for through movement between Chicago and Denver-Colorado Springs and not to or from intermediate points.

REFERENCE NOTES

▲—Eastbound train departs from Santa Fe station, Colorado Springs. Westbound train arrives at Rio Grande station, Colorado Springs.
●—Slumbercoach passengers need purchase only coach (not 1st class) ticket, plus modest room charge. See page 29 for Slumbercoach room charges.
a—Stops to let off revenue passengers from Omaha and beyond. Will not carry passengers locally from Aurora to Chicago.
c—Stops to let off revenue passengers from Burlington and east.
d—Stops to let off revenue passengers from Denver and beyond; and to receive revenue passengers for Lincoln and east when notified at Holdrege.
x—Stops to let off revenue passengers from Chicago or to receive for Denver or beyond.

ZEPHYR EQUIPMENT

The following lists equipment built and operated on the various Zephyr streamliners, including the California Zephyr cars which were often used in other Zephyr trains and specials. The length shown is that over the buffers.

Type	Numbers and/or Names	Built	Original Service
Articulated Trains			
Power Baggage Mail	9900	1934	Pioneer Zephyr
Baggage	505	1934	
Observation Coach Parlor	570	1934	
Power Baggage	9901, 9902	1935	Twin
Diner Coach	101, 525	1935	Zephyr
Observation Coach	102, 571	1935	
Power Baggage Mail	9903 Injun Joe	1935	Mark Twain Zephyr
Baggage	506 Becky Thatcher	1935	
Dinette Coach	551 Huckleberry Finn	1935	
Observation Coach	572 Tom Sawyer		
Power Baggage	9904 Pegasus	1936	Twin Zephyr
	9905 Zephyrus		
Baggage Lounge (Aux. Power)	960 Venus		
Coach	4626 Vesta		
Coach	4627 Minerva		
Diner	150 Ceres		
Parlor	4625 Diana		
Obs. Parlor	225 June		
Baggage Lounge (Aux. Power)	961 Apollo		
Coach	4629 Neptune		
Coach	4630 Mars		
Diner	151 Vulcan		
Parlor	4628 Mercury		
Obs. Parlor	226 Jupiter		

Type	Numbers and/or Names	Built	Original Service
Diesel Unit	9906 Silver King	1936	Denver Zephyr
Diesel Unit	9906 Silver Queen		
Baggage Mail (Aux. Power)	950 Silver Courier		
Baggage Dorm-Lounge	980 Silver Lining		
Coach	4631 Silver City		
Coach	4632 Silver Lake		
Diner	152 Silver Grill		
12 sec. Slpr	410 Silver State		
12 sec. Slpr	411 Silver Tip		
12 sec. Slpr	412 Silver Arrow		
6 Bedroom, 3 Compt, 1 DR	440 Silver Sides		
Observation Parlor	230 Silver Flash		
Diesel Unit	9907 Silver Knight	1936	Denver Zephyr
Diesel Unit	9907 Silver Princess		
Baggage Mail (Aux. Power)	951 Silver Herald		
Baggage Dorm Lounge	981 Silver Bar		
Coach	4633 Silver Spruce		
Coach	4634 Silver Plume		
Diner	153 Silver Service		
12 sec. Slpr	413 Silver Skates		
12 sec. Slpr	414 Silver Screen		
12 sec. Slpr	415 Silver Tone		
6 bedroom, 3 Compt, 1 DR	441 Silver Threads		
Observation Parlor	231 Silver Streak		
Coach	550 (For train 9900)	1935	Pioneer Zephyr
Diner Coach	4850 Psyche (For 9904)	1937	Twin Zephyr
	4851 Cupid (For 9905)		
Dinette Coach	500	1938	
Dinette Coach	4852 Silver Beam (For 9906)	1938	Denver Zephyr
	4853 Silver Bell (For 9907)		
Coach	100	1939	
4 Chambrette 4 Roomette 4 Bedroom 1 Compt 1 Draw. Rm Slpr.	445 Silver Slipper (For 9906)	1939	Denver Zephyr
	446 Silver Moon (For 9907)	1939	

Non-Articulated Equipment

Type	Numbers and/or Names	Length	Seating Cap'y	Built	Original Service
Diesel Baggage	9908 Silver Charger	84'-0"	80	1939	General Pershing Zephyr
Coach	4705 Silver Leaf	80'-2"	52		
Coach	4706 Silver Eagle	89'-0"	46		
Observation Diner Parlor	301 Silver Star				
Baggage	900 Silver Light	73'-2"		1940	Silver Streak Zephyr
Baggage Mail	1600 Silver Sheen	73'-2"		1940	
Coach	4703 Silver Gleam	84'-0"	60		
Coach	4704 Silver Glow	84'-0"	60		
Observation	300 Silver Spirit	89'-0"	46		
Baggage	901 Silver Chest	88'-8"		1940	Aksarben Zephyr (First One) and the Zephyr Pool
Baggage	902 Silver Express	88'-8"			
Baggage Mail	1501 Silver Mail	73'-2" (30' Mail)			
Coach	4707 Silver Birch	80'-2"	60		
Coach	4708 Silver Brook	80'-2"	60		
Coach	4709 Silver Castle	80'-2"	60		
Coach	4710 Silver Cloud	80'-2"	60		
Coach	4711 Silver Crest	80'-2"	60		
Coach	4712 Silver Crown	80'-2"	52		
Coach	4713 Silver Forest	80'-2"	60		
Coach	4714 Silver Alchemy	80'-2"	60		
Coach	4715 Silver Cascade	80'-2"	60		
Observation	302 Silver Pours	89'-0"	46		
Diner Parlor	303 Silver Fountain	89'-0"	46		
Baggage Tavern	800 Silver Buffet	85'-0"		1947	Twin Cities
	801 Silver Salon	85'-0"			
Dome Coach	4723 Silver Bluff	85'-0"	50		
	4724 Silver Glade	85'-0"	50		
	4725 Silver Island	85'-0"	54		
	4726 Silver River	85'-0"	54		
	4727 Silver Stream	85'-0"	54		
	4728 Silver Wave	85'-0"	54		
	4729 Silver Scene	85'-0"	54		
	4730 Silver Vision	85'-0"	54		
Diner	196 Silver Silver	85'-0"	48	1948	
	197 Silver Feast	85'-0"	48		
Parlor	340 Silver Parlor	85'-0"	31+	1949	
	341 Silver Chair	85'-0"	31+		
Dome Parlor	360 Silver View	85'-0"	30+	1947	
	361 Silver Vista	85'-0"	30+		
Dome Coach	4714 Silver Dome	80'-2"		1945	
	4709 Silver Castle	80'-2"		1949	

(4714 and 4709 were rebuilt in the years shown and operated on the Twin Cities Zephyr, and other trains.)

Type	Numbers and/or Names	Length	Seating Cap'y	Built	Original Service
Baggage	903 Silver Door	72'-8"		1948	California Zephyr
	904 Silver Buffalo	72'-8"			
	905 Silver Coyote	72'-8"			
Dome Coach	4716 Silver Bridle	85'-0"	46	1948	
	4717 Silver Lodge	85'-0"	46		
	4718 Silver Lariat	85'-0"	46		
	4719 Silver Ranch	85'-0"	46		
	4720 Silver Rifle	85'-0"	46		
	4721 Silver Saddle	85'-0"	46		
	4722 Silver Stirrup	85'-0"	46		
Dome Buffet Lounge Dorm	250 Silver Club	85'-0"		1948	
	251 Silver Lounge	85'-0"			
	252 Silver Roundup	85'-0"			
Diner	193 Silver Cafe	85'-0"	48	1948	
	194 Silver Diner	85'-0"	48		
	195 Silver Restaurant	85'-0"	48		
10 Rmt 6 Bdrm Sleeper	423 Silver Point	85'-0"	22	1948	
	424 Silver Shore	85'-0"	22		
	425 Silver Butte	85'-0"	22		
	426 Silver Cliff	85'-0"	22		
	427 Silver Falls	85'-0"	22		
	428 Silver Valley	85'-0"	22		
16 section Sleeper	400 Silver Maple	85'-0"	32	1948	
	401 Silver Larch	85'-0"	32		
3 Bdrm, 1 DR Dome Obs Lnge	375 Silver Horizon	85'-0"	9	1948	
	376 Silver Penthouse	85'-0"	9		
	377 Silver Solarium	85'-0"	9		
Baggage-RPO	1604 Silver Pouch	73'-10" (30' Mail)		1952	Kansas City and American Royal Zephyrs
Coach	4731 Silver Shaft	85'-0"	50		
	4732 Silver Shield	85'-0"	50		
	4733 Silver Spear	85'-0"	50		
	4734 Silver Sword	85'-0"	50		
Dome Buffet Coach	320 Silver Garden	85'-0"			
	321 Silver Patio	85'-0"			
Diner	198 Silver Cuisine	85'-0"	48	1952	
	199 Silver Inn	85'-0"	48		
Dome Obs Parlor	365 Silver Terrace	85'-0"	30+	1952	
	366 Silver Tower	85'-0"	30+		
10 Rmt 6 DBR Sleeper	431 Silver Dale	85'-0"	22	1952	
	432 Silver Isle	85'-0"	22		
	433 Silver Meadow	85'-0"	22		
	434 Silver Plain	85'-0"	22		
	435 Silver Prairie	85'-0"	22		
	436 Silver Slope	85'-0"	22		
6 Sec 6 Rmt 4 DBR Slpr	460 Silver Flower	85'-0"	26	1952	
	461 Silver Gladiola	85'-60"	26		
	462 Silver Hyacinth	85'-0"	26		
	463 Silver Iris	85'-0"	26		
	464 Silver Orchid	85'-0"	26		
	465 Silver Tulip	85'-0"	26		

Type	Numbers and/or Names		Length	Seating Cap'y	Built	Original Service
6 Bdrm, 5 Cmpt. Sleeper	450 451 452	Silver Dove Silver Quail Silver Thrush	85'-0" 85'-0" 85'-0"	22 22 22	1952	California Zephyr
Diner	200	Silver Diner	85'-0"	48	1952	Aksarben
10 Rmt, 6 DBR Sleeper	429 430	Silver Craig Silver Chasm	85'-0" 85'-0"	22 22	1952	and Calif.
16 Sec. Slpr	402	Silver Cedar	85'-0"	32		Zephyrs
3 Bdrm, 1 DR	376	Silver Lookout	85'-0"	9		
Coach	4737 4738 4739 4740 4741	Silver Bit Silver Blanket Silver Halter Silver Cinch Silver Rein	85'-0" 85'-0" 85'-0" 85'-0" 85'-0"	50 50 50 50 50	1956	Denver Zephyr
Dome Coach	4735 4736	Silver Buckle Silver Brand	85'-0" 85'-0"	46 46		
Dome Coffee Shop Dorm	253 254	Silver Cup Silver Kettle	85'-0" 85'-0"			
Diner	201 202	Silver Chef Silver Tureen	85'-0" 85'-0"			
24 SR, 8 DBR Slumbercoach	4900 4901 4902 4903	Silver Siesta Silver Slumber Silver Rest Silver Repose	85'-0" 85'-0" 85'-0" 85'-0"	40 40 40 40	1956	
10 Rmt, 6 DBR Sleeper	485 486 487 488 489 490 491 492 493	Silver Terrain Silver Plateau Silver Hollow Silver Boulder Silver Channel Silver Vale Silver Ravine Silver Basin Silver Ridge	85'-0" 85'-0" 85'-0" 85'-0" 85'-0" 85'-0" 85'-0" 85'-0" 85'-0"	22 22 22 22 22 22 22 22 22	1956	
6 Bdrm, 5 Cmpt	453 454	Silver Swan Silver Pelican	85'-80" 85'-0"	22 22		
Dome Obs. Lnge Parlor	235 236	Silver Chateau Silver Veranda	85'-0" 85'-0"			
Coach	4700 4701 4702	Silver Chariot Silver Trail Silver Spring	84'-0" 84'-0" 84'-0"	56 58 56	1938	Zephyr Pool
Diner	190 191 192	Silver Pheasant Silver Inn Silver Spoon	83'-8" 83'-8" 83'-8"	36 36 36	1938	
Coach	6000	Silver Pendulum	85'-6"	60	1940	
Baggage	906 907 908	Silver Argo Silver Olympus Silver Treasure	72'-8" 72'-8" 72'-8"		1948	
Mail Baggage	1602 1603	Silver Post Silver Page	85'-0" 85'-0"	(30' mail) (30' mail)	1948 1948	

It is Pre-vista dome days, and train No. 24, the eastbound Afternoon Zephyr departs St. Paul on September 2, 1945 with a burst of speed that will soon have it on the 60 mark and it is not yet to Dayton's Bluff yard. Note the mixture of streamlined and articulated equipment as well as the shovel nose diesel MU'd with an "E" type B unit. (A. Robert Johnson)

Chapter 5
TRANSCONTINENTAL
STREAMLINERS

On a good many railroads the transcontinental streamliner was the fleet leader or flag bearer of the passenger train fleet. However, on the Burlington Route, there was not one such train but a grand total of five transcontinental streamliners; and the road participated in the operation of several other transcontinental trains that were not streamliners.

The transcon streamliner fleet added substantially to the territory served by CB&Q trains even though a good deal of their mileage was over rail lines not owned or operated by Burlington. This in turn underscored even more the slogan "Everywhere West."

However the fact that CB&Q operated five such trains was not of itself so unusual. Many other roads such as the Union Pacific, Santa Fe and Southern Pacific actually operated more streamliners. The big difference with the Burlington Route's operation was the vast number of co-operating railroads and the varied color schemes. The Burlington operated through trains with the Great Northern, Northern Pacific, Spokane, Portland & Seattle Ry., Rio Grande, and Western Pacific Railroads. The Southern Pacific Railroad came the closest to the CB&Q's operation with co-operative arrangements with the Union Pacific, Rock Island, Chicago & North Western (or Milwaukee Road) and the Wabash (later the Norfolk & Western). The CB&Q was involved in more thru train contracts than any other railroad in the country.

This in turn led to varied color schemes. Not all silver cars on the CB&Q were of CB&Q ownership. Many were Rio Grande, Western Pacific, Pennsylvania or Northern Pacific. Not all CB&Q cars were silver. Many were GN's Omaha Orange and Pullman (and later Big Sky Blue), Northern Pacific's two tone green and some were even painted in the Illinois Central color scheme for winter season Pullman dome operation.

Philosophies differed from train to train too. The Empire Builder was completely different from the California Zephyr, which was different still from the North Coast Limited. The Mainstreeter and Western Star had still different philosophies and atmospheres. Each of these streamliners will now be covered separately in this chapter according to their placement in service. As one would expect, the Empire Builder was first.

The Empire Builder

The first post war streamliner in the west was the Empire Builder, which was placed in service on February 23, 1947. The Burlington Route handled the train between Chicago and St. Paul, while the Great Northern operated the beautiful orange and green between St. Paul and Seattle. The Spokane, Portland and Seattle Railway handled the Chicago-Portland section between Spokane and Portland. The train continued to operate in that fashion until Amtrak day in May, 1971.

The 1947 edition of the Empire Builder consisted of:

    1 mail and baggage car
    1 60 seat coach
    3 Day-nite coaches (one car to Portland)
    1 dormitory coffee shop lounge car
    1 dining car
    2 16 duplex roomette, 4 double bedroom cars
    2 4 section, 8 duplex roomette, 4 double bedroom sleeping cars
    1 2 double bedroom, 1 drawing room observation lounge car

This twelve car consist was typical of the winter season make up with an additional sleeping car of the 4-8-4 type during heavier travel seasons. Additional cars were added at St. Paul, but by and large the above consist was standard between the years 1947 to 1951 on the CB&Q. The schedule too remained relatively stable with train No. 49 departing Chicago at 1:00 p.m. and arriving St. Paul at 7:45 p.m., and No. 44 departing St. Paul at 7:15 a.m. arriving Chicago at 2:00 p.m. CB&Q's Empire Builder carried the numbers 49 and 44 until the late 1950s.

Out of the original equipment order, the CB&Q owned one mail and baggage car (1104), one 60 seat coach (1114), three 48 seat coaches (1132 to 1134), one dormitory coffee shop (1144), one dining car (1154), two 16-4 sleepers (1178, 1179), two 4-8-4 sleepers (1167, 1168), and one 2-1 Obs. Lounge car (1194) for one complete train set. All were sub-lettered CB&Q and carried the train name in the letter board. Needless to say, the train was simply beautiful and the CB&Q always assigned silver E-7s (and later E-8s and E-9s) to the head-end between Chicago and St. Paul.

The Burlington's Empire Builder, No. 44, breezes through Lisle, Illinois on July 27, 1951 at 80 miles per hour with 15 cars. For many years, the Empire Builder shared honors with the Zephyrs for the World Speed Crown for its 84.4 miles per hour average speed sprint along the Mississippi River. The two Burlington "E" units certainly look as though they were quite capable of such over the road action. (George-Paterson Collection)

In 1951, the Great Northern elected to completely re-equip the Empire Builder. The CB&Q did not participate in the original purchase of any equipment in the 1951 train, which was placed in service on June 3rd. This train was even more beautiful than the first. The consist included:

    1 mail and baggage car
    1 baggage-dormitory car
    1 60 seat chair car
    3 48 seat chair cars
    1 coffee shop lounge car, the "Ranch Car."
    1 River series Sleeper (4 sections, 1 compartment, 7 duplex roomettes and 3 double bedrooms)
    1 Pass series sleeper (6 roomettes, 5 double bedrooms, and 2 compartments)
    1 dining car
    1 River series sleeper
    2 Pass series sleepers
    1 Mountain series Observation lounge car

This 14 car consist was standard on the CB&Q between Chicago and St. Paul. Again the train name was carried in the letter board but none of the cars carried the sub lettering "CB&Q" in the corners of the new equipment. The 1951 train continued to depart Chicago at 1:00 p.m. and arrive at St. Paul at 7:45 p.m. Eastbound departure of No. 44 remained at 7:15 a.m. with a 2:00 p.m. arrival at Chicago.

For two years the equipment ownership was almost exclusively Great Northern. Some of the CB&Q cars of the 1947 Empire Builder ran in the new train from time to time, but the basic philosophy was not to mix them. Besides, the 1947 equipment had been assigned to the new Western Star which required six sets of equipment for its Chicago-Seattle-Portland assignment.

This equipment arrangement, however, became unsatisfactory to the CB&Q due to wheelage charges. The Burlington was, in effect, contributing very little to balancing the equipment responsibility for its segment of the operation between Chicago and St. Paul. Therefore in order to balance ownership of the train, GN sold to Burlington in 1953 one baggage and one mail car, one baggage-dormitory car, three chair cars, one "Ranch" car, one dining car, six sleeping cars and one observation lounge car. The Burlington Route literally purchased one whole set of the Empire Builder. The cars were promptly re-sublettered "CB&Q" but not renumbered. Also during 1953, the CB&Q sold to the Great Northern one of the 1947 mail and baggage cars and one coach.

1955 brought the addition of dome cars to the Empire Builder. The Burlington purchased 3 dome coaches and 1 dome lounge car. At the same time, the Mountain series observation lounge cars were reassigned to the Western Star replacing the former River series observation cars. The 1947 cars were rebuilt with 4 double bedrooms, 1 compartment, 6 roomettes and a small lounge in the observation room without beverage service. The six cars were renamed in the Coulee series.

Also by 1955 the Empire Builder departed Chicago at 2:00 p.m. and arrived St. Paul at 8:40 p.m. Eastbound was still a 7:15 a.m. to 2:00 p.m. run for the 427 mile rin.

By 1959, the Empire Builder was as popular as ever and during the summer season carried 1 baggage and mail car, 1 dormitory-baggage, 4 coaches (including 3 dome coaches), 1 "Ranch" car, 1 dining car and 6 sleeping cars plus the "Great Dome" lounge car for Pullman passengers only. This was a grand total of 15 cars between Chicago and St. Paul and the consist was usually expanded west of the Twin Cities.

However, traffic was beginning to slip away. In 1961, the Empire Builder was combined with the Afternoon Zephyr between Chicago and St. Paul;

and with the North Coast Limited between St. Paul and Chicago. No. 31 now departed Chicago at 3:00 PM with a 9:45 arrival in St. Paul during the off season. Eastbound No. 32 still maintained the 7:15 AM to 2:00 PM schedule. However, the consist was beginning to become rather dismal. The November, 1964 time table reveals that the Empire Builder consisted of the following equipment: (Westbound No. 31)

    1   mail and baggage car
    1   dormitory-baggage car
    2   Afternoon Zephyr dome coaches
    1   Zephyr dining car
    1   Zephyr Dome parlor car
    2   dome coaches
    1   "Ranch" car
    1   dining car
    2   sleeping cars

The 12 car train carried but 8 cars for the Empire Builder. The pattern was set for further consolidations for in 1968. The EB was consolidated still further with the North Coast between Chicago and

It's shortly after 7:00 am on a sunny May, 1948 St. Paul morning. An E-5/E-7 lash up has replaced the Great Northern E-7's, and No. 44 has backed out of Union Depot. The switch tender is lining the connection behind the depot roundhouse and immediately the pride of the northwest will roll toward the Milwaukee Road tracks, which will be used for the initial 18 miles of its run to Lake Michigan. (Jim Scribbins)

Although the Q painted much of their equimpent to match GN and NP equipment, only in one instance did the owning roads purchase a car that matched CB&Q's color scheme. Northern Pacific slumbercoaches, which operated on the Denver Zephyr as well as the Mainstreeter and North Coast Limited, were that exception to the rule. (Tom Hoff Collection)

The CZ, as she was often called, was conceived during a time streamliners were the rage throughout the USA. Jet airliners were being studied and tested by the British, but domestic air lines were as yet giving only lip service to the idea. Meanwhile, the railroads were still experiencing full passenger loads and the race was on for not only the fastest but the finest in passenger equipment. And so in 1947, the Burlington, Rio Grande and the Western Pacific finalized plans for a "Domeliner" that would replace the Exposition Flyer. The master craftsmen at the Budd Company were given the job of constructing the 69 cars that would be used to assemble 6 eleven car sets for the daily Chicago-San Francisco service. (In the original order there were three extra 10 roomette, 6 double bedroom sleeping cars. One of these, the Silver Rapids, was owned by the Pennsylvania Railroad for transcontinental New York-San Francisco service. The Rio Grande also purchased an additional 16 section sleeper. In 1952, six 6 double bedroom, 5 comparment sleepers were placed in service. At the same time, the CB&Q purchased an additional observation car. Altogether 77 CZ cars were constructed—all built by the Budd Company—with 34 of the cars being owned by the CB&Q.

When the California Zephyr was first placed in service in 1949, and throughout most of the 1950s, 17 and 18 were basically eleven car trains throughout

If you were standing on top of the Savanna Palisades on October 26, 1963, you would have seen the combined Empire Builder-North Coast Limited racing toward Chicago with 20 cars. A very impressive train! (William S. Kuba)

CB&Q passenger extra 9981 West charges out of the Union Station en route to St. Paul over Milwaukee Road trackage. The combined North Coast Limited and Empire Builder is being re-routed because of floods on the Mississippi River in April, 1965. (William A. Raia)

the entire year. However, during the summers and Christmas-New Year's Holiday seasons, the train not infrequently carried an additional coach and one or two extra sleepers. The typical consist prior to 1952 was one baggage car, three dome coaches (designated CZ 20, CZ 21 and CZ 22), one dome buffet lounge dormitory, one dining car, two 10 roomette, 6 double bedroom sleepers (CZ 14, CZ 15), one 16 section sleeper (CZ 11) and finally the 3 double bedroom, drawing room sleeper observation lounge car (CZ 10).

As mentioned previously, the three railroads invested in 6 six double bedroom, 5 compartment sleepers in 1952 and placed them in the consist of the train, designating them CZ 16. The sixteen section sleepers continued to operate, first on a year around basis, and then on a seasonal basis through 1962. From 1962 on, only room sleepers operated on a regular basis on the California Zephyr.

The summer time tables also listed a flat top coach as part of the regular train consist, usually designated CZ 23. Summer consists were often 13

The California Zephyr was one of the most popular trains in the USA, not only from a rail fan view point, but by the general public as well. Originally trains 17 and 18 were pulled by three unit F-3 sets, probably because they had a somewhat slower schedule (by Q standards, anyway) than did the Denver Zephyr. This photo shows the train during its first summer of operation, the train that was "scheduled for scenery" holds the center track between Congress Park and LaGrange. (Jim Scribbins)

All California Zephyr equipment carried the name in the letter board for all to see, with the initials of the owning road in the corners. The Silver Sage was owned by the Western Pacific. (Harold K. Vollrath Collection)

cars or higher reducing to the standard 11 during the rest of the year.

Dining on the California Zephyr was a memorable experience. Advance dinner reservations were required, which eliminated waiting in line for a table. The menu featured a choice of traditional favorites as well as regional delicacies cooked to the passenger's order. Several dishes on the CZ had an Italian flavor because this type of cooking was once featured. Examples of dinners included Antipasto, Chicken Cacciatori, Ravioli and Spahetti and Veal Scalopine A La Parmesan. The seating capacity of the dining room ranged from 40 to 48 passengers depending upon the number of two seat tables in the car.

During the 21 years of operation, there were three types of Pullman sleepers in service on 17 and 18. The most prevalent were the 10-6 type cars. However, the exteriors of the cars did not show the word "Pullman" anywhere. The letter board proudly displayed the name "California Zephyr." It was the last train to carry its name on the letter boards. (The Empire Builder was the second last.) The sub lettering in the car corners denoted railroad ownership. For most of the CZ's career, three 10-6 sleepers were operated in the consist of the train.

The 16 section sleepers contained only berth accommodations. There were men's and women's dressing rooms at opposite ends of the car. The addition of a narrow partition parallel to the aisle at the edge of each permanent headboard gave a feeling of privacy to the sections in these cars.

The six double bedroom, five compartment sleepers were similar to the 10-6 cars with the exception of five compartments instead of 10 roomettes. The passenger capacity of 22 was the same for both cars.

Bringing up the rear of this superb train was the 3 double bedroom, 1 drawing room, dome observation lounge car. This Pullman operated car was the fifth dome in the train.

Besides the five vista domes, the CZ had several features. Each train was staffed with a hostess called a "Zephyrette." The train was purposely scheduled to travel through the Rockies and the Sierra Nevadas in daylight. On the WP, the Zephyr crossed the Sierras at Beckworth Pass and then it followed the Feather River for many miles. The scenery and the unspoiled wilderness in Colorado and California were part of the train's great selling points.

The trains were also equipped with radio and public address systems. Two 2 spool wire reprdocuers gave 12 hours continuous entertainment. There was also a telephone system by which members of the train crew could communicate between certain points in the train.

An interesting sidelight concerning the train consist took place during the first few months of the new

The 10 roomette, 6 double bedroom sleeper was the most popular sleeper operated on the CZ. The Silver Gorge was owned by the Rio Grande, but all sleepers were operated by Pullman even though there were no external indications. (Sy Dykhouse)

CZ observation cars were the only dome lounge observation sleepers constructed for U.S. service. Only Canadian Pacific's dome observation sleepers for the Canadian equaled them. (Sy Dykhouse)

operation. When the "CZ" was first placed in service, the dome buffet lounge car—intended primarily for use of the coach passengers—was placed behind the three coaches and ahead of the two bedroom-roomette cars. The full diner, two sleepers and observation car followed. In service, this arrangement tended to draw passengers from the two sleepers forward into the buffet car for liquor service. The presence of passengers enjoying refreshments changed the atmosphere of the car to that of a club lounge car and dissuaded coach passengers from partaking of the a la carte buffet snack service. This placed an additional burden on the dining car which was being taxed by heavier than anticipated patronage. The consist of the train was then rearranged so that the full diner was between the buffet and the sleepers. This arrangement continued until the end of CZ service in 1970. This new

Silver Crescent carries the markers as CZ 17 heads into the sunset through West Hinsdale, Illinois in October, 1965. It as well as four domes up front are evidence why 17 and 18 were "the most talked about trains in America." (Jim Scribbins)

positioning influenced the Pullman passengers to move to the observation lounge for beverage service. Coach patronage to the buffet snack service increased as the refreshment trade shifted to the rear of the train.

On June 1, 1949, cold plate meals from the small one man buffet kitchen were handled by the substitution of paper plate services except for coffee, cereals and liquor relieving the cook of most of his dishwashing duties.

After the CZ had been in operation for three months, the accountants released figures that showed the profit picture. The train was earning $1.29 per train mile, or in other words the CZ was placing 36.5% of the gross revenue in the net income column. Three years later, the CZ was earning $1.19 per train mile. The three railroads were earning approximately $800,000 per year on their $18 million investment. However, this investment did not include such items as coach yard facilities or ticket offices.

In March, 1959 when the CZ was 10 years old, she had carried an average passenger load of 89.4% the year around. The train had also run more than 18,500,000 miles and carried more than 1,500,000 passengers. However from the late 1950's on, the CZ operated at a profit only during the summer seasons, and by the late 1960's the world famous train operated at a loss on a year around basis. For 3½ years the ICC investigated the CZ's situation and in March, 1970, trains 17 and 18 were withdrawn from service as the California Zephyr. For approximately 1 year, a California Service was operated over the BN lines to Denver, and the D&RWG to Ogden, Utah where a connection was made with the City of San

Francisco over Southern Pacific rails. The super domeliner had lost the battle of the times. The world's most talked about train had become an item of history.

As this is being written in 1975, Amtrak operates the San Francisco Zephyr over former CB&Q rails between Chicago and Denver. Beyond Denver the Union Pacific and Southern Pacific do the honors. The only hint of the once famous train is Rio Grange's Rio Grande Zephyr, a day train between Salt Lake City and Denver. The California Zephyr operated for a grand total of 21 years, and its equipment has been sold to Amtrak and Auto-Train.

The Western Star

When the 1951 edition of the Empire Builder went into service, the Great Northern transferred the 1947 equipment to a new streamliner between Chicago, Seattle and Portland. With the new train, the GN often advertised "two great trains each way daily." The new "Star" replaced the old Oriental Limited and operated on an overnight basis, between Chicago and St. Paul. For the Burlington this meant a complete streamliner equipped with an observation lounge sleeper, 3 sleeping cars, dining car, coffee shop dormitory car and 3 to 4 day-nite coaches plus head-end equipment. The train consist usually included 11 cars and operated as train No. 53 Chicago to St. Paul.

No. 53 departed Chicago at 10:50 PM and arrived in St. Paul at 7:15 AM. She operated independently on the westbound run, however the Star was combined with the Black Hawk on the eastbound run.

The combined train, running as No. 54, departed St. Paul at 11:30 PM and arrived in Chicago at 7:20 AM. The eastbound "Star" carried the same equipment with the addition of two CB&Q Pullmans, two Black Hawk coaches and 1 buffet lounge car. No. 54 was never less than 15 cars even during the non-vacation periods. This type of operation with the Western Star continued from 1951 until 1954. By 1955, the Western Star, the NP's Mainstreeter and the Black Hawk were combined into one train in each direction between Chicago and St. Paul.

The November, 1955 CB&Q time tables listed the Western Star section consisting of two sleepers (one each for Portland and Seattle) and two coaches, again one each for Portland and Seattle. The summer time consist would expand this by one coach and one Pullman. Head end equipment usually consisted of one or two baggage cars. These types of consists were the standard operating procedures throughout the 1950's. Except for some two section operation of CB&Q trains 47 and 48, the Western Star was always carried in the consist of the Black Hawk.

The first major change in the operating technique was the speeding up of the Western Star over Great Northern trackage. Up to seven hours had been cut from the schedule between St. Paul and Seattle. Consequently, the eastbound Western Star arrived in St. Paul at 3:20 PM effective with the June, 1960 time tables. Previous arrival times were around 10:45 PM. Therefore, passengers generally did not wait for the overnight Black Hawk, but transferred to the Afternoon Zephyr departing St. Paul at about 4:00 PM arriving in Chicago at 10:40 PM. From that time, only one coach and one sleeper operated between Chicago and St. Paul (plus one head end car) for the Western Star. Depending upon traffic requirements, an extra sleeper and/or coach did sometimes operate but not as a general rule. The sleeper and coach on the eastbound run laid over in St. Paul for the departure of No. 48, but only a few passengers elected to stay in St. Paul for a morning arrival in Chicago. The westbound operation continued in the same manner as had been done so since 1951.

Western Star passengers made use of the Black Hawk's dining lounge car for food and beverage service.

Patronage declined substantially on the combined train between Chicago and St. Paul, and the Burlington Route discontinued the Black Hawk in 1970. However, the through Chicago-Seattle sleeper of the Western Star had been discontinued in 1968. The through coach was discontinued in 1969, so in effect, the Burlington Route's participation in the operation of the Western Star had ended about one year before the Black Hawk was taken off. The CB&Q's Western Star operated for a grand total of 18 years.

The Mainstreeter

The last transcontinental streamliner to go into service on the CB&Q was the Northern Pacific's Mainstreeter. She went into service replacing the old schedule of the North Coast Limited in 1952. Originally she could hardly be called a streamliner, but a very fine train indeed. Her original consist included the following cars:

 1 8 section buffet lounge sleeper
 1 6 section 6 double bedroom sleeper
 2 coaches
 2 head end cars

On the westbound run, she was combined with the Black Hawk, but eastbound she operated independently. She also carried a dining car from St. Paul to Chicago, whereas westbound passengers made use of the buffet lounge or the Black Hawk's dining car. Originally she departed Chicago at 11:00 PM and arrived in St. Paul at 7:35 AM. Eastbound departure from St. Paul was at 11:45 PM with an 8:00 AM arrival in Chicago. All independent operation of the train had ceased by 1955. By this time the consist of the Mainstreeter over the CB&Q had been reduced to one streamlined sleeper, one day-nite coach and one head-end car. There was to be no change in the operation of the Mainstreeter until the Fall, 1964 time table change. At that time, a slumbercoach replaced both the through sleeper and through coach. It marked for the first time that coach passengers en route between Chicago and Seattle had to change trains at St. Paul. The following summer of 1965, through coach service was again provided but by September the through service was again withdrawn. Only the through Chicago-Seattle slumbercoach remained, and by 1970 when the Black Hawk was discontinued, it was the only car representing the Mainstreeter on the CB&Q. The Mainstreeter had actually outlasted the Western Star between Chicago and the Twin Cities. Mainstreeter service to Chicago was withdrawn in 1970 with the demise of the Black Hawk.

Chapter 6
COMMUTER TRAINS

The Chicago, Burlington and Quincy Railroad Company operated one of the finest commuter train services in the country, and we might add that the present Burlington Northern still does. The commuter or suburban service began about 1869 when the very first trains were operated for the purpose of carrying passengers to Chicago in the morning and back home in the evening. By 1895 there were 25 trains each way between Chicago and Downers Grove. The scheduled running time was 43 minutes for the 21 mile run. CB&Q trains shared depot facilities with the Illinois Central and Michigan Central on the east side of down town Chicago in those early days.

In 1881 the CB&Q began to use the original Union Station on the west side of downtown Chicago. Also during this time, the Burlington did much to sell the benefits of living in suburbia. People flocked from Chicago on that advice, and this in turn helped build the suburban traffic during the period 1875 to 1900.

Rolling stock and motive power consisted of small open end coaches and American type 4-4-0s prior to the 1890s. Between 1889 and 1893, the CB&Q constructed five 0-6-2T suburban engines (500 to 504) that supplemented the 4-4-0s. Both types of engines were replaced by ten-wheelers by 1910. These 4-6-0s were capable of achieving 80 miles per hour in a short distance. They were perfect for commuter service, and they were the mainstay for such service until the 1930s, when they were replaced by 4-6-2 Pacific type steam locomotives.

By 1920 a number of the wooden coaches were replaced by steel cars but many open end cars would remain in service until 1950.

The 1930s were a grim period of time for the Nation, and this was followed by World War II. Little progress was made in upgrading CB&Q suburban service for over twenty years.

Service between Chicago and Downers Grove, and Chicago and Aurora was about evenly split in terms of the number of trains operated. Post World War II years saw an increase in the number of people moving to the suburbs. The CB&Q was caught in a two way squeeze. On the one hand, inflation was creating problems with operating costs and yet there was an increase in patronage. To add more trains in the triple track suburban territory would not have been practical, nor was it possible to operate longer trains because of the length of station platforms. Clearly changes had to be made in the basic operating techniques of the service.

The Burlington began to look around to see what other suburban roads were doing with the passenger seating capacity of equipment. The Long Island employed a double deck car with a staggered two-level seating arrangement. The design led to some further developments with the Budd Company, who came up with a car design that permitted comfortable seating on two levels. The new design became known as the gallery car, and it solved three problems for the Company. First, the Burlington was able to increase the capacity of the trains without expanding the length of the trains. Second, the Chicago Union Station charged a rental fee based on a per car basis and the Company was able to haul more commuters without an increase in Union Station fees. Finally, the 14th Street coach yard in Chicago did not need to be increased (there wasn't any room anyway). to handle additional passenger equipment for the increase in suburban business. The first of the new gallery cars went into service in September, 1950. Thirty were purchased that year, and another 30 were added by 1957.

The streamlined gallery cars were not the only car equipment changes being made. All of the standard cars still in service were given roller bearings,

Pacific No. 2816 wheels a three car commuter train by Naperville, Illinois in a typical 1940 fashion. (William A. Raia)

tightlock couplers, new floors and seats, vestibules, new lighting and air conditioning. The cars were repainted inside and out with the exteriors sporting a green and tan scheme with a silver roof. But that was only the beginning.

The steam power, which had been in operation since the 1930s, began to be replaced by new diesel locomotives. On September 26, 1952, the last steam powered commuter trains arrived and departed both Chicago and Downers Grove. Also on that day, the Downers Grove suburban yard was closed and all trains were operated between Chicago and Aurora. This had the effect of doubling service west of Downers Grove to Aurora, which was highly beneficial for the entire suburban operation.

The overall number of trains had been increased too. For example in 1951 before the service changes, 10 trains arrived in Chicago between 7:30 and 8:30 a.m. carrying about 8000 passengers. In 1964, 14 trains were scheduled to arrive during that hour with about 14,000 passengers. Note the difference, which is reflected in the increased capacity of the gallery cars.

Dieselization came in the form of General Motors' Electro-Motive Division E-7s, E-8s and E-9s. These locomotives were serviced in Aurora, and prior to the days of push pull engines and were turned there also.

The push pull trains arrived in 1965, and brought a number of efficiencies to the suburban operation. Except for the power cars, all standard passenger equipment was retired and taken out of service. the CB&Q could point out with pride that their service was one of very few in the world that was virtually all streamlined. The efficient and safe operation developed by the CB&Q has continued since the Burlington Northern merger. The route of the double deck silver commuter streamliners is still one of the best in the world.

As the Twentieth Century neared its mid-point, the character of the Chicago-Aurora commuter service began to exhibit change: the westbound Pacifics at LaGrange Road, 2802 and 2812 are both class S-1a even though one sports a feedwater heater between its stack and headlight, and the open platform cars trailing them in August, 1949 were the only ones operating in the area. (Jim Scribbins)

And things were changing: conventional main line coaches with fully enclosed vestibules were beginning to be assigned to the "scoots" and six of them follow highest numbered S-2 2949 in LaGrange. (Jim Scribbins)

An eastbound Zephyr kicks up the dust as she flies by the Downers Grove suburban train yard during the year 1945. Note the open end coaches, many of which were later rebuilt with enclosed vestibules and air conditioning. (Russ Porter)

CB&Q Pacific No. 2931 lays over between commuter runs in Downers Grove, Illinois in 1950. This yard was later closed. (Collection of Russ Porter)

In the early 1950's, the "Q" assigned long distance "E" units to suburban trains during the Chicago lay over time of the diesels, as witness the 9924A arriving in LaGrange. Could it be that this unit is something special? Although it has the nose and grill placement of an E-7, it lacks vertical louvers behind the cab. (Jim Scribbins)

Approaching Chicago Union Station is an inbound late-afternoon train which can boast new re-built ex-open enders, green and brown coaches with cream window trim and gray roofs. Two are lettered "Suburban Service" in the same manner in which more prestigeous vehicles flaunted individual names. In the Pennsy coach yard are first class cars for the Golden Triangle, then undergoing a comprehensive modernization. The 4-6-2's in these summer 1949 scenes were all scrapped approximately two years later. (Jim Scribbins)

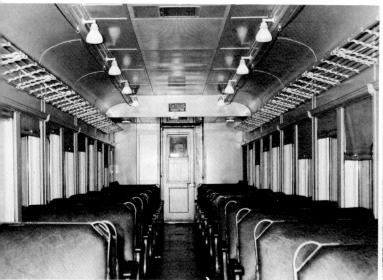

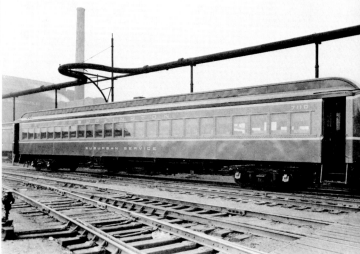

The power cars contained walkover seats as well as baggage racks the entire length of the coach section. Although the cars were post-war rebuilds, they continued to be lit with milk glass globes, which gave the air conditioned cars a combination 1920s/1940s atmosphere. The power cars housed a diesel generator set to suppy electric power for the train lighting and air conditioning. (Jim Scribbins)

Suburban coach No. 7110 carried a temporary modified green and brown color scheme, which included a wrap around the ends. The ex-open ender was air conditioned and included cushioned walk over seating. (Burlington Northern)

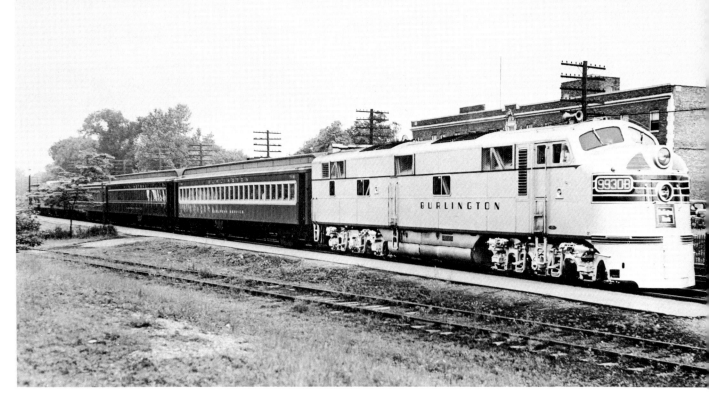

It is June 27, 1949, and the 9930B leads a train of newly rebuilt equipment out of Downers Grove enroute to Chicago. The reader should note the difference in the color arrangements of the first coach as compared to the photo of the 7110 shown previously. (Burlington Northern)

While the open-enders were being rebuilt, new double deck streamlined coaches were arriving from the Budd Company. Semi-streamlined power cars were also part of each train consist, with either double deck or the rebuilt single level coaches. This photo shows a typical non-rush hour suburban run en route from Chicago to Aurora, Illinois. (William A. Raia)

The power cars were always coupled to the west end of the trains, as shown with this eastbound train en route to Chicago on July 27, 1951 with a threatening thunder storm about to cut loose. (George-Paterson Collection)

Some power cars were also equipped with a baggage compartment. (Sy Dykhouse)

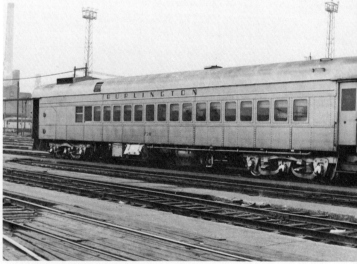

While other cars were full coaches. (Sy Dykhouse)

Burlington gallery No. 741 was photographed at Aurora during CB&Q's centennial celebration of suburban service. The circular decal to the left of the door commemorated the event. (Jim Scribbins)

The comfort index of the gallery cars is very high for the distance traveled by Chicago-Aurora commuters. The two level seating concept was pioneered by the Burlington and Budd partnership and has since been adopted by the major Chicago commuter carrying railroads. (Jim Scribbins)

The final step in Burlington commuter service was the implementation of the push-pull concept, pioneered by the Chicago & North Western. Here car No. 792 leads an inbound suburban train into Chicago: trains were pushed into Chicago, and pulled en route to the suburbs. (Burlington Northern)

99

Chapter 7
Freight and Mixed Trains

The Burlington Route was, and is, a granger route. Indeed for most of its life as a separate railroad well over 55% of its total annual tonnages and revenues came from farm and food products. And being a granger road, one can easily visualize a big 4-8-4 steam locomotive or red and grey diesel units high balling a mile long freight over the prairies on superbly constructed track, track so good that it was difficult to find even a stone of ballast out of place. Or if you wanted a change of pace, smaller steam power and/or single unit diesel locomotives traveled over light rail trackage pulling a short train with either a caboose or a combine carrying the markers. Either way, one could see the entire train, and see it for miles in both directions. Although main line freights were consistently long, the branch line freights varied in length from a handfull of cars most of the year to as many as 40 or 50 during harvest time, depending of course which line one was thinking about.

The CB&Q was very concerned about the performance of its freight trains. For example, in 1926 the CB&Q found that its less than carload lot freight that was distributed from peddler cars was becoming less profitable. They found that such peddling involved an alarming amount of shortages and a staggering amount of overtime was paid out to the way freight crews. Claims were very heavy and were increasing; and when the claim investigation was completed, the company was still in the dark as to what happened.

The CB&Q launched a study into the problem and found that the peddler cars were the principal cause of the trouble. It was decided to abolish the peddler by consolidating the freight at a centrally located transfer into as many straight cars as tonnage would warrant.

The CB&Q conducted a study and found that the railroad was strewn with merchandise cars, and that peddlers were taking as long as four to five days to deliver freight to destination. They found that the cars were being opened from 3 to 16 stations, and that the cars were exposed to pilferage and a great deal of damage was caused by train men who failed to even down the cargo after the car was at a station. Therefore, the Burlington set up a consolidation plan

which permitted the CB&Q to cut the delivery times for LCL freight to second morning delivery from any point to any point.

With farm and food products making up a major proportion of the CB&Q's freight business, the company left no stone unturned in promoting farming and in the education of farming techniques. One of the combination educational/promotional techniques was farm specials of various types. Widely used in the 1920's, the special trains concentrated on hogs, potatoes, sugar beets or in one particular case in 1926, a poultry train. A total of 206,205 people passed through such a poultry train in 98 towns in Nebraska and Kansas from March 1 to April 8 during that year. This was an average of 2000 per town.

The train was made up of 9 cars. The first was a dynamo baggage car containing chicken feed, bulletins and supplies. The second was a coach with exhibits portraying the necessity of sanitation in successful poultry raising. The third was a standard live poultry transit car with exhibits in the stateroom. The fourth was a flat car on which were mounted two standard Nebraska poultry houses in actual operation, one with baby chicks and the other with growing pullets. The fifth car, a coach, contained live poultry exhibits to demonstrate the value of good breeding stock. The sixth car showed the value of producing only high quality poultry products for the market, the value of grading eggs, correct packing, eggs in cold storage and an exhibit of dressed poultry showing market classifications. The seventh car was a 12 section Pullman while the next one was a cafe car and the ninth and last a business car.

The local communities also arranged special features for the arrival of the train. These included poultry shows, egg shows (in which 1,729 dozen eggs were entered), poultry poster contests in the schools, essay contests, band concerts, glee clubs, parades, chicken chasing contests, special sales days, poultry window displays and a red headed girls contest. In many towns the boys in the high schools built poultry houses from lumber furnished by lumber dealers. These were sold at public auction, the proceeds above the cost of materials going to the

Freight traffic is the bread and butter of all railroads, and even though the Q was a pro-passenger operator, the same was true for that system. The Route scheduled their freights even during the days of steam, such as No. 81 rolling along the Mississippi River at DeSoto, Wisconsin, behind steam locomotive No. 5622, Class 0-5-a, a powerful 4-8-4. (Burlington Northern)

boys. At Curtis an egg throwing contest was staged while at Campbell 5000 eggs were fried for egg sandwiches.

The train visited three towns daily, starting its program at 9:00 AM and closing the train at 11 at night. Speakers were sent to the schools and the school children taken through the train. While the school children were being instructed, lectures were given to the local farmers at town halls. 46,193 people attended these lectures at the town halls, while 30,000 school children attended the special classes.

We don't see such trains anymore because the county agricultural agents now carry out such education/promotional ventures. The ultimate objective of the CB&Q was increased farm traffic, and the Burlington was not the only road to operate such specials. One could see them on the Great Northern, Northern Pacific, Union Pacific and most other lines throughout the west and mid-west.

Sales promotions and educational projects would have done little to increase and retain freight traffic if the Burlington did not work to improve the operating procedures. In 1923 the CB&Q scheduled freight from Chicago to Denver in three and one-half days. By 1938, they had reduced this to less than two days. In 1923 it took two days for a carload to move from Chicago to Paducah, Kentucky. Fifteen years

later that had been reduced to less than 24 hours. During that 15 year period, many schedules had been speeded up as much as 60%. However, they were not satisfied with that and in 1941, a new set of schedules went into effect.

The CB&Q participated in new schedules that cut a day from Chicago and St. Louis to all Pacific Coast destinations. Also in 1941, the road established first morning delivery from Chicago to such stations as LaCrosse, Wisconsin, St. Joseph, Missouri, and Ottumwa, Iowa between 300 and 450 miles distant. Also first evening arrival at Billings, Montana on merchandise from Denver with early second morning delivery at Billings and by truck service to considerable area round Billings.

Other schedule reductions included 2 hours, Chicago-Kansas City; 12 hours, St. Louis-Denver; and as much as 20 hours from St. Louis to Montana points.

1941 schedules also revealed fast overnight service for long distances from Galesburg, Illinois to Lincoln, Nebraska, 372 miles; from Lincoln to Denver, 479 miles; and from Kansas City to East St. Louis, 350 miles. A particularly fast train (for that time) was No. 62 from Denver to Chicago, 1034 miles in 33 hours or an average speed of about 32 miles per hour. We will discuss this freight again later in this chapter, which handled a heavy volume of

Time freight No. 97 highballs through Lisle, Illinois, on July 27, 1951 en route to St. Paul with 68 cars at 45 miles per hour. (George-Paterson Collection)

perishables and livestock, a substantial portion of which was through business requiring a fast, on time schedule to protect market requirements.

There were many other improvements during the year 1941, which could not have been timed more carefully with the advent of World War II. Some of these improvements included a co-ordinated rail-truck service (The CB&Q tried very hard to develop a balanced transportation system, but government and ICC rulings prevented much progress. However, the CB&Q was a leader in rail-highway transport co-ordination.); the installation of a teletype tracing service for shippers and receivers; the provision of a direct telephone service between important stations and terminals; the construction of new market terminals and team tracks at Denver, Kansas City and St. Louis; new diesel electric power for switching services and the purchase of new equipment including special types such as 65 foot mill type gondolas, covered hoppers, automobile parts box cars, auto device cars, longer flat cars and many other types of rolling stock.

The World War taxed the CB&Q to the utmost with train traffic hitting levels far above the previous depression years. The fact that the CB&Q, and other railroads, were able to handle the expanded traffic safely and efficiently stands as a testimonial to the ability of the American Railroads to be flexible and capable of handling any and all emergencies. Although the War prevented the CB&Q from initia-tint new innovations, the company was quietly making plans for the return to peace time operations.

One such plan was the development of new refrigerator cars.

As we mentioned previously, the CB&Q conducted several research projects during the war but without the implementation or field testing. Two refrigerator cars were constructed at the Plattsmouth, Nebraska, shops of the Burlington Refrigerator Express Company in late 1945, just after the war. Each car incorporated several new ideas in the protection of perishables during transit. The two cars tested new devices such as fan-type air circulation, overhead ice bunkers, heaters and several other features. The cars were used in a research and testing program conducted under the direction of a committee representing shippers, the Association of American Railroads, the United States Department of Agriculture, refrigerator car owners and other groups. The committee expected to develop recommendations for an improved all purpose refrigerator car, which eventually led to the further development of mechanical refrigerator cars.

The research, however, was not restricted to new freight car concepts because even the best car will not earn a dime if the service procedures are not appropriate for shipper needs.

One of the biggest post-war projects was the opening of the "direct route" freight line between Kansas City and St. Louis in 1949. This new route produced a substantial increase in the volume of through freight between those two important gateways as well as marked improvements in through freight service between St. Joseph and St.

The Q provided way freight service over every mile of line. Such a train is shown here pedaling through Lisle, Ill., with a 2-8-2 for power and 34 cars. (George-Paterson Collection)

Louis. (This route change was mentioned briefly in Chapter 1.)

For many years, the CB&Q operated two routes between Kansas City and St. Louis, one via its own circuitous route through Cameron and Hannibal, and the other an interline service with the Alton (later the Gulf, Mobile & Ohio and now the Illinois Central Gulf) via Mexico, Missouri. On September 26, 1949, the CB&Q obtained trackage rights over the GM&O between Kansas City and Mexico, and transferred all of its through Kansas City-St. Louis service to the new route.

One of the problems of the previous routings and operations was that a large portion of the available and potential traffic between the two gateways was "bridge" traffic between points east and southeast of St. Louis and points southwest, west and northwest of Kansas City and St. Joseph or vice versa. The pre-improvement leaving and arrival times of the important western connections on the Santa Fe and Union Pacific at Kansas City and St. Joseph varied in such a manner that the CB&Q could not operate a single train between Cameron and St. Louis, handling both Kansas City and St. Joseph cars, and still maintain close connections at both cities.

For many years the CB&Q operated an interline service between Kansas City and St. Louis via the

GM&O. This operation required a change of power and crews at Mexico as well as complete inspections of the train. A substantial amount of switching was also required to combine the Burlington's St. Louis traffic with the GM&O's traffic to or from points east of Mexico. As a result even though the combined route was shorter than either the GMO's or CB&Q's route between the two cities, schedules were long and performance exceptionally poor. As one might guess, each road preferred to handle traffic over its own circuitous route, the GM&O via Roodhouse, Illinois and the Burlington by way of Cameron and Hannibal, rather than divide the revenues via the shorter interline route. This condition produced a gradual diminution of traffic over the interline route to the point by as early as 1946 that through traffic had to be handled in what amounted to connecting local trains. Thus the "Q" switched its entire solicitation efforts to its own longer route, which in turn produced even more problems and in turn traffic and revenues continued to decline.

The operations via the longer route provided that the Kansas City cars were handled on St. Joseph-St. Louis trains because there was insufficient volume to justify operating separate trains. This meant that the eastbound train had to be run to connect with the latest arrival from the west, which in 1946 to 1949, happened to be at St. Joseph. This meant that the Kansas City cars had to wait extra hours before starting east. Westbound the train had to be scheduled for the first westbound departures, which happened to be at Kansas City, and the result was that St. Joseph cars had to leave St. Louis earlier (or wait until the next day) and lay over in St. Joseph. This service was also integrated with schedules to and from Chicago which further complicated operations.

This had to change particularly because of the rapid post-war industrial and economic development of the west and southwest in those years. Kansas City and St. Joseph increased in importance as gateways for that growing area. The opportunities for offering the needed improvements in service to both St. Louis and Chicago via Hannibal was restricted by the physical limitations of the single track line between Palymra and Kansas City-St. Joseph, particularly west of Brookfield and south of Cameron. The operation of additional trains over that route would have posed serious difficulties.

To correct this proble, the CB&Q sought an agreement with the GM&O for the new route. Secondly, the company improved the trackage between Palmyra and Brookfield and began construction of the Kansas City short cut mentioned previously in Chapter 1.

The CB&Q obtained trackage rights and began operating through freights with its own power and crews, and retained all of the revenue from terminal to terminal. The Burlington further agreed to improve the GM&O's trackage to heavy duty high speed standards. A pro rata share of this improvement cost was paid by the CB&Q as a part of its rental and use fees. New 112 and 115 pound rail was laid and the entire line was raised 4 to 6 inches on new chat ballast. Centralized Traffic Control was installed between Kansas City and Slater, Missouri and the automatic block signal system was upgraded substantially from Slater to Mexico.

The Company inaugurated four completely new time freights. Inasmuch as the CB&Q simply has trackage rights between Kansas City and Mexico, the road could operate through trains only, with local service between Kansas City and Mexico handled exclusively by the GM&O. These new freights operated on fast non-stop schedules. the CB&Q continued the operation of its local train between St. Louis and Mexico. Another innovation

Train No. 68, en route to Chicago, charges through Lisle, Illinois with 118 cars at 40 miles per h our on July 27, 1951. (George-Paterson Collection)

The 5509 shakes the countryside as it rolls through the Greenwood, Nebraska area between Lincoln and Omaha on the Lincoln Division in August, 1955. (Harold K. Vollrath Collection)

as of the September 26, 1949 date was the through operation of cabooses from Kansas City to East St. Louis yard, without switching out at the intermediate crew terminal at Mexico as was the regular operating practice previously. This operation began a new look at pooling cabooses and the result was that eavantually all cabooses were run through.

The new Kansas City trains were operated on the schedules shown in the table and were run through to East St. Louis, using the Burlington's own line crossing of the Mississippi River at Alton, Illinois. The connections into St. Louis were provided by transfers to and from West Alton.

The direct route trains handled only Kansas City traffic to and from western and southern connections at Kansas City. St. Joseph traffic was not handled through Kansas City because better schedules and connections were possible through an independent operation through Cameron.

The St. Joe-St. Louis trains made possible later closing and earlier delivery times at St. Louis and East St. Louis. Improvements in this service over the old line were an important by-product of the new "direct route" between KC and East St. Louis. The St. Louis-St. Joe trains operated non-stop between West Alton, Missouri, and Hannibal, where they set out and picked up cars to and from Galesburg and all

points via Galesburg, including Chicago, Twin Cities, Rock Island, Davenport, Moline and points north of Quincy. All of the cars were blocked according to destinations, so the setout and pickups required less than 60 minutes most of the time. The trains then operated non-stop between Hannibal and St. Joseph.

All of the St. Joe trains operated into and out of St. Louis. No. 72's cars to southern and eastbound connections to East St. Louis were handled in Second No. 72 which originated at Hannibal and ran directly into East St. Louis by way of Alton. No. 68 had a shuttle train connection from West Alton to East St. Louis. Westbound trains No. 61 originated in St. Louis, while No. 71 originated at East St. Louis. No. 71 operated non-stop to Hannibal where it was combined with No. 61.

These major revisions in freight service were only a prelude for the new service that was to be introduced by the CB&Q in 1953 when the new route between Kansas City and Chicago went into service.

We seldom hear of freight trains being christened, and we seldom hear of a freight train being named. However, with the opening of the Kansas City Short Cut in 1953, the CB&Q celebrated the event with "Red" Grange (who wore the number 77 and was known Nationwide among football fans as the

"We were waiting for 25, the North Coast Limited, and had located a good spot beneath a wooded bluff north of Prairie du Chien when the unmistakable sound of steam was heard in the distance," says photographer/author Jim Scribbins. Around the bend popped a headlight, and it was the 5621—first of the 0-5-a class outshopped by West Burlington in 1938—leading a train "wrong main" to enable the Limited to overtake it. This was the last time we saw Q steam in non-excursion service. October, 1956. (Jim Scribbins)

"Galloping Ghost") christening train No. 77, the top time freight between Chicago and Kansas City. Prior to 1953, No. 77 took from 18 to 20 hours to run from Chicago to Kansas City. With the new high speed railroad line, the CB&Q promptly sliced the time of No. 77 by 6 hours to a scheduled running time of 13 hours, 30 minutes which was later reduced still further by another 10 minutes. In 1962, the overnight schedule of 77 departed Chicago at 8:00 p.m. and arrived in Kansas City at 9:20 a.m. The eastbound time freight, No. 80, was not as fast as 77, departing

Kansas City at 8:00 p.m. and arriving in Chicago at 1:00 p.m. the next day. Eastbound traffic required more set outs at important intermediate terminals.

The CB&Q sought continuously to upgrade its freight service in all areas throughout its history. This was particularly true with livestock and piggyback traffic. The former eventually dwindled to almost nothing, while piggyback traffic on the other hand grew continuously since 1941, and continues to grow today for Burlington Northern. Let's take a look at these two areas.

The railroads have always been most adaptable to unusual shipments, and this photo shows a special 17 car train of wine from San Francisco rolling through Denver behind the 5010, Class 0-1, a 2-8-2. (Burlington Northern)

Time freight 82 pauses at Eola, Illinois (en route from St. Paul to Chicago) to set out cars for the Elgin, Joliet & Eastern Ry. (Russ Porter)

Livestock Traffic

Ever since the CB&Q expanded into Iowa, Nebraska and Kansas, the company was a key element in American meat production. Livestock moved from the western states to Kansas City, St. Paul and Chicago literally in train load lots. Stock movements occurred in seasonal surges in the spring and fall. Also when the range began to dry up, steers were moved to Iowa feed lots for finishing off. In other words, putting on the beef and the little layer of fat that made the meat tender and tasty.

The rules and regulations concerning livestock in transit required that animals be unloaded and fed and watered after they had been in transit for 28 hours. Livestock could not be confined to cars in excess of 28 hours, unless at the written request of stockmen, which had to be attached to the waybill. Then transit confinement could be extended to 36 hours except during exceptionally hot weather. Also hot weather meant that hogs would need to be watered more often than 28 hours.

This was a costly operation for the railroads, and the only answer was fast freight service for livestock. For the CB&Q this meant running the fastest livestock train in America. Their No. 62, which we mentioned earlier, ran from Denver to Chicago in a little over 31 hours as far back as 1941, and was scheduled for 28 hours in 1963. No. 62 wheeled the distance from Denver to Akron, Colorado, 112 miles in 2 hours, 19 minutes. This type

With the set out completed, No. 82, with the massive and impressive 4-8-4 numbered 5615 strides off with a white column of smoke to complete her run to Chicago. Eola is an important interchange point with the EJ&E for freight routed "Around, Not Thru Chicago" by the J's own admission. (Russ Porter)

A very important ingredient on any railroad are the switch engines that assemble or disassemble freight trains, and deliver or pick up in terminal areas. The 0-6-0 No. 509 switches in the Rockford, Illinois area in April, 1954. (W. S. Kuba)

107

Beginning in 1929, the "Q" invested in a small fleet of gas-electric switchers. The fleet, numbered from 9100 to 9120, could perform not only the same work as steam switchers, but for about 50% of the steam costs. The 9120 was the last of the fleet and was sold to the Illinois Midland Railroad in 1959. This Whitcomb built switcher is shown here at Millington, Illinois, on the Montgomery and Zearing Subdivision of the Chicago and Aurora Divisions in 1958. (Russ Porter)

To the "FT" units must go the credit of revolutionizing freight train performance. The "FT" started a trend of good looking locomotive power, and the Burlington scheme fit very well with "F" unit contours. The 107-D is shown here in a diesel shop near Chicago in 1961. Built in 1944, the unit is still in suberb looking condition, a tribute to Burlington's maintenance policy. (Russ Porter)

CB&Q No. 67, a high speed Chicago-Kansas City time freight passes through Mendota, Illinois on the Chicago and Aurora Division. The four matched "F" units give the head-end of the time freight a streamlined appearance. Very appropriate for such a train. The year is 1961. (Russ Porter)

of timing was typical from one subdivision to another. The timing would have been faster in 1941 except for the changing of cabooses and motive power at division points. To give an example of the faster times with diesels, RAILWAY AGE (October 21, 1963) reported that one of the fastest long-distance freight train movements in history was undertaken by a joint Union Pacific-Burlington special all livestock train of 75 cars with 2500 head of prime Hereford yearlings that made the 966 mile run from Hanna, Wyoming, to Galesburg, Illinois, in 21 hours, 50 minutes.

However the high speed of the livestock trains was not enough. To improve efficiencies of the operations, the CB&Q took delivery of 100 fifty foot double deck stock cars in 1963. These were the largest cars in the Burlington's fleet and the first to be equipped with roller bearings.

In 1966, the CB&Q experimented with livestock containers. The road constructed a 50 foot slatted container that could be mounted on a 53 foot flat car and transform that car into a 70,000 pound capacity stock car. A trial run of the container was made on November 23rd from the CB&Q stockyards at Lincoln to the road's stockyards at Montgomery, Illinois. Aboard were 89 head of calves weighing 34,170 pounds. On the second trip, a typical load of 133 head of cattle and calves weighing 66,633 pounds was handled from Lincoln to Galesburg. The tests showed that the loading and unloading of the cattle, plus the performance of the car while in transit was satisfactory. The objective was to reduce expenses with idle stock cars during the slack periods of the year. The containers could be stored while the flat car remained in revenue service.

However as the packing plants moved out to the ranges, stock traffic dwindled to virtually nothing. An era has come to an end in America, and along with it, the drover's car. The drover's car provided accommodations for the stockmen riding through with their four legged charges. These men remained with the animals until their destination was reached, and they were responsible for caring for the animals and always on the lookout for cripples or sick animals. The drover's car was usually an old coach that had seen its better days. It was fitted with bunks, stove, pantry, kitchen and oil lamps. The stockmen brought their own food, skillets, coffeepots and other eating utensils. While on board, the men would spit, argue, eat and be on the watch for their group of livestock. The bunks provided an area for what sleep the men did get, because leisure time was generally spent playing cards. These cars carried a million stories, some true and almost all exaggerated. Now in 1975, such equipment is no longer in operation on the Burlington or any railroad for that matter. Many a man that has spent miles and miles in such cars, now sits around at night and spins yarns about the adventure on the drover's cars.

Extra 124-D east goes into the eastbound hold track at Eola, Illinois with two F-3s and two FTs. The eastbound train must await a clear track ahead before continuing on to Cicero yard on the outskirts of Chicago. The year—1961. (Russ Porter)

An eastbound freight passes the platforms of the modern Ottumwa, Iowa depot behind a trio of F3s in September, 1960. (Jim Scribbins)

West (approaching) and eastbound freights meet just off the east edge of the depot in Ottumwa, September 1960. The livery sired by the F's was adapted for the streamlined waycars. (Jim Scribbins)

Train 88 pumps up air before departing Savannah, Ill. (W. S. Kuba)

Train No. 82 passes Lisle, Illinois in July, 1951 at 35 mph with 128 cars, all from its Great Northern and Northern Pacific connections in St. Paul. (Harold K. Vollrath Collection)

Just 37 miles out of Denver, an extra west barrels through Keensburg, Colorado en route to the mile high city in the Rockies, with 103 cars. (George-Paterson Collection)

Piggyback Service

Of all the innovations presently in operation on North American railroads, piggyback service has to rank as one of the best performers for it combines the advantages of highway and rail together for mutual benefit for all concerned. The Burlington inaugurated piggyback service between Chicago and Kansas City on January 8, 1941. That early plan involved the National Transport Company which made arrangements with truckers operating between and in the two cities. National provided the facilities for loading and unloading trailers on and off flat cars. The loaded piggyback flats departed Chicago at 10:30 p.m. and arrived in Kansas City at 4:30 p.m. the next afternoon. Eastbound departures from Kansas City were at 6:00 p.m. with arrival in Chicago at 1:00 p.m.

This truck load freight was all that was handled by the CB&Q from 1941 through 1954. Growth was minimal. However, the CB&Q served all major terminals with piggyback service by 1956.

The company had only 29 flats in piggyback service in 1954, but by 1956 this had been expanded to almost 150.

Up to 1954, the CB&Q never handled more than 10 trailers in one day, and less than 3000 trailers per year. By 1957, it was over 15,000 trailers per year and this grew to nearly 70,000 annually by 1966. It continued to grow substantially by the merger date in March, 1970; and it continues to grow in 1975 on the Burlington Northern.

Mixed Trains

The mixed freight and passenger train was a popular way to operate trains in the early days of railroading, but as traffic built up such trains diminished in importance. That is, until the depression of the 1930's. And then did the mixed train come back in full bloom as it turned out to be a very efficient way to reduce train, locomotive and crew miles and costs and still maintain service. Sometimes without even downgrading or impairing service.

The Burlington Route was no exception, and the granger roads seemed to operate more mixed trains than railroads in other parts of the USA. The midwest and the prairie was the home for the mixed train, just as Indiana and Ohio were home to the interurbans.

The Burlington operated, and still does, a vast number of branch lines throughout Iowa, Kansas, Nebraska, Missouri and Illinois. Almost every line had one or two mixed trains in each direction daily, with a few tri-weekly and bi-weekly trains throughout the system. A number of mixed trains operated on the main lines.

Equipment for the mixed came in the form of down graded passenger equipment. The cars functioned not only as a coach, but also as a caboose. Most mixed trains were equipped with a combine, but others carried a coach and baggage car while still others were equipped with just a caboose, sometimes with a side door.

110

The mixed train lasted until the merger date, but most were gone before 1969. The last time such trains were listed in the public time tables was the November, 1966-April 1967 edition. The mixed train was just one more part of Americana and railroading that we no longer have with us.

The Caboose

Cabooses were known as way cars on the CB&Q. The wood cars were painted a dark or box car red with white lettering. As with most railroad cabooses, they were nothing to brag about. They were stricly functional, but did provide the crews with a home away from home and the conductor with an office while on duty.

The year 1953, however, changed all that. The new way cars, 35 in all, that were delivered that year were brightly painted with aluminum with a broad stripe of Scotchlite along each side, including a 4 x 5 foot BURLINGTON ROUTE insignia. The new all steel cars provided riding comfort with Waugh cushion underframes. The cars were equipped with electric lights and Motorola VHF two-way radio powered by Leece-Neville alternators. A Mars oscillating red light was mounted at the roof line at each end of the car as an added safety feature. The light flashed on automatically when the train line air pressure declined to 20 pounds or less. If operation of the light was desired with more than 20 pound brake pipe pressure, it could be operated manually.

These new cabooses in the 13500 series started a new trend which eventually led to the purchase of extended vision cupola cabooses, all painted in the bright aluminum with the red striping. They were a superb and novel bit of public relations because who could miss the brightly painted cars. They certainly put a gleaming period on the end of CB&Q freights system wide.

Time freight 77, the Galloping Ghost, speeds through the Summit Cut on Burlington's Kansas City Short-cut. Not only did the short cut chop time for the new Zephyrs, but also many hours off the schedules for thru Chicago-KC freights. (Burlington Northern)

It is only 8 days after the shortest day of the year in 1966, when GP-20 No. 901 leads a three unit combo on symbol freight C.D. out of Cicero yard en route from Chicago to Denver. (William A. Raia)

Many branch line freights were powered by switch engines, partly because of the ease of operation in either direction. (William A. Raia)

This photo typifies the CB&Q freight service just prior to the merger. Virtually all time freight or high speed freight was handled by second generation high horsepower hood units. The red and grey set off the bright white letters "Burlington" in such a way that no one could miss the "Burlington Route." (William A. Raia)

A westbound freight departs Cicero yard in December, 1966. (William A. Raia)

A southbound local powered by a SD-7 and a GP-20 is about to cross the Rock Island trackage at Coloma, Illinois. (William S. Kuba)

Train 88 passes Portage Tower, Illinois (south of East Dubuque) where the ICG separates from the former CB&Q and Chicago Great Western trackage. The date is May 28, 1966. (William S. Kuba)

Five Burlington and UP GP-30's and 35's lead a run thru freight by Cheyenne and on to Sherman Hill on UP trackage. The photo was taken on June 20, 1964 from the C&S overpass. (William S. Kuba)

114

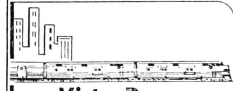

Chariton-Indianola

65 Ex. Sat. -Sun. Mixed	Miles	READ DOWN	Table No. 42	READ UP	66 Ex. Sat. -Sun. Mixed
AM					PM
11.59	0	Lv. Chariton, Ia. 1, 38	Ar		3 45
12.30	14	Lacona			3 15
1.00	22	Milo			2 55
2.00	33	Ar. Indianola	Lv		2 30
PM					PM

Red Oak-Griswold

93 Ex. Sat. -Sun. Mixed	Miles	READ DOWN	Table No. 44	READ UP	94 Ex. Sat. -Sun. Mixed
AM					PM
11.45	0	Lv. Red Oak, Ia. 1, 41A	Ar		3 35
1.05	13	Elliott			2 30
1.30	19	Ar. Griswold	Lv		2 05
PM					PM

McCook-Imperial

	Miles	READ DOWN	Table No. 44-A	READ UP	
			Mt. Standard Time		
	0	McCook, Nebr. 1			
	11	Culbertson, 1			
	20	Beverly			
	29	Palisade			
	36	Hamlet			
	44	Wauneta			
	60	Imperial			
		Mixed Train Service. Consult Agent.			

REFERENCE NOTES

f — Flag stop.

⊡ Train-auto service available at this point

* — Will not operate New Year's Day, Washington's Birthday, Memorial Day, Independence Day, Labor Day, Thanksgiving and Christmas

MIXED TRAIN SERVICE
Consult Agent for Details

Rushville-Fairview

Mls.	Table No. 44-B
0	Rushville, Ill.
8	Ray
15	Vermont, 7
22	Ipava
32	Lewistown, 7
41	Cuba
46	Fiatt
51	Fairview

Quincy-Kirksville

Mls.	Table No. 45
0	Quincy, Ill. 3, 8
5	Taylor, Mo.
9	Maywood
13	Durham
16	Ewing
24	Lewistown
30	LaBelle
35	Knox
45	Edina
52	Hurdland
56	Brashear
62	Bullion
68	Kirksville, Mo.

Corning-Villisca

Mls.	Table No. 46
0	Corning, Mo., 9
7	Fairfax
15	Tarkio
22	Westboro, Mo.
27	Northboro, Ia.
33	Coin
39	Page Centre
..	Shambaugh
46	Clarinda
54	Hepburn
61	Villisca, 1

Creston-Cumberland

Mls.	Table No. 46-A
0	Creston, Ia. 1, 28
8	Spaulding
13	Orient
21	Greenfield
29	Fontanelle
36	Bridgewater
41	Massena
47	Cumberland

Rio-Monmouth-Vermont

Mls.	Table No. 47
0	Rio, Ill. 7
4	N. Henderson
9	Alexis
15	Gerlaw
21	Monmouth, 1
33	Roseville
38	Swan Creek
40	Youngstown
44	Walnut Grove
50	Bushnell, 3
59	Adair
64	Table Grove
69	Vermont, 7

Buda-Elmwood

Mls.	Table No. 44-C
0	Buda, Ill., 1
8	Lombardville
11	Bradford
16	Castleton
21	Wyoming
27	Duncan
32	Monica
38	Brimfield
45	Elmwood, 18

Burlington-Washington

Mls.	Table No. 49
0	Burlington, Ia. 1, 8, 37
9	Latty
12	Sperry
15	Mediapolis
21	Roscoe
24	Yarmouth
28	Mt. Union
34	Winfield
40	Wyman
44	Crawfordsville
47	Havre
50	Washington

Bigelow-Skidmore

Mls.	Table No. 50
0	Bigelow, Mo. 9
3	Mound City
14	Maitland
21	Skidmore

Cameron-N. Kansas City

Miles	Table No. 51
0	Cameron, Mo. 3A
5	Keystone
9	Turney
16	Lathrop
23	Holt
29	Kearney
34	Chandler
39	Liberty
45	Birmingham
47	Randolph
51	North Kansas City

By the mid-1960's, 85 foot flats were the answer for piggyback and accommodated two trailers each. This westbound freight was photographed near Lisle, Illinois, on October 11, 1964. (Burlington Northern)

Symbol freight GDI was (and is) a thru Burlington-Union Pacific freight interchanged at Grand Island, Nebraska. The GDI is shown here with UP power only on its westbound run. (William S. Kuba)

Three New York Central units lead a single Q unit on a thru freight (97) just east of Savanna, Illinois, on September 30, 1967. (William S. Kuba)

Mikado No. 807 departs Denver in October, 1957 with a livestock special for the eastern markets. (Photo by R. R. Wallin, W. S. Kuba collection)

Mikado 5065 heads up a stock train extra at Lincoln, Nebraska, in October, 1953. (Harold K. Vollrath)

Newer steel cabooses on the CB&Q featured streamlined colors and cupola but nearly identical window configuration of the wood cars. (Harold K. Vollrath collection)

The new extended vision way car (as the Q termed its cabooses) was one of several types of freight equipment displayed at the Aurora station for the May, 1964 Centennial event. (Jim Scribbins)

Piggyback had a very modest start on the Q, and originally trailers were carried on flat cars that could be easily converted for regular flat car use. This photo shows a train in the mid-1950's carrying about 20 trailers as it passes Aurora, Illinois en route from the Twin Cities to Chicago. (Burlington Northern)

Although the Q used the ordinary ramps for loading and unloading trailers, it soon became evident that something new was needed to handle the trailers that arrived at the terminal backwards. It was an expensive proposition to switch out the backward cars and have them turned around for unloading. Consequently, the CB&Q invested in a traveling crane to load, unload and even classify trailers. This photo was taken at Cicero yard. (Burlington Northern)

WESTWARD AND SOUTHWARD FROM CHICAGO

	*ACD (Example)	CD-CG1 (Example)	77 (Example)	61 (Example)
Lv Chicago......	6:00 AM Tue...	10:30 AM Mon.....	8:00 PM Mon. (1)(3).	10:30 PM Mon.
Ar Galesburg...		1:35 PM Mon.....	11:05 PM Mon...	1:45 AM Tue.
Ar Moline...		11:15 PM Mon. (3)...	,.....	11:15 PM Tue. (3)
Ar Rock Island...		11:45 PM Mon. (3)		11:45 PM Tue. (3)
Ar Davenport...		12:15 AM Tue. (1)		12:15 AM Wed. (1)
Ar Clinton...		4:30 AM Tue. (1)		4:30 AM Wed. (1)
Ar Peoria...		1:00 AM Tue.		9:15 AM Tue. (2)
Lv Peoria...		1:45 AM Mon.		11:00 AM Mon. (2)
Ar Burlington...		7:00 AM Tue.		7:00 AM Tue.
Ar Keokuk...		11:59 AM Tue. (1)		11:59 AM Tue. (1)
Ar Ottumwa...		4:30 PM Tue.		7:00 AM Tue.
Ar Creston...		6:55 PM Tue.		9:50 AM Tue.
Ar Des Moines...		3:05 AM Wed.		3:05 AM Wed.
Ar Omaha...		5:35 PM Tue.		10:15 PM Tue.
Ar Council Bluffs...	(67)11:30 AM Tue.			7:30 PM Tue.
Ar Lincoln...		10:55 PM Tue.		1:40 AM Tue.
Ar Grand Island...	10:55 PM Tue.	3:25 AM Tue.		#10:55 PM Tue.
Ar Hastings...		1:40 AM Wed.		5:00 PM Tue.
Ar McCook...		4:40 AM Wed.		8:20 PM Tue.
Ar Denver...	3:45 AM Wed.	10:00 AM Tue.		2:30 AM Wed.
Ar Centralia...		1:00 PM Tue.		1:00 PM Tue.
Ar Paducah...		7:00 PM Tue.		7:00 PM Tue.
Ar W. Quincy...		2:50 AM Tue.	2:50 AM Tue.	12:01 PM Tue.
Ar Hannibal...		1:00 PM Tue.		1:00 PM Tue.
Ar St. Louis...		9:00 PM Tue.		9:00 PM Tue.
Ar E. St. Louis...		12:01 PM Tue.		12:01 PM Tue.
Ar Kansas City...	(67)12:30 PM Tue.		9:20 AM Tue.	12:15 PM Wed.
Ar St. Joseph...		12:15 PM Tue.		12:15 PM Wed.
Ar Sioux City...		1:30 PM Tue.		6:30 AM Wed. (4)
Ar Alliance...		2:30 AM Wed.		2:30 AM Wed.
Ar Edgemont...		7:40 AM Wed.		7:40 AM Wed.
Ar Sheridan...		2:15 PM Wed.		2:15 PM Wed.
Ar Casper...		2:30 AM Thur.		2:30 AM Thur.
Ar Scottsbluff...		6:05 PM Wed.		6:05 PM Wed.
Ar Cheyenne (C&S)...		10:30 AM Wed.		10:30 AM Thur.
Ar Laurel (Billings)...		9:00 PM Wed.		9:00 PM Wed.

*Operates from Chicago Friday, Saturday, Sunday and Tuesday only.

#Connects with Adv GI-67 at Lincoln Fri., Sat., Sun., Tue.; other days connects with GI-67, arriving Grand Island 3:25 AM following morning.

NORTHWARD FROM ST. LOUIS, E. ST. LOUIS AND PADUCAH

	71 & 97 (Example)	62 (Example)	66 (Example)
Lv St. Louis...	(97) 11:00 PM Mon...		
Lv E. St. Louis...	(71) 11:00 PM Mon...	11:45 AM Mon...	
Lv Paducah...			8:00 AM Mon.
Ar Galesburg...	7:30 AM Tue.	7:45 PM Mon.	9:30 PM Mon.
Lv Hannibal...	4:40 AM Tue.		
Ar Keokuk...	7:45 AM Tue. (1)		11:59 PM Tue. (1)
Ar W. Quincy...	5:37 AM Tue.		12:01 PM Tue.
Ar Burlington...	9:30 AM Tue.	7:00 AM Tue.	7:00 AM Tue.
Ar Peoria...	1:00 AM Wed.	9:15 AM Tue. (2)	9:15 AM Tue. (2)
Ar Chicago...	1:30 PM Tue.	1:00 PM Tue.	1:00 PM Tue.
Ar Moline...	11:15 PM Tue. (3)	11:15 PM Tue. (3)	11:15 PM Tue. (3)
Ar Rock Island...	11:45 PM Tue. (3)	11:45 PM Tue. (3)	11:45 PM Tue. (3)
Ar Davenport...	12:15 AM Wed. (1)	12:15 AM Wed. (1)	12:15 AM Wed. (1)
Ar Clinton...	4:30 AM Wed. (1)	4:30 AM Wed. (1)	4:30 AM Wed. (1)
Ar East Dubuque...	3:30 AM Wed.	3:30 AM Wed.	3:30 AM Wed.
Ar No. La Crosse...	9:00 PM Tue.	9:00 PM Tue.	9:00 PM Tue.
Ar St. Paul-Minneapolis (Dayton Bluff)...	2:00 AM Wed.	2:00 AM Wed.	2:00 AM Wed.
Ar Kansas City...			12:30 AM Tue.
Ar Ottumwa...	4:30 AM Tue.	10:00 AM Tue.	10:00 AM Tue.
Ar Creston...	6:55 PM Tue.	2:15 PM Tue.	2:15 PM Tue.
Ar Des Moines...	3:05 AM Wed. (1)	3:05 AM Wed. (1)	3:05 AM Wed. (1)
Ar Omaha...			10:15 PM Tue.

WESTWARD FROM ST. LOUIS, EAST ST. LOUIS

	97 and 71 (Example)		97 & 71 (Example)
Lv St. Louis...	(97) 11:00 PM Mon.	Ar Hastings...	1:40 AM Wed.
Lv East St. Louis...	(71) 11:00 PM Mon.	Ar McCook...	4:40 AM Wed.
Lv Hannibal...	5:00 AM Tue.	Ar Denver...	@3:45 AM Wed.
Ar St. Joseph...	10:40 AM Tue.	Ar Alliance...	2:30 AM Wed.
Ar Omaha...	10:15 PM Tue.	Ar Edgemont...	7:40 AM Wed.
Ar Council Bluffs...	11:30 AM Wed.	Ar Sheridan...	2:15 PM Wed.
Ar Sioux City...	1:30 PM Wed.	Ar Laurel (Billings)...	9:00 PM Wed.
Ar Lincoln...	3:00 PM Tue.	Ar Casper...	2:30 AM Thur.
Ar Grand Island...	#10:55 PM Tue.	Ar Scottsbluff...	6:05 PM Wed.
continued next column)		Ar Cheyenne (C&S)...	10:30 AM Thur.

#Connects with Adv GI-67 at Lincoln Fri., Sat., Sun., Tue.; other days connects with GI-67 arriving Grand Island 3:25 AM following morning.

@ Connects with ACD at Lincoln Fri., Sat., Sun., Tue.; other days connects with 61 arriving Denver 2:30 AM same morning.

WESTWARD AND NORTHWARD FROM KANSAS CITY AND ST. JOSEPH

	61 (Example)	71 (Example)	67 (Example)	75 (Example)
Lv Kansas City...	8:00 AM Tue.	10:30 AM Tue.(1)	9:00 PM Mon.	6:30 PM Mon.
Ar St. Joseph...	9:45 AM Tue.	12:15 PM Tue.	11:00 PM Mon.	8:30 PM Mon.
Lv St. Joseph...	10:15 AM Tue.	2:00 PM Tue.	11:30 PM Mon.	9:00 PM Mon.
Ar Omaha...		10:15 PM Tue.		5:35 PM Tue.
Ar Council Bluffs...		7:30 PM Tue.		11:30 AM Tue.
Ar Sioux City...	6:30 AM Wed(4).	1:30 PM Wed.	6:30 AM Wed(4).	1:30 PM Tue.
Ar Lincoln...	2:40 PM Tue.		5:00 AM Tue.	
Ar Grand Island...	#10:55 PM Tue.		#10:55 PM Tue.	
Ar Hastings...	1:40 AM Wed.		5:00 PM Tue.	
Ar McCook...	4:40 AM Wed.		8:20 PM Tue.	
Ar Denver...	@3:45 AM Wed.		2:30 AM Wed.	
Ar Alliance...	2:30 AM Wed.		2:30 AM Wed.	
Ar Edgemont...	7:40 AM Wed.		7:40 AM Wed.	
Ar Sheridan...	2:15 PM Wed.		2:15 PM Wed.	
Ar Billings (Laurel)...	9:00 PM Wed.		9:00 PM Wed.	
Ar Casper...	2:30 AM Thur.		2:30 AM Thur.	
Ar Scottsbluff...	6:05 PM Wed.		6:05 PM Wed.	
Ar Cheyenne (C&S)...	10:30 AM Thur.		10:30 AM Thur.	

#Connects with Adv GI-67 at Lincoln Fri., Sat., Sun., Tue.; other days connects with GI-67 arriving Grand Island 3:25 AM following morning.

@ Connects with ACD at Lincoln Fri., Sat., Sun., Tue.; other days connects with CD arriving Denver 10:00 AM same morning.

WESTWARD FROM SIOUX CITY, COUNCIL BLUFFS AND OMAHA

	85 & 75 (Example)	88 & 73 (Example)	CB-67 (Example)
Lv Sioux City...	(85) 11:00 PM Mon. (1)	(88) 11:00 AM Mon.	
Lv Council Bluffs...			4:00 PM Mon.
Lv Omaha...	(75) 5:35 PM Tue. (1)	(73) 5:00 PM Mon.	
Ar Lincoln...	(85) 4:45 AM Tue. (2)	(73) 7:30 PM Mon.	6:00 PM Mon.
Ar Lincoln...	(75) 9:00 AM Tue.		
Ar Grand Island...	3:25 AM Wed.	3:25 AM Tue.	3:25 AM Tue.
Ar Hastings...	5:00 PM Tue.	1:40 AM Tue.	1:40 AM Tue.
Ar McCook...	8:20 PM Tue.	4:40 AM Tue.	4:40 AM Tue.
Ar Denver...	2:30 AM Wed.	10:00 AM Tue.	10:00 AM Tue.
Ar Cheyenne (C&S)...	10:30 AM Thur.	10:30 AM Wed.	10:30 AM Wed.
Ar Alliance...	2:30 AM Wed.	1:45 PM Tue.	1:45 PM Tue.
Ar Edgemont...	7:40 AM Wed.	7:40 AM Wed.	7:40 AM Wed.
Ar Sheridan...	2:15 PM Wed.	2:15 PM Wed.	2:15 PM Wed.
Ar Billings (Laurel)...	9:00 PM Wed.	9:00 PM Wed.	9:00 PM Wed.
Ar Scottsbluff...	6:05 PM Wed.	6:05 PM Wed.	6:05 PM Wed.
Ar Casper...	2:30 AM Thur.	2:30 AM Wed.	2:30 AM Wed

NORTHWARD TO ST. PAUL AND MINNEAPOLIS

	97 (Example)	83 (Example)	81 (Example)
Lv Chicago...	11:00 AM Mon.	6:40 PM Mon.	8:00 PM Mon.
Ar Rockford...		5:30 AM Tue. (1)	
Lv Rockford...		7:30 AM Tue. (3)	
Ar Savanna...	2:15 PM Mon.	10:00 PM Mon.	2:00 AM Tue.
Lv Peoria...	1:45 AM Mon.		11:00 AM Mon. (2)
Lv Galesburg...	10:30 AM Mon.		9:30 PM Mon.
Lv Savanna...	3:30 AM Mon.	10:15 PM Mon.	5:00 AM Tue.
Ar E. Dubuque...			6:00 AM Tue.
Ar N. La Crosse...	9:00 AM Mon.		11:00 AM Tue.
Ar E. Winona...			1:00 PM Tue.
Ar Dayton Bluff (Twin Cities)...	2:00 AM Tue.	6:00 AM Tue.	5:00 PM Tue.

BETWEEN CHICAGO AND LA SALLE

85 (Example)			86 (Example)
Lv 8:00 PM Mon. (3)...	Chicago...	Ar 3:00 AM Tue. (2)	
	Aurora (Eola)...	Ar 2:00 AM Tue. (2)	
Ar 3:15 AM Tue....	Ottawa...	Lv 9:45 PM Mon. (1)	
Ar 4:40 AM Tue. (1)...	Streator...	Lv 8:30 PM Mon. (1)	
Ar 6:30 AM Tue. (1)...	LaSalle...	Lv 6:30 PM Mon. (1)	

FROM QUAD CITIES

	64 (Example)
Lv Davenport...	5:30 PM Mon. (1)
Lv Rock Island...	6:00 PM Mon. (1)
Lv Moline...	6:15 PM Mon. (1)
Lv East Moline...	6:30 PM Mon. (1)
Ar Galesburg...	1:00 AM Tue. (2)
Ar Savanna...	3:00 AM Tue. (2)
Ar Chicago...	8:00 AM Tue. (2)

NORTHWARD FROM TEXAS CITIES

	76 (Example)	98 (Example)	72 (Example)
Lv Galveston (F.W.D.)...		10:00 PM Sun.	
Ar Houston...		12:01 AM Mon.	
Lv Houston...	6:30 PM Mon.	6:45 AM Mon.	
Ar Dallas...	4:35 AM Tue.	4:50 PM Mon.	
Ar Ft. Worth...	8:30 AM Tue.	8:30 PM Mon.	
Lv Ft. Worth...	11:15 AM Tue.	(76) 11:15 AM Tue.	5:00 PM Mon.
Lv Wichita Falls...	3:45 PM Tue.	3:45 PM Tue.	9:00 PM Tue.
Lv Amarillo...	11:50 PM Tue.	11:50 PM Tue.	8:10 AM Wed.
Lv Dalhart...	3:10 AM Wed.	3:10 AM Wed.	10:40 AM Wed.
Lv Texline (C&S)...	4:10 AM Wed.	4:10 AM Wed.	11:30 AM Wed.
Lv Pueblo...	3:30 PM Wed.	3:30 PM Wed.	4:30 AM Thur.
Ar Denver...	8:30 PM Wed.	8:30 PM Wed.	9:00 AM Thur.

NORTHWARD FROM DENVER

	77-75 (Example)	72 (Example)
Lv Denver (C&S)...	(77) 5:00 AM Thur. (C.B.& Q.)	11:30 PM Mon.
Ar Cheyenne...	10:30 AM Thur.	
Ar Casper (C.B.&Q.)...	(75) 2:30 AM Fri.	Via Alliance...
Ar Alliance...		2:30 AM Tue.
Ar Edgemont...		7:40 AM Wed.
Ar Sheridan...		2:15 PM Wed.
Ar Billings (Laurel)...	9:00 PM Fri.	9:00 PM Wed.

BETWEEN KANSAS CITY AND ST. LOUIS-E. ST. LOUIS

60 (Example)			65-97 (Example)
Lv 8:00 PM Mon...	Kansas City...		Ar 7:15 AM Tue.
Ar 6:15 AM Tue...	St. Louis...	(97)	Lv 11:00 PM Mon.
Ar 6:30 AM Tue...	E. St. Louis...	(65)	Lv 9:15 PM Mon.

(1) Except Sunday. (2) Except Monday. (3) Except Saturday. (4) Except Tuesday

Mar. 1, 1962   Subject to change without notice.

LINGTON & QUINCY R. R. CO.
THROUGH FREIGHT SERVICE

EASTWARD FROM DENVER AND GRAND ISLAND

	66 (Example)	68 (Example)	62 (Example)	GI-68 (Example)
Lv Denver	11:30 AM Mon.	8:00 PM Mon.	10:30 PM Mon.	
Ar McCook	5:35 PM Mon.	1:30 AM Tue.	4:25 AM Tue.	
Ar Hastings	11:00 PM Mon.	5:25 AM Tue.	8:15 AM Tue.	
Lv Grand Island				3:30 AM Tue.
Ar Lincoln	3:15 AM Tue.	7:35 AM Tue.	10:25 AM Tue.	5:30 AM Tue.
Ar Omaha			4:30 AM Wed.	
Ar Council Bluffs		3:30 PM Tue.	11:30 AM Wed.	
Ar St. Joseph		1:45 Tue.	2:00 A.M. Wed.	11:50 Tue.
Ar Kansas City		4:30 PM Tue.	4:30 AM Wed.	4:30 PM Tue.
Ar Hannibal		12:30 AM Wed.	1:00 PM Wed.	5:00 PM Tue.
Ar St. Louis		9:00 PM Tue.	9:00 PM Wed.	9:00 PM Tue.
Ar E. St. Louis		9:00 PM Tue.	12:01 AM Wed.	9:00 PM Tue.
Ar Sioux City		6:30 AM Wed. (4)	6:30 AM Wed. (4)	
Ar Des Moines		3:05 AM Thur.	3:05 AM Thur.	
Ar Creston		2:10 PM Tue.	3:40 PM Tue.	11:45 AM Tue.
Ar Ottumwa		4:45 PM Tue.	6:20 PM Tue.	2:15 Tue.
Ar Burlington		7:00 AM Wed.	7:00 AM Wed.	7:00 AM Wed.
Ar Keokuk		11:59 AM Wed. (1)	11:59 AM Wed. (1)	
Ar W. Quincy		2:50 AM Wed.	12:01 AM Wed.	
Ar Galesburg		7:25 Tue.	9:20 Wed.	5:50 Tue.
Ar Chicago		1:30 AM Wed.	3:40 AM Wed.	11:45 PM Wed.
Ar Paducah		7:00 PM Wed.	7:00 PM Wed.	7:00 PM Wed.
Ar Peoria		1:00 PM Wed.	9:15 AM Wed. (2)	1:00 AM Wed.
Ar Moline		11:15 PM Wed. (3)	11:15 PM Wed. (3)	
Ar Rock Island		11:45 PM Wed. (3)	11:45 PM Wed. (3)	
Ar Davenport		12:15 AM Thur. (1)	12:15 AM Thur. (1)	
Ar Clinton		4:30 AM Thur. (1)	4:30 AM Thur. (1)	
Ar E. Dubuque		3:30 AM Thur.	3:30 AM Thur.	
Ar No. LaCrosse		9:00 PM Wed.	9:00 PM Wed.	
Ar E. Winona		12:15 PM Thur.	12:15 PM Thur.	
Ar St. Paul (Dayton Minneapolis Bluff)		2:00 AM Thur.	2:00 AM Thur.	2:00 AM Thur.

EASTWARD FROM SIOUX CITY, OMAHA AND COUNCIL BLUFFS

	88-70 (Example)	72-74 (Example)	85 (Example)
Lv Sioux City	(88) 11:00 AM Mon.		11:00 PM Mon. (1)
Lv Omaha	(70) 5:00 PM Mon. (1)	(72) 4:30 AM Mon.	
Lv So. Omaha	(70) 6:15 PM Mon. (1)	(72) 2:40 AM Mon.	
Lv Council Bluffs	(70) 4:30 PM Mon.	(74) 10:30 AM Mon.	
Ar Creston	10:15 PM Mon.	2:10 PM Mon.	2:10 Tue.
Ar Des Moines	3:05 AM Wed.	3:05 AM Mon.	3:05 AM Tue.
Ar Ottumwa	1:45 AM Tue.	4:45 PM Mon.	4:45 Tue.
Ar Burlington	11:00 PM Tue.	7:00 AM Tue.	7:00 AM Wed.
Ar Keokuk	11:59 AM Wed. (1)	11:59 AM Tue. (1)	11:59 AM Wed. (1)
Ar Galesburg	5:30 AM Tue.	7:25 PM Tue.	7:25 PM Tue.
Ar W. Quincy	6:55 PM Tue.	12:01 PM Wed.	12:01 PM Wed.
Ar Hannibal	5:00 PM Tue.	1:00 PM Tue.	5:00 PM Tue.
Ar St. Louis	9:00 PM Tue.	9:00 PM Wed.	9:00 PM Wed.
Ar E. St. Louis	9:00 PM Tue.	12:01 AM Wed.	9:00 PM Wed.
Ar Paducah	7:00 PM Wed.	7:00 PM Wed.	7:00 PM Wed.
Ar Moline	11:15 PM Tue. (3)	11:15 PM Tue. (3)	11:15 PM Wed. (3)
Ar Rock Island	11:45 PM Tue. (3)	11:45 PM Tue. (3)	11:45 PM Wed. (3)
Ar Davenport	12:15 AM Wed. (1)	12:15 AM Wed. (1)	12:15 AM Thur. (1)
Ar Clinton	4:30 AM Wed. (1)	4:30 AM Wed. (1)	4:30 AM Thur. (1)
Ar E. Dubuque	3:30 AM Wed.	3:30 AM Wed.	3:30 AM Thur.
Ar Peoria	9:15 AM Tue. (2)	1:00 AM Tue.	1:00 AM Wed.
Ar Chicago	1:00 PM Tue.	1:30 AM Tue.	1:30 AM Wed.

SOUTHWARD FROM SIOUX CITY, OMAHA AND COUNCIL BLUFFS

	88-82-74-70 (Example)	72 (Example)	85 (Example)
Lv Sioux City	(88) 11:00 AM Mon.		11:00 PM Mon. (1)
Lv Sioux City	(82) 6:00 PM Mon.		
Lv Omaha	(70) 5:00 PM Mon. (1)	4:30 AM Mon.	
Lv So. Moline	(70) 6:15 PM Mon. (1)	2:40 AM Mon.	
Lv Council Bluffs	(70) 4:30 PM Mon.		
Lv Council Bluffs	(74) 10:30 AM Mon.		
Ar St Joseph	3:15 Tue.	2:00 AM Mon.	1:45 Tue.
Ar Kansas City	5:30 Tue.	4:30 AM Tue.	4:30 Tue.
Ar Hannibal	5:00 PM Tue.	12:30 AM Tue.	5:00 Tue.
Ar West Quincy		2:00 AM Wed.	2:00 AM Wed.
Ar St. Louis	9:00 PM Tue.	6:15 AM Tue.	9:00 PM Tue.
Ar E. St. Louis	9:00 PM Tue.	7:00 AM Tue.	9:00 PM Tue.

EASTWARD FROM KANSAS CITY AND ST. JOSEPH

	74 (Example)	70-72-80 (Example)
Lv Kansas City	11:00 AM Tue.	(70) 8:00 PM Mon.
Lv St. Joseph		(72) 5:00 PM Mon. (1) (3)
Ar Keokuk	7:45 AM Wed.(1)	7:45 AM Tue. (1)
Ar Burlington	7:00 AM Wed.	9:30 AM Tue.
Ar St. Louis		6:15 AM Tue.
Ar E. St. Louis		(80) 7:00 AM Tue.
Ar Paducah	7:00 PM Wed.	7:00 PM Wed.
Ar W. Quincy	4:15 PM Tue.	2:00 AM Tue.
Ar Galesburg	7:00 PM Tue.	6:00 AM Tue.
Ar Moline	11:15 PM Wed. (3)	11:15 PM Tue. (3)
Ar Rock Island	11:45 PM Wed. (3)	11:45 PM Tue. (3)
Ar Davenport	12:15 AM Thurs. (1)	12:15 AM Wed. (1)
Ar Clinton	4:30 AM Thurs. (1)	4:30 AM Wed. (1)
Ar E. Dubuque	3:30 AM Wed.	3:30 AM Wed.
Ar Peoria	1:00 AM Wed.	9:15 AM Wed. (2)
Ar Chicago	1:30 AM Wed.	1:00 PM Tue.
Ar N. La Crosse	9:00 PM Wed.	9:00 PM Tue.
Ar St. Paul (Dayton Minneapolis Bluff)	2:00 AM Thurs.	2:00 AM Wed.

SOUTHWARD FROM MINNEAPOLIS AND ST. PAUL

	80-88 (Example)	82 (Example)
Lv Minneapolis (Dayton St. Paul Bluff)	(80) 12:01 AM Tue.	9:30 PM Mon.
	(88) 11:45 AM Tue.	
Ar E. Winona	(80) 6:30 AM Tue.	
Ar N. La Crosse	(88) 3:10 PM Tue.	1:30 AM Tue.
Ar E. Dubuque	(80) 12:15 AM Wed.	
Ar Chicago	12:15 AM Wed.	12:30 Tue.
Ar Moline	5:15 AM Wed.	5:15 AM Wed.
Ar Rock Island	5:30 AM Wed.	5:30 AM Wed.
Ar Davenport	6:30 AM Wed.	6:30 AM Wed.
Ar Galesburg	1:00 AM Wed.	1:00 PM Tue.
Ar Peoria	9:15 AM Wed. (2)	1:00 AM Wed.
Ar W. Quincy	12:01 AM Wed.	2:50 AM Wed.
Ar Hannibal	1:00 AM Wed.	1:00 PM Wed.
Ar Keokuk	11:59 AM Wed. (1)	11:59 AM Wed. (1)
Ar Burlington	7:00 AM Wed.	7:00 AM Wed.
Ar Ottumwa	10:00 AM Wed.	10:00 AM Wed.
Ar Creston	2:15 PM Wed.	2:15 PM Wed.
Ar Lincoln	10:55 AM Wed.	1:40 AM Wed.
Ar Grand Island	3:25 AM Thur.	3:25 AM Thur.
Ar Hastings	1:40 AM Thur.	5:00 AM Thur.
Ar McCook	4:40 AM Thur.	8:20 AM Thur.
Ar Denver	10:00 AM Thur.	2:30 AM Thur.
Ar Alliance	2:30 AM Fri.	2:30 AM Thur.
Ar Scottsbluff	6:05 PM Fri.	6:05 PM Thur.
Ar Casper	2:30 AM Sat.	2:30 AM Fri.
Ar Paducah	7:00 PM Wed.	7:00 PM Wed.
Ar E. St. Louis	12:01 PM Wed.	12:01 PM Wed.
Ar St. Louis	9:00 PM Wed.	9:00 PM Wed.
Ar Kansas City	12:30 AM Thur.	9:20 AM Wed.

EASTWARD FROM BILLINGS AND CASPER

	80 (Example)	78 (Example)
Lv Billings (Laurel)	11:00 AM Mon.	1:00 PM Mon.
Lv Greybull		6:00 PM Mon.
Lv Bonneville		10:25 PM Mo.
Lv Sheridan	5:05 PM Mon.	
Lv Edgemont	1:00 AM Tue.	
Lv Casper		4:30 AM Tue.
Ar Wendover		8:00 AM Tue.
Lv Scottsbluff		11:15 AM Tue.
Lv Alliance	7:00 AM Tue.	3:45 PM Tue.
Ar Lincoln	7:30 PM Tue.	3:30 AM Wed.
Ar Omaha	3:05 AM Wed.	3:05 AM Thur.
Ar Council Bluffs	3:30 AM Wed.	3:30 AM Wed.
Ar Sioux City	6:30 AM Wed. (4)	6:30 AM Thur. (4)
Ar St. Joseph	2:00 AM Wed.	1:45 AM Wed.
Ar Kansas City	4:30 AM Wed.	4:30 AM Wed.
Ar Hannibal	5:00 PM Wed.	12:30 AM Thur.
Ar Keokuk	11:59 AM Thur. (1)	11:59 AM Thur. (1)
Ar St. Louis	9:00 PM Wed.	6:15 AM Thur.
Ar E. St. Louis	9:00 PM Wed.	7:00 AM Thur.
Ar Des Moines	3:05 AM Thur.	3:05 AM Thur.
Ar Creston	2:10 PM Wed.	3:40 PM Wed.
Ar Ottumwa	4:45 PM Wed.	6:20 PM Wed.
Ar Burlington	7:00 AM Thur.	7:00 AM Thur.
Ar W. Quincy	12:01 PM Thur.	12:01 PM Thur.
Ar Galesburg	7:25 PM Wed.	9:20 PM Wed.
Ar Peoria	1:00 PM Wed.	9:15 AM Thur. (2)
Ar Paducah	7:00 PM Thur.	7:00 PM Thur.
Ar Moline	11:15 PM Thur. (3)	11:15 PM Thur. (3)
Ar Rock Island	11:45 PM Thur. (3)	11:45 PM Thur. (3)
Ar Davenport	12:15 AM Fri. (1)	12:15 AM Fri. (1)
Ar Clinton	4:30 AM Fri. (1)	4:30 AM Fri. (1)
Ar E. Dubuque	3:30 AM Fri.	3:30 AM Fri.
Ar Chicago	1:30 AM Thur.	3:40 AM Fri.

SOUTHWARD FROM BILLINGS AND DENVER

	80-71-73 (Example)	78-75-95 (Example)
Lv Billings (Laurel)	(80) 11:00 AM Mon. (78)	1:00 PM Mon.
Lv Casper		4:30 AM Tue.
Ar Wendover		8:00 AM Tue.
Lv Wendover (C&M)		8:40 AM Tue.
Lv Sheridan	5:05 PM Mon.	
Lv Edgemont	1:00 AM Tue.	
Lv Alliance	(71) 4:00 PM Tue.	
Lv Cheyenne		3:30 PM Tue.
Ar Denver	7:00 AM Wed.	8:00 PM Tue.
Lv Denver (C&S)	(73) 8:15 PM Wed. (75)	5:30 AM Wed.
Ar Pueblo	12:15 AM Thur.	9:45 AM Wed.
Ar Trinidad	5:45 AM Thur.	3:30 PM Wed.
Lv Texline (FWD)	12:15 PM Thur.	9:50 PM Wed.
Lv Dalhart	1:10 PM Thur.	11:03 PM Wed.
Lv Amarillo	4:30 PM Thur.	2:30 AM Thur.
Ar Wichita Falls	11:45 PM Thur.	9:40 AM Thur.
Ar Ft. Worth	3:30 AM Fri.	1:30 PM Thur.
Ar Dallas	6:30 AM Fri. (95)	7:00 PM Thur.
Ar Houston	6:00 PM Fri.	5:00 AM Fri.
Ar Galveston	6:30 PM Sat.	

SHIP BURLINGTON
Everywhere West

COORDINATED SCHEDULES
CONVENIENT TERMINALS
DEPENDABLE SERVICE

MODERN EQUIPMENT
SMOOTH ROADBED
INTERESTED PERSONNEL

The CB&Q operated a number of 40 foot passenger cars in both mail or baggage coach configurations. The cars operated either in mixed train service or branch line local service. Note that 3003 has been re-stenciled "Railway Express Agency" at the RPO section of the car. The cars also functioned as cabooses. (Russ Porter)

CB&Q

Cabooses
(Way Cars)

Road Number	Body Type	Year Built	Inside Length
13690 to 13714	Steel	1969	30' 0"
13678 to 13689	Steel	1968	30' 0"
13640 to 13677	Steel	1967	30' 8"
13590 to 13639	Steel	1964	30' 8"
13560 to 13589	Steel	1959	37' 11"
13525 to 13559	Steel	1958	30' 2"
14497	Wood	1908	
14004 to 14344	Wood	1868–1894	30' 0"
14534 to 14634	Wood	1885	28' 0"
14351 to 14359	Wood	1868–1894	30' 0"
14357 to 14406	Wood	1906–1907	30' 0"
14652 to 14660	Wood	1907	28' 0"
14662 to 14684	Wood	1907	30' 0"
14411 to 14473	Wood	1910–1911	30' 0"
13986 to 13996	Wood	1912–1914	30' 0"
13926 to 13978	Wood	1914	30' 0"
13906 to 13919	Wood	1915	30' 0"
13858 to 13903	Wood	1917	30' 0"
13808 to 13841	Wood	1918	30' 0"
13741 to 13800	Wood	1920–1923	30' 0"
14700	Wood	1959	15' 7"
13500 to 13524	Steel	1930	30' 2"

This is a listing or summary of the CB&Q caboose fleet in operation during the last 25 years of Burlington history.

This car was a typical wood caboose and was equipped with passenger car type trucks. (Harold K. Vollrath collection)

Chapter 8
COAL TRAINS

When one thinks of the Burlington Route, or the Milwaukee Road or Chicago & North Western for that matter, he or she thinks of a railroad running west and north of Chicago. Little thought is given to the fact that these three railroads served the Southern Illinois or Southern Indiana coal fields. In the case of the Burlington, she reached down from Galesburg to Beardstown, Litchfield, Centralia in Southern Illinois and snuck across the Ohio River to Puducah, Kentucky. Why that sounds like Illinois Central country, doesn't it? One could say that it was (and is) as strange for the CB&Q to reach into Kentucky as it is for the Illinois Central (now Illinois Central Gulf) to be in Omaha, Nebraska or Sioux Falls, South Dakota.

The Burlington operated a line between Galesburg and St. Louis, Missouri, ever since the 1880s. However they did not elect to enter into the mining country until 1903 when they purchased the 111 mile bankrupt Jacksonville and St. Louis Railroad. The line originally operated between Jacksonville and Centralia, Illinois. Upon purchase, the CB&Q immediately constructed a 10 mile connection between Jacksonville and Concord. Concord is 10 miles south of Beardstown on the Galeburg-St. Louis Line or about 100 miles north of St. Louis. In 1905 the old J&StL was extended south from Centralia to Herrin, 53 miles and several spurs were constructed to serve several mines. A further extension was built from Herrin to Paducah, Kentucky, to serve as a connection with lines south of the Ohio River. The line was built primarily to serve as a connection for merchandise traffic.

The construction of the railroad south from Centralia presented a number of economic problems for the CB&Q. It turned out that the condition of the railroad lines was not suitable for the heavy train loading that would be required for an economical operation. A marketing cost study was made of the cost of production at the mines, and of the rail-water rates via the lakes. It was found that in order for the mining companies to be able to sell the coal in the Twin Cities region on a competitive basis, the highest freight rate possible was $2.10 per ton, Herrin to St. Paul, 648 miles or 3.2 mills per ton mile.

(Railway Age, February 7, 1931, page 316.) The reader should also take note here that the Burlington Route was conducting marketing and cost studies as early as 1910.

However, the condition of the railroad was such that the coal could not have been handled at such a rate as described above. The entire line from Jacksonville to Galesburg was built with frequent grades of over 1% against the northbound loaded movement of coal. Therefore, the CB&Q rebuilt the entire railroad to a low grade line with a maximum of 0.3% grades against the loaded movement. Thus the entire section of railroad from Southern Illinois to St. Paul did not have a single grade greater than 0.3%. The result was a superb and highly efficient railroad. These reconstruction projects were largely completed by 1912-1913. The CB&Q was able to charge the rate previously mentioned, and the result was that the coal traffic began to grow. In fact, much of the line from Herrin to Galesburg was double tracked by or before 1917.

Later developments in the coal rates prohibited the handling of coal into the Twin Cities from Southern Illinois on a profitable pasis. However a sufficient business had been developed to Chicago and other points in Missouri, Iowa and Nebraska and the coal movement continued to be very heavy.

In 1930, the CB&Q served 52 mines in the Southern Illinois coal field. However as the Depression dragged on, the number of operating mines dropped 50% in 1931 and still more closed, at least temporarily, as the hardest years up to 1935 rolled by. Nevertheless, traffic before, during and after the war was still heavy and was a highly interesting operation. Also the movement was seasonal with peak tonnages moving during the winter and summer, with the winter movement being the heavier of the two. The fall and spring were generally slack times.

The train operations were particularly interesting during the days when steam motive power was king. The mine runs operated from Centralia to the mines setting out empties and picking up loads. The principal runs (during the early 1930s) were between

Class M-2a, a 2-10-2 built by Baldwin in 1915, leads a northbound loaded coal train at Bushnell, Illinois. Almost the entire train is made up of gondolas. The photo was taken on August 26, 1942. (Burlington Northern)

Centralia to West Frankfort (49 miles one way) and return; to Herrin and return (52 miles), Christopher and return (41 miles) and Ziegler and return (47 miles). Switch engines were operated at each of these points to serve the mine loading tracks and to make up the trains for the run to Centralia. These switch engines averaged 16 hours continuous duty daily. Later the engine terminals at West Frankfort and Ziegler were closed with the power from those locations being serviced at Herrin and Christopher respectively. Coal from the smaller mines was brought in by shorter mine runs or by local freights, which took merchandise and empties south and brought back coal trains. The operations at that time were so arranged as to get the coal moving north by no later than nine o'clock on the morning following the loading. In fact, much of it was picked up and taken to Centralia during the day on which it was loaded.

The concentration point for the Southern Illinois coal was Centralia. All coal was classified according to type and by mine, and was made up into outgoing trains at that point. The Centralia yard in 1931 consisted of 53 miles of track with a capacity of 2,400 cars. The majority of the carloads and empties handled was coal cars. Also, the empties moving south through Centralia yard were separated into 12 classifications before they moved to the mines. From Centralia the loaded trains were moved to Galesburg, with a stop at Beardstown to change crews and to cut out any bad orders or short loads that may have been on the train. The Beardstown yard had a capacity of 2400 cars and was used principally for the classification of general freight.

Trains were powered by the M-4 Texas type (2-10-4) steam locomotives during the late 1920s and 1930s throughout the world war until dieselization. These engines were capable of handling 8800 tons unassisted, and they did the job well day in and day out. In the February 7, 1931 issue of RAILWAY AGE, a detailed description of a coal train powered by type M-4 No. 6326 was written up. Let's slip back now to October 8th and 9th in the year 1930 and see how coal trains were handled with steam at that time.

A mine run extra was called for shortly after 4:00 a.m. at Centralia. Extra 6326 South departed Centralia at 4:20 a.m. with 121 empties, arriving at West Frankfort at 7:30 a.m. The 6326 was then turned and made ready for a northbound coal train. She departed West Frankfort at 9:45 a.m. with 129 loads, 8,842 tons and arrived at Centralia at 12:45 p.m. making the 49.4 mile trip in exactly three hours non-stop.

At Centralia the engine was serviced and departed northbound at 3:20 PM with 122 loads, 8,817 tons. The extra stopped for water at Litchfield, 56.6 miles at 6:52 PM and departed at 7:00 PM arriving at Virden, 24.5 miles at 8:15 PM. At Virden an hour's stop was made to permit the crew to eat and to take coal and water. Leaving Virden at 9:15 PM, the train ran to Beardstown, 54.5 miles non-stop arriving at 12:25 AM on October 9th. There were no bad orders or shorts to set out, and the same engine, after servicing departed with the same train at 2:25 AM arriving at Bushnell, 44.5 miles at 6:20 AM, where a stop was made for coal, water and meals. Departing Bushnell at 7:15 AM, the train arrived Galesburg, 29 miles at 9:30 AM.

The 6326 departed Galesburg on the return trip at 11:15 AM with 29 loads and 38 empties, 1,920 tons, arriving at Beardstown at 2:45 PM. She departed Beardstown at 4:45 PM with 125 empties, 2,500 tons arriving at Centralia at 11:15 PM, thus completing a trip of 513 miles. The running time of the tonnage coal train from West Frankfort to Galesburg, 255.5 miles was 23 hours, 45 minutes. If one deducts the 7 hours, 56 minutes for engine servicing, water, fuel and crew meals, the total running time was 15 hours, 49 minutes. The average speed was 16.5 miles per hour.

These steam locomotives were operated with a high degree of utilization. Only diesel locomotives have been able to exceed the utilization described in the above paragraphs.

The M-4 steam locomotives were superb machines, with a coal capacity of 27 tons and a water capacity of 21,500 gallons. The CB&Q assigned 18 M-4's to the coal service in 1930. There were also 16 M-2's with a coal capacity of 20.8 tons and a water capacity of 12,000 gallons. The M-4's went into service in May, 1929. They made a substantial impact on train length and in the improvement of motive power utilization. They had a tractive power of 90,000 pounds and weighed 353-820 pounds on the drivers. The total weight of the engine and tender was 897,910 pounds or nearly 449 tons.

The coal capacity of 27 tons and the water capacity of 21,500 gallons on the new M-4's were very important factors in eliminating stops, which was (and still is) of paramount importance if heavy tonnage trains are to be handled efficiently. For

A mixed freight and coal train ambles through Ayres, Illinois en route to Beardstown on July 16, 1955 with 52 cars. (George-Paterson Collection)

The 6311 wheels a heavy coal train with a mixed consist of gondolas and hopper cars into Centralia, Illinois in the year 1948. (William S. Raia)

example, the nearly 50 mile run from West Frankfort to Centralia could be run without stopping for any reason whatever. This non-stop feature however, was not the only factor in avoiding delays.

The old Beardstown division with its north-south running encountered an unusual number of crossings with other railroads. Every crossing was interlocked (except for three) and since that time (1931) nearly all crossings have been equipped with automatic interlocking facilities. Spring switches were also provided at the entrances to double track and at the south end of the sidings at Concord, Jacksonville, Franklin, Lowder, Girard, Atwater, Litchifield, Walshville, Sorento, Ayers, Smithboro, Keyesport and the north end of the siding at Cambon. This eliminated stopping of the northbound loaded coal trains for throwing switches.

In 1931, two first class (passenger) trains a day in each direction were operated over most of the territory in which the coal trains operated. These passenger runs were taken care of by gas-electric cars and it was most unusual to stop the coal trains for them. This was accomplished by operating the motor cars against the current of traffic to run around the coal drags. These movements were handled by train order only.

Another problem with heavy train loading was the difficulty of operating with full tonnage in the winter time. Deep cuts were especially trouble makers since the frost gathers there and remains until late in the morning, thus causing an extremely adverse rail condition that frequently stalled the trains. This trouble was eliminated during the days of steam with a device that sprayed hot water from the boiler on the rails. This device enabled the CB&Q to maintain its tonnage rating during the winter without having the heavy trains stall on frosty or bad track.

Diesels replaced the steam power on the coal trains after World War II. Coal continued to play an important part in the CB&Q's traffic pattern right through 1969, the last full year before the merger. Annual tonnages ranged from about 8 to 12 million per year, or in terms of carloads of 175,000 to 180,000 per year. Despite the fact that coal made up from 17 to 22% of the CB&Q's annual tonnage, the revenue earned from coal traffic was only 5 to 7% of the total revenue.

A big 2-10-2 No. 6122 powers a loaded coal train into Centralia, Illinois in 1948. The Southern Illinois coal drag includes two wooden box cars on the head-end, and it was not unusual for box cars to be loaded with coal. A wood coal door was placed inside the outside door and it created a big bin out of the car. It functioned in the same way as a grain door. Box cars assigned to coal service were usually on their last days of service. (William S. Raia)

The traffic patterns described earlier in this chapter continued to hold true right through 1969, but changes began to take place in 1965. At that time plans were being made to operate a new unit train for Union Electric's huge Sioux generating station at Machens, Missouri just north of St. Louis. Approximately 3 million tons of coal annually moved by CB&Q (and now BN) from the old Ben mine at North Benton, Illinois. For this service, the CB&Q built 210 aluminum hopper cars of 105 ton capacity at the Havelock shops.

Originally coal did not move south to Kentucky, but in the late 1960's, the CB&Q began operation of unit coal trains for the Tennessee Valley Authority's generating station at Chiles, Kentucky just across the Ohio River from Illinois. Approximately 2 million tons annually were handled by the CB&Q, and this continues at the present time with Burlington Northern.

Still another important Southern Illinois coal unit train operation began in 1968. This time it was coal moving to the Wisconsin Electric Power Company at Milwaukee on a joint CB&Q (later BN)-Chicago & North Western routing. This coal moved on the Burlington from Sesser to Virden, Illinois. From that point C&NW power handled the train to and from Milwaukee. Approximately 1 million tons annually were handled with this operation.

Conditions continue to change with coal traffic, not only from Southern Illinois but Wyoming and Montana as well. Coal traffic on the Burlington Northern is a very exciting operation, but that is another story. It will suffice to say that very few people realize that the Burlington Route, or the Burlington Northern, was and is a very important coal railroad. Move over C&O and N&W!

The huge roundhouse at Galesburg served not only the coal lines to Southern Illinois, but also the main line between Chicago and Denver. The big 2-10-4 on the turntable is being readied for a coal train. It is interesting to note that while the Burlington chose 2-10-4's for their coal traffic, neighboring Chicago & North Western chose 2-8-4's. (Burlington Northern)

A northbound coal train, with a few box cars mixed in for good measure, moves through the Centralia, Illinois coal yards in April, 1948. (Frank Smarz, Kuba Collection)

Burlington's huge 2-10-4's, such as the 6323 shown here at Galesburg, Illinois in 1948, were assigned to heavy coal trains from Southern Illinois. This heavy steam power was the most efficient motive power assigned to the coal district until diesels replaced these well designed machines. (Russ Porter)

The 5617 powers a mixed coal and drag freight by Wataga, Illinois just north of Galesburg on the line to Savanna, Illinois. (Harold K. Vollrath Collection)

The CB&Q assigned special duty (type SD) units for the Southern Illinois coal traffic after the demise of the mighty 2-10-4's. Coal traffic continued to be significant through the dieselization era, and unit train operations appeared on the scene in the late 1960's. At the same time, one of the Q's most advanced coal hoppers, the "Silver Sides" aluminum 100 ton capacity, hit the rails. A unit train of "Silver Sides" is shown here unloading at the Union Electric plant at Machens, Missouri in 1969— less than a year to merger day. (Burlington Northern)

Chapter 9
BURLINGTON ROUTE
SUBSIDIARIES

As with all major railroad systems, the Chicago, Burlington and quincy Railroad Company was not just simply the CB&Q. In addition to the parent company, the Colorado & Southern Railway Company was part of the Burlington Route, which owned nearly 75% of the C&S. The Colorado & Southern was incorporated in Colorado in late 1898 and on January 11, 1899 took over the properties of the Union Pacific, Denver & Gulf Railway and the Denver, Leadville & Gunnison Railway. The C&S extends from Orin Junction, Wyoming, where a connection was made with the Burlington, southward through Cheyenne, Denver, Pueblo, Trinidad to Texline where a connection is made with the Fort Worth & Denver Railway forming a through line to Galveston. The total mileage of the C&S is 708 miles in the states of Wyoming, Colorado and New Mexico.

The Colorado & Southern Railway, in turn, owns 99.9% of the Fort Worth & Denver Railway. This company was incorporated under the laws of Texas, appropriately, on May 26, 1873, as the Fort Worth and Denver City Railway and was reorganized in 1896. The company operates over 1200 miles of line, all in the state of Texas, from Texline to Galveston. The Fort Worth & Denver and Colorado & Southern Railways have operated trains as if the line were one railroad from the Gulf Coast to Wyoming. Each line has its own management.

Passenger service on the C&S-FW&D was very "Burlington-ish" and was an excellent way of travel from Wyoming to the Gulf Coast. The finest of the standard trains was the old Colorado Special. The train ran with a variety of head-end cars, one or two coaches, dining car and two or three sleepers. The train was replaced in 1940 by the Texas Zephyr, which was a most interesting train with a combination of streamlined and standard equipment.

The TZ went into service between Denver and Dallas in August, 1940. The new train was equipped with two diesel units, 1 baggage mail car, 1 baggage dormitory coach, 2 coaches, 1 dinette coach, 1 eight section, five double bedroom sleeper; 1 twelve section, one drawing room sleeper and 1 ten section, 1 drawing room and 1 compartment sleeper and 1 diner lounge observation car. The three sleepers had been rebuilt with semi-streamlined roofs and were

the only standard cars in the consist. The observation cars contained a 32 seat dining room and a 23 seat lounge in the rear of the car.

The train was such a success, that the C&S and FW&D installed an Advance Texas Zephyr with standard equipment in 1940. This lasted until 1941, and World War II interrupted further progress on the route.

The first Texas Zephyr continued to operate, and was a very popular train, from 1940 to 1956. At that time, the C&S and FW&D replaced the original train with the 1936 edition of the Denver Zephyr. The second Texas Zephyr set of equipment operated in the Dallas-Denver service until trains 1 and 2 were discontinued in 1967. The original Denver Zephyr sets had operated almost continuously for 31 years, and Denver was always one of their terminals.

The Texas Zephyr was not the only joint passenger train service of the Fort Worth & Denver Railway. The reader will recall that one of the Twin Zephyrs went into service as the Texas Rocket between Houston and Fort Worth, while the other ran as the Sam Houston Zephyr. The Twins were running again together in *Twin service,* on a twice daily operation between Fort Worth and Houston in "Twin" railroad service the Rock Island and FW&D. The Sam Houston Zephyr operated as trains 3 and 4, while the Rock Island's Texas Rocket ran as trains 17 and 18. The two trains ran the 283 miles in 5 hours between Fort Worth and Houston. They ran with an overall scheduled speed of 62.5 miles per hour, and the revenue per train mile was $1.00 and $1.09 for the Zephyr and the Rocket respectively through 1941. By this time, the Zephyr had been in service since 1936, while the Rocket had been in operation since 1938. At the same time, the Texas Zephyr was grossing $1.41 per train mile.

It is interesting to note that the average passengers per train mile were 63 for Sam Houston Zephyr, 70 for the Texas Rocket and 54 for the Texas Zephyr. Note the difference in the number of passengers and wide difference in revenue for the short and long distance trains.

The joint service between the FW&D and the Rock Island continued through the 1960s. The Rock Island replaced the Texas Rocket service with the Twin Star Rocket, operated between Minneapolis and Houston

The flagship of the Colorado & Southern-Fort Worth & Denver Zephyr fleet, the Texas Zephyr, arrives in Denver on September 20, 1948, as a Union Pacific yard goat and three Rio Grande road engines await in the clear. It is almost as though all activity ceases as the great streamliner glides to a halt after her long run from the Lone Star State. (Elmer Treloar)

with the joint service Fort Worth-Houston. The train was so named because it connected the North Star State, Minnesota and the Lone Star State, Texas. This train was a luxury train in all respects. The Rocket, however, was discontinued in 1964, and the Sam Houston Zephyr was discontinued in 1965. The original joint Rock Island-Fort Worth and Denver service, started in 1938, had been discontinued after 26 years of cooperative efforts in passenger service. Passengers had abandoned the trains for the automobile.

The joint FW&D—RI service reminded one of the pool services offered by the UP-NP-GN between Seattle and Portland where three railroads operated over the same trackage.

Before closing this section on C&S-FW&D passenger service, it should be mentioned that the Sam Houston Zephyr ran with conventional Zephyr equipment from 1944 on. It offered coach seats as well as dining parlor car, which ran as Car A in both directions.

Color schemes on all equipment were painted in the Burlington Route scheme with the initials C&S or FW&D designating ownership. The two roads adopted the CB&Q's silver color scheme for passenger service, and the red and grey or grey and black schemes on diesel freight power. This has continued through to the present day with the Burlington Northern Green and black being adopted with the sub-initials C&S or FW&D designating

ownership. As with the Burlington Route insignia, the C&S and FW&D now sport the big BN on all power, and as new cars are ordered (or older ones repainted) the BN insignia is applied.

The C&S and FW&D were not merged into the Burlington Northern system, and have retained their separate identities. They continue to work in much the same way as they did before, with the exception of passenger service. As of 1975, Amtrak does not operate any passenger trains over the C&S or FW&D. However, the line is the only direct route between Colorado and the Gulf Coast. The two roads participate in through freight train service from the Gulf Coast to Seattle, which is one of the longest freight schedules in the USA. The distance from Galveston to Seattle is 2,745 miles and 77 and 78 make the run in about 136 hours.

Although operations are separate with the BN, C&S and FW&D owning and operating their own trains and equipment, they are fully integrated. C&S motive power often shows up in the Twin Cities area as well as Seattle on the through trains.

The two railroads are all that is left of the names of the previous Burlington Route System. In some ways, from a nostalgic point of view, it is too bad that C&S and FW&D equipment could not retain the Burlington Route insignia. However, it cannot and for understandable reasons. The C&S and FW&D are fine railroads, and are a credit to the American Railroad industry.

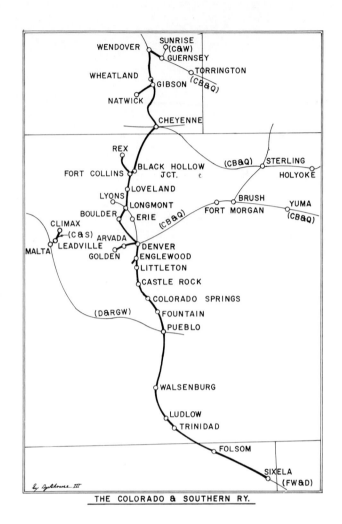

THE COLORADO & SOUTHERN RY.

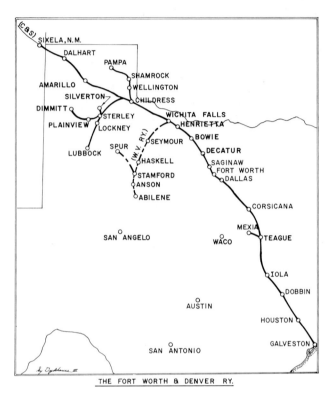

THE FORT WORTH & DENVER RY.

CB&Q 537, a 2-8-0, is indeed an unusual engine. The exchange of motive power extended to narrow gauge equipment with this CB&Q engine switching with the way freight at Breckenridge, Colorado on the C&S. (Harold K. Vollrath Collection)

Colorado & Southern 102 heads up an ancient combine and coach at Denver before knuckle couplers had been installed, but notice the air brake hose on the pilot. (Harold K. Vollrath Collection)

Narrow gauge C&S 70 steams softly between runs at the Denver roundhouse in May, 1939. 1939 was just one year after extensive abandonment took place. In that year less than 50 miles of narrow gauge remained of what was once the remarkable Denver, South Park & Pacific. (Harold K. Vollrath Collection)

Narrow gauge C&S No. 8 powers a local passenger train at Breckenridge, Colorado in July, 1936. (Harold K. Vollrath Collection)

Colorado & Southern motive power did not always stay on home rails. For example, in August, 1939 C&S 331 was assigned to local passenger trains 141 and 142 between Edgemont, South Dakota and Deadwood and Lead. (Harold K. Vollrath Collection)

C&S train No. 28 zips along at Kelker, Colorado on July 20, 1952 with 7 cars at 50 miles per hour. (George-Paterson Collection)

Another day, and No. 28 has only four cars, shown here at Lascar, Colorado. (George-Paterson Collection)

Fort Worth & Denver train 7 nears Irving, Texas in December, 1953. The long consist reflects holiday travelers. (Harold K. Vollrath Collection)

Fort Worth & Denver train 7 arrives in Dallas, Texas in May, 1936. The five car train had departed Denver the previous morning, and carried a diner as far as Amarillo and an observation sleeper to Fort Worth. An additional coach was also picked up at Amarillo for the final leg of the 24 hour run to Dallas. The consist here includes three coaches, one head-end car and one 12 section, 1 drawing room sleeper. (Harold K. Vollrath Collection)

The **Sam Houston Zephyr** zips by Irving, Texas. The three car speedster had long been displaced on its original Twin Cities run when this photo was taken in March, 1948. (Harold K. Vollrath Collection)

The **C&S-FW&D Texas Zephyr** must rank as one of the Burlington Route's most nostalgic trains. The first Zephyr carried a mixture of streamlined and rebuilt standard equipment. There is something about such a train when the equipment does not exactly match. The TZ did not have the glamor of say a Broadway or a Super Chief, but it had a touch of something that made it a very popular train. FW&D 2 is shown here departing Fort Worth in September, 1953. (Harold K. Vollrath Collection)

The Texas Zephyr shares the Denver depot with the Rocky Mountain Rocket in August, 1940. (Harold K. Vollrath Collection)

C&S train 1, the Texas Zephyr, speeds by Castle Rock, Colorado in July, 1951 with 11 cars. (George-Paterson Collection)

C&S 2-10-2 No. 900 steams softly on the night of July 29, 1958 prior to departure with a freight out of Denver. (R. R. Wallin, Kuba Collection)

FW&D switcher No. 50 performs switching duties at Fort Worth, Texas in August, 1923. (Harold K. Vollrath Collection)

C&S 641 equipped with a large snow plow for service on the Leadville line in mountain territory, Colorado. (Harold K. Vollrath Collection)

One of the most common types of freight power on the FW&D were the 450 series of oil burners. This particular engine was photographed on May 21, 1957 during its lease to the Texas & Pacific for high water service—where diesels fear to tread. (Harold K. Vollrath Collection)

Typical freight power on the C&S were these 800 series Mikados shown here in Denver in August, 1953. (Harold K. Vollrath Collection)

Among the heaviest power on the C&S were the 900 series 2-10-2's such as the 907 shown here double heading with an Electro-Motive Special Duty road-switcher at Denver in January, 1954. (Harold K. Vollrath Collection)

An extra south moves by Monument, Colorado in July, 1951 with 45 cars at 30 miles per hour. (George-Paterson Collection)

FW&D No. 407 chugs through Stamford, Texas with a heavy freight in August, 1954. (George-Paterson Collection)

A C&S extra south to Pueblo has picked up orders at Palmer Lake, Colrado and is moving south with 46 cars on July 19, 1951. (George-Paterson Collection)

Another extra south charges past Palmer Lake, Colorado with 41 cars in tow. (George-Paterson Collection)

C&S train No. 75, en route from Denver to Houston, ambles along at 30 miles per hour with 52 cars near Palmer Lake, Colorado in July, 1951. (Harold K. Vollrath Collection)

Diesels 701A, B, C and D speed 75 by Lascar, Colorado in July, 1952 with 74 cars. (George-Paterson Collection)

C&S No. 831 leads a northbound freight by Palmer Lake on September 29, 1962. (William S. Kuba)

The C&S and Santa Fe share facilities in the Denver area, and consequently, switchers wore the Burlington scheme and carried initials for the C&S and AT&SF. (William S. Kuba)

And now with the Burlington Northern, the same conditions hold true. Only the colors have changed, but the dual road initials remain. (Sy Dykhouse)

This four wheeled caboose displays the C&S insignia of years gone by. (Sy Dykhouse)

Later, cabooses wore the insignia of the Burlington Route but the initials remained reflecting true ownership and road. (Harold K. Vollrath Collection)

The final development of cabooses and color schemes was the adoption of the silver and extended vision concept. The red striping was left off this modern FW&D way car, No. 154.

Diesel powered freight trains on the Leadville-Climax spur on mountainous Colorado are a far cry from the C&S narrow gauge lines of yesteryear. (Burlington Northern)

DENVER-AMARILLO-FT. WORTH-DALLAS-HOUSTON

No. 7-3 Daily	No. 7	No. 1 TEXAS ZEPHYR	Mls.	Table M COLORADO & SOUTHERN LINES	No. 2 TEXAS ZEPHYR	No. 8	No. 4-2 Daily
PM	PM	PM			AM	PM	PM
	8.00	12.45	0	Lv. Denver, Colo. (M.T.).Ar	6.30	6 05	
	9.44	2.27	74	Lv....Colorado Springs..Ar	4.50	4 20	
	11.14	3 24	118	Lv.....Pueblo, Colo.....Ar	4.00	2 45	
	6.30	9 49	384	Ar..Dalhart, Tex. (C.T.) Lv	11 12	9 52	
⊡ 2.25			465	Ar.......El Paso.......Lv	⊡ 9 20	● 10 30	
	8 05	11 19	465	Ar.....Amarillo.....Lv	9 30	8.05	
	12 50	4 01	687	Ar....Wichita Falls Lv	5 04	1 45	
	3 30	6 25	801	Ar.....Fort Worth.....Lv	2 40	10 45	
4 00	4 00	6.50	801	Lv.....Fort Worth.....Ar	2 10	10 15	2 10
4 40	4 40	7.35	834	Ar........Dallas........Lv	1 30	9 30	1 30
5 00	# 5 00	◊ 9.55	0	Lv........Dallas........Ar	#12 47	◊ 8 50	12.47
9 25	# 9 25	◊ 2.15	250	Ar.......Houston......Lv	# 8 30	◊ 4 45	8 30
PM	PM	PM			AM	PM	AM

SOUTHBOUND—No. 7

Standard Sleeper
Denver to Ft. Worth-Dallas
8 Sec., 5 D.B.R.

Observation-Dining Lounge Car
Pueblo to Ft. Worth

Reclining Chair Coaches
Denver to Ft. Worth-Dallas

NORTHBOUND—No. 8

Standard Sleeper
Dallas-Ft. Worth to Denver
8 Sec., 5 D.B.R.

Observation-Dining Lounge Car
Ft. Worth to Pueblo

Reclining Chair Coaches
Dallas-Ft. Worth to Denver

TEXAS ZEPHYRS

SOUTHBOUND—No. 1

Observation Lounge-Parlor Car
Denver to Dallas (20)
Sleeping Cars
Denver to Ft. Worth-Dallas
Sections, Roomettes, Duplex Single Rooms, Bedrooms singly or en suite, Compartments and Drawing Rooms (21, 22, 23) Occupy in Dallas to 8.00 AM
Dining Car—Denver to Dallas
Refreshment Service
Reclining Chair Coaches (Foot Rests)
Denver to Dallas

NORTHBOUND—No. 2

Observation Lounge-Parlor Car
Dallas to Denver (20)
Sleeping Cars
Dallas-Ft. Worth to Denver
Sections, Roomettes, Duplex Single Rooms, Bedrooms singly or en suite, Compartments and Drawing Rooms (21, 22, 23)
Dining Car—Dallas to Denver
Refreshment Service
Reclining Chair Coaches (Foot Rests)
Dallas to Denver

Checked baggage may be handled locally on Texas Zephyr between the following stations in Texas: Dallas, Fort Worth, Wichita Falls, Vernon, Quanah, Childress, Memphis, Amarillo, Dalhart; but is not handled locally between Denver, Colorado Springs, Pueblo, Walsenburg, Trinidad and Clayton.

SAM HOUSTON ZEPHYR

SOUTHBOUND—No. 3

Observation Parlor-Dining Car (A)
Reclining Chair Coaches
Ft. Worth to Houston
(On No. 7 Ft. Worth to Dallas)

NORTHBOUND—No. 4

Observation Parlor-Dining Car (A)
Reclining Chair Coaches
Houston to Ft. Worth
(On No. 2 Dallas to Ft. Worth)

TWIN STAR ROCKET

SOUTHBOUND—No. 507

Parlor Car
Ft. Worth-Dallas to Houston
Dining Car—For all meals
Reclining Chair Coaches
Ft. Worth-Dallas to Houston

NORTHBOUND—No. 508

Parlor Car
Houston to Dallas-Ft. Worth
Dining Car—For all meals
Reclining Chair Coaches
Houston to Dallas-Ft. Worth

REFERENCE NOTES

‡ Cody Bus Line. Rail tickets honored. Arrives and departs from CB&Q railroad station in Denver. ♀ Bus connection. ⊙ Connection. ‖ Meal stop.
● Via C.R.I.&P.—Sou. Pac. between Santa Rosa, N. Mex. and El Paso. D.B.R.—Double Bedroom. D.R.—Drawing Room. Rmet.—Roomette Sec.—Section

◊ Twin Star Rocket between Dallas and Houston. # Sam Houston Zephyr.

NOTE: Tickets in either direction reading via C.R.I.&P., G.C.&S.F. and M-K-T between Houston and Dallas or Ft. Worth, including tickets between Houston and Dallas via So. Pac., will be honored optionally via F.W.&D.

Chapter 10
And Now It's
Burlington Northern

On March 2, 1970, what could probably be classed as the greatest railroad merger in United States history took place. On that day, the Chicago, Burlington & Quincy Railroad was joined with the Great Northern and Northern Pacific Railways to form what has been called "A New Kind of American Railroad," the BURLINGTON NORTHERN. It was in many ways a natural name for a natural merger. The Great Northern, the Northern Pacific and the Burlington Route were very closely related, not only through stock ownership but in operating procedures as well. The new name linked the word "Northern" with the word "Burlington" and with one swoop combined with two words the system of railways that heretofore had been called "The Northern Lines" collectively.

Throughout the territory of the Burlington Route, people continued to call the railroad, "The Burlington." And interestingly enough, captains on

Great Lakes ore carriers oftenrefer to the ore docks at Allouez, Wisconsin as the Burlington docks. (This former Great Northern iron ore transloading facility is the largest of its kind in the entire world). Other people simply refer to the new company as "BN." However, the name "Burlington" has stuck and continues to be used throughout the entire system. No matter what one chooses to call the new company, there is no question about it but that the former 8,700 mile Burlington Route with its parents Great Northern and Northern Pacific has been transformed into the 23,800 mile Burlington Northern. Thus the Burlington Route experienced another name change as well as adding two more major railroads to the 204 companies that had previously been consolidated to make up the Burlington Route. Therefore it is fitting that we take a look at the latest stage in the growth and development of the "BURLINGTON."

During the first few months of the merger, Burlington Northern became more and more obvious as motive power began to flow throughout the huge new system. Here former Burlington power rolls a time freight by East Glacier Park Station, Montana on former Great Northern trackage. (Elmer Treloar)

This photo demonstrates the modern Burlington Northern with high horsepower, highly fuel efficient motive power as fast freight train 77 threads through spectacular Wind River Canyon in Wyoming on its 2600 mile run from Galveston, Texas to Seattle, Washington—the longest single system scheduled freight run in the U.S. The train is the northbound section of BN's 5 day service between the Pacific Northwest and the Gulf Coast. This service involves trains operating over the BN as well as the Colorado & Southern and the Fort Worth & Denver Railways. (Burlington Northern)

During the initial merger days, power of the NP and GN remained for a while in their original color schemes, but could be found all over the original Burlington Route. These three units are heading north out of LaCrosse, Wisconsin. (Burlington Northern)

F units are still in service on the BN in 1976, and this two unit combo could possibly still be seen today. In this case, it is September, 1970 and the westbound freight is near Plattsmouth, Nebraska. (William S. Kuba)

BN operates fast piggyback trains between Chicago and Seattle. Here is train 3 rounding the curves at Maiden Rock along the shore of Lake Pepin south of the Twin Cities. (Burlington Northern)

Coal is fast becoming one of BN's most important traffic items. This train is headed for Havanna, Illinois, after leaving the Decker Coal Company mine at Decker, Montana. Not only is the tonnage increasing, but the coal traffic is almost all long haul. (Burlington Northern)

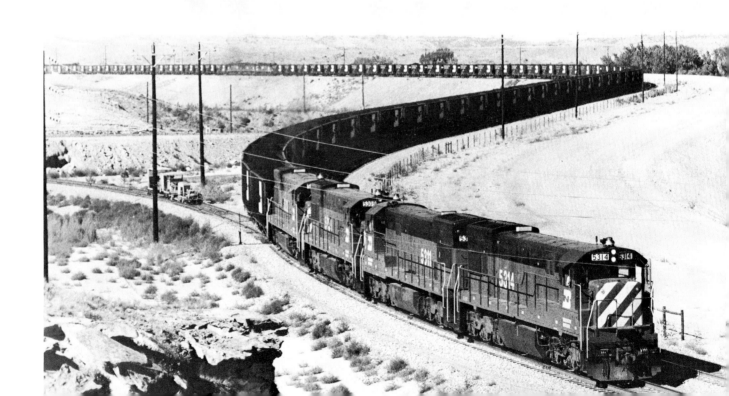

A coal train begins loading at the speed of one half mile per hour for a loading rate of 5000 tons/hour at the Decker Coal Company mine tipple at Decker, Montana. (Burlington Northern)

Coal hoppers in BN unit trains carry up to 100 tons of the black stuff. Highly efficient equipment, the cars proudly carry the system logo, "BN". (Burlington Northern)

Two BN freights are headed into Galesburg yard from the east. BN 3018 is passing CB&Q 977 as the latter is being held out of the yard temporarily. (William S. Kuba)

BN runs through freights with many different roads. This photo shows a westbound thru freight with UP power passing the BN terminal at Galesburg. Note the coaling tower in the background, and also the UP's passenger Geep-30 as the center unit of the three unit consist. Such passenger units were the only ones ever constructed. (William S. Kuba)

BN-UP thru freight enters Lincoln yard on September 26, 1970, just a few short months after the merger date. (William S. Kuba)

General Electric units are operated on the coal trains, such as this eastbound train crossing the Missouri River bridge west of Pacific Junction on October 8, 1972. (William S. Kuba)

An eastbound loaded coal train passes West Burlington, Iowa in mid-1975. (William S. Kuba)

An eastbound Milwaukee Road-Burlington Northern pool coal train en route to a Wisconsin Power plant passes St. Paul in August, 1975. Note the pooled power. (William S. Kuba)

L&N run through freight No. 135 leaves Galesburg yard with 3 L&N units in August, 1972. (Burlington Northern)

A westbound freight arrives at Daytons Bluff yard in St. Paul with a mixed consist of empty ore cars and piggyback from the St. Louis area. The ore cars are en route vack to the Mesabi Range for more all-rail ore. (William S. Kuba)

BN has been working to constantly upgrade much of the trackage, such as this work train unloading welded rail near Lisle, Illinois. (Burlington Northern)

Burlington Northern's electronic freight car classification yard at Kansas City was constructed at the cost of $10 million. The two mile long yard contains 75 miles of track. The main classification tracks have a capacity of 1680 cars and receiving and departure tracks hold 2,284 cars. Yard features include air-conditioned offices, television scanner, two-way radio and talk-back communications sytems; mercury-vapor lighting for night operations, and a weigh-in-motion track scale. The yard also has a "piggyback" and container handling facility and a modern car repair center. A computer controls the speed of cars descending the hump and operates the track switches, routing cars into any of 42 classification tracks. (Burlington Northern)

A view of the interior of the Kansas City hump tower showing various types of contols and the closed circuit TV system. (Burlington Northern)

Cicero yard was the key Chicago yard for the CB&Q, and is now even more important for the Burlington Northern. (Burlington Northern)

Smaller yards, such as North La Crosse, Wisconsin, still are important although most classification work is now carried out in Galesburg, Minot, Northtown (St. Paul-Minneapolis) and Cicero. (Burlington Northern)

The engine terminal at Galesburg now services green and black diesels instead of the red and grey scheme of the CB&Q. (Burlington Northern)

BN is one of the world's largest grain carriers. There is much specialized equipment to handle rail cargo, such as this car dumper unloading a box car at a Kansas City, Missouri terminal elevator. Approximately 1400 cars are loaded with a total of 3.8 million bushels of grain each day on the 25,000 mile system. (Burlington Northern)

Co-ordination is the key word here at Kansas City with a very efficient piggyback and container terminal. The piggybacker in the photo can transfer a trailer or container to or from a flat car in less than two minutes. A very effective marriage of highway and railway transportation. (Burlington Northern)

Burlington Northern is also part of the iron ore traffic movement from the Mesabi Range to the port of Allouez, Wisconsin for transloading into Great Lakes carriers. The Edward J. Ryerson is shown arriving at the former Great Northern ore dock No. 1. (Burlington Northern)

Burlington Northern commuter trains await placement in the Union jstation for the evening rush, while the San Francisco Zephyr is prepared for the trip to the west coast in the background. (Burlington Northern)

Passenger service prior to May 1, 1971 was more extensive than it is now. This photo shows the combined Empire Builder and North Coast Limited departing Chicago just after the merger in May, 1970, and a year before Amtrak. (John H. Kuehl)

BN train 25, the combined North Coast/Empire Builder is being backed into the Chicago Union Station. The train includes equipment from the original California Zephyr. The train to the left is No. 11, the combined California and Nebrasks Zephyr. The time is February, 1971. (Patrick C. Dorin Collection)

161

A BN commuter train departs Chicago with the skyline in the background and Amtrak equipment on the right in the former Pennsylvania Railroad coach yards. (Burlington Northern)

BN has, however, maintained two coaches as part of its passenger car fleet for special services. Often, Amtrak leases the equipment for service on BN lines.

BN painted at least one Great Dome lounge in the BN green and white, #1395, "River View"—a former CB&Q car. BN did not retain a single dome lounge car. (John H. Kuehl)

St. Croix River is operated for special train services. The car includes 8 duplex roomettes, 2 double bedrooms, buffet and dining room lounge sections. Interior wording is in both French and English reflecting former Great Northern/Canadian National Railway operation on the Winnipeg Limited and other CN trains. The car is in a special DM&IR train in September, 1974 at Knife River, Minnesota.

Great Northern operated special baggage cars with rear end brakeman compartments for mail train service. The BN painted at least one of these cars in the green and white, shown here at the Minneapolis Depot in September, 1973.

Interestingly enough 3 sleeping cars have been retained for special services, and often are loaned out to other railroads for special train operations. This particular car, Big Horn Pass, happens to be in the consist of a Duluth, Missabe & Iron Range Railway special between Duluth and Two Harbors, Minnesota.

The Illinois Zephyr is one of two passenger trains operated by Amtrak over former CB&Q trackage. The Illinois Zephyr zips along near Wataga, Illinois with a two car consist in June 25, 1972. The popularity of the train has increased the consist to four bi-level cars in 1975. (William S. Kuba)

With three Budd built domes in its center, BN 32, the Empire Builder noses on the stone arch bridge as it leaves Minneapolis April 26, 1971. Represented in its consist are the original "Builder" orange and Pullman green, GN Big Sky Blue and BN green and white. (Jim Scribbins)

This photo above all reflects the many changes in railroading on the former CB&Q. Instead of the red and grey road-switchers, we have the green SD-40 No. 6816. The yellow Rail Box car shows as the bright as ever advertising the new nationwide box car pool. Instead of CB&Q silver "E" units, we have instead silver Amtrak SDP-40Fs powering a San Francisco Zephyr instead of a California Zephyr or a Denver Zephyr. Despite the loss of some old and faithful friends, the changes seem to indicate a new and bright future for the BURLINGTON NORTHERN. (BN Photo)

Although **BN has** a sizeable passenger fleet, they are sometimes obliged to borrow equipment from Amtrak (and sometimes from the Union Pacific) for special trains. These former Southern Pacific articulated coaches are in service on a special train at Moose Lake, Minnesota in July, 1974.

The San Francisco Zephyr is one of three transcontinental trains operated by Amtrak over BN trackage, but the SFZ is the only run of the three on former Q routes. The Empire Builder and North Coast, alas, operate not on the BN but over the Milwaukee Road to and from St. Paul. The North Coast even reflects the new hybrid operation with the name North Coast Hiawatha. The SFZ is shown here at Burlington, Iowa in September, 1975. She is a very popular train. (William S. Kuba)

STATION INDEX

Everywhere West | Burlington Route

🚗 Train-Auto Service available at these Burlington points •BURLINGTON STATIONS WITH AGENTS ♁ Freight Service only

TO FIND THE SERVICE TO OR FROM ANY GIVEN POINT

First, locate the station in the index; opposite the station are the numbers of the time tables in which the service is shown (the numbers opposite the station in the time table refer to other tables in which service to or from that station is shown).

Stations shown in black-faced type in the various schedule tables are terminal cities, junction or division points.

Italics indicate important points to and from which there is connecting service.

Table No.

Abbott, Neb. 12
♁•Abilene, Tex. 🚗 81
•Abingdon, Ill. 3
•Adair, Ill. 47
•Adams, Neb. 12
♁•Adrian, Ill. 75A
•Afton, Ia. 1, 36
Agency City, Ia. 1
•Akron, Colo. 1
•Albany, Mo. 38
Albany Jct., Mo. 38
•Albia, Ia. 1, 35
•Aledo, Ill. 72A
•Alexandria, Mo. 8, 27
•Alexis, Ill. 47
•Allen, Neb. 57
•Alliance, Neb. 12, 13, 14
•Alma, Neb. 61
•Alma, Wis. 2
•Almena, Kan. 71
•Alpha, Ill. 7, 72A
•Alsey, Ill. 7
•Altona, Ill. 1
•Alvord, Tex. 78
•Amarillo, Tex. 🚗 78
•Amazonia, Mo. 9, 28
♁•Amboy, Ill. 74
•Amherst, Colo. 52
Anabel, Mo. 3
Anderson, Ia. 29
•Angora, Neb. 13
•Annada, Mo. 8
•Anselmo, Neb. 12
•Ansley, Neb. 12
♁•Anson, Tex. 81
Antioch, Neb. 12
•Arapahoe, Neb. 1
Arbela, Mo. 27
Arcadia, Neb. 53
Archer, Neb. 53
Ardmore, S. D. 12
•Arenzville, Ill. 7
Argyle, S. D. 37
Arkoe, Mo. 28
Arlington, Ill. 1
•Arminto, Wyo. 16
Armour, Mo. 9
Arno, Wyo. 12
Arpee, Ill. 72A
Arvada, Wyo. 12
Ashburn, Mo. 8
•Ashby, Neb. 12
•Ashland, Neb., 1, 10, 55, 56
Ashton, Mo. 27
Ashton, Neb. 53
♁•Aspermont, Tex. 80
•Astoria, Ill. 7
•Atchison, Kan., 🚗 3, 3A, 9, 12
Atlanta, Neb. 1
•Atwood, Colo. 14
•Atwood, Kan. 70
•Auburn, Neb. 67A
•Augusta, Ill. 3, 3A
•Aurora, Ill. 🚗 1, 2, 3, 3A, 21, 23, 72
•Aurora, Neb., 12, 53, 58
Avery, Ia. 1
•Avon, Ill. 3
•Axtell, Neb. 1
Ayr Jct., Neb. 59

Bader, Ill. 7
•Bagley, Wis. 2
Ballantine, Mont. 12
Bardwell, Tex. 79
•Barnard, Mo. 28
Barrow, Ill. 7
•Barstow, Ill. 7, 74
Bartlett, Ia. 9
•Bartley, Neb. 1
♁Basco, Ill. 75A
•Basin, Wyo. 16
Batavia, Ill. ♁
•Batavia, Ia. 1
•Bayard, Neb. 13
•Bay City, Wis. 2
Beardsley, Kan. 70
•Beardstown, Ill. 7
•Beatrice, Neb. 11, 69
•Beaver City, Neb. 70
•Bedford, Ia. 28
Belden, Neb. 57
Bellevue, Neb. 55
•Bellingham, Wash. (GN) A
•Bellwood, Neb. 41
•Belmont, Ill. 23
•Belmont, Neb. 12
•Belton, Mont. (GN) A
Belvidere, Neb. 66
•Benedict, Neb. 67
•Benkelman, Neb. 1
•Bennet, Neb. 64
Berne, S. D. 37
•Berthoud, Colo. 16
•Bertrand, Neb. 52
•Berwyn, Ill. 23
Berwyn, Neb. 12
•Bethany, Mo. 38
Bettendorf, Ia. 7
•Beverly, Mo. 9
Beverly, Neb. 44A
•Bevier, Mo. 3, 3A
•Bigelow, Mo. 9, 50
•Biggsville, Ill. 1
Big Rock, Ill. 2
•Billings, Mont. 🚗 12, 14, 16, 17
•Billings, Mont. (NP) B
Bingham, Neb. 12
•Bird City, Kan. 70
Birmingham, Mo. 51
Bishop, Wyo. 16
•Bismarck, N. Dak. (NP) B
Bixby, Neb. 67B
•Bladen, Neb. 69
Blakeman, Kan. 70
•Bloomfield, Ia. 33
Bloomington, Neb. 61
•Blue Hill, Neb. 69, 76
Blue Springs, Neb. 11
Bluff Hall, Ill. 25
Blythedale, Mo. 38
Bogard, Mo. 39
Bolckow, Mo. 28
♁•Bomarton, Tex. 81
Bond, Colo. (D&RGW) C
•Bonneville, Wyo. 16
Bostwick, Neb. 61
•Boulder, Colo. 16, 16A
•Bowie, Tex. 78
Boynton, Mo. 39
•Bozeman, Mont. (NP) B
•Bradford, Ill. 44C
•Bradshaw, Neb. 12
Brandon, Neb. 52
•Branson, Colo. 78
Brashear, Mo. 45
•Breckenridge, Mo. 3A
Breslau, Neb. 57
•Bridgeport, Neb. 13, 14
Bridgewater, Ia. 46A
Brighton, Ill. 7
Brimfield, Ill. 44C
•Bristol, Ill. 1
•Broken Bow, Neb. 12
•Brookfield, Ill. 23
•Brookfield, Mo. 3, 3A, 39
Brooks, Ia. 1
Browning, Ill. 7
•Browning, Mo. 39
Brownville, Neb. 64
•Bruning, Neb. 66
•Brunswick, Neb. 57
•Brush, Colo. 1, 14
Bryant, Ill. 7
Buckingham, Colo. 52
•Bucklin, Mo. 3, 3A
Bucknum, Wyo. 16
•Buda, Ill. 1, 3, 3A, 44C
♁Buell, Mo. 75C
Bullion, Mo. 45
Burchard, Neb. 11
Burdock, S. D. 12
♁Burgess Jct., Ill. 72
•Burlington, Ia. 🚗 1, 8, 12, 33, 49, 75A
Burress, Neb. 65
•Burwell, Neb. 54
Busch, Mo. 8
•Bushnell, Ill. 3, 47
•Bussey, Ia. 35
•Butte, Mont. (NP) B
•Byron, Neb. 61

•**C**airo, Neb. 12
•Callao, Mo. 3
•Camanche, Ia. 7
Cambria, Ia. 38
•Cambridge, Neb. 1
Cameron, Ill. 1
•Cameron, Mo. 3A, 51
Campbell, Neb. 69
Camp Grant, Ill. 20
•Camp Point, Ill. 3
•Canton, Ill. 7
•Canton, Mo. 8
•Cantril, Ia. 33
♁Carman, Ill. 75A
Carpenter, Wyo. 52
•Carrollton, Mo. 39
Carson, Ia. 30
♁•Carthage, Ill. 75A
•Casper, Wyo. 🚗 12, 13, 16
Cassa, Wyo. 13, 16
•Cassville, Wis. 2
Castleton, Ill. 44C
Cedar Bluffs, Kan. 70
Cedar Creek, Neb. 55
Cedar Rapids, Ia. (CRI&P) K
•Cedarwood, Colo. 78
•Centerville, Ia. 27
•Central City, Neb. 53
♁•Centralia, Ill. 75B
♁Cereal, Tex. 82
•Chadwick, Ill. 2
•Chalco, Neb. 10
•Chana, Ill. 2
•Channing, Tex. 78
•Chapin, Ill. 7
•Chariton, Ia. 1, 38, 42
Chatham, Wyo. 16
Cheneys, Neb. 64
•Chester, Neb. 61
•Cheyenne, Wyo. 🚗 16, 52
•Chicago, Ill., 🚗 1, 2, 3, 3A, 12, 13, 21, 23, 28, 33, 35, 38, 41A
•Childress, Tex. 78, 83
♁Chiles, Ky. (*via P&I*) 75B
Chillicothe, Ia. 1
•Chillicothe, Mo. 3A
•Chillicothe, Tex. 78
♁•Christopher, Ill. 75B
•Chugwater, Wyo. 16
•Cicero, Ill. 23
•Clarence, Mo. 3, 3A
•Clarendon, Tex. 78
•Clarendon Hills, Ill. 23
•Clarinda, Ia. 46
Clarkson, Ia. 35
•Clarksville, Mo. 8
•Claude, Tex. 78
Clay Center, Neb. 67B
•Clayton, N. Mex. 78
•Clearfield, Ia. 28
•Clearmont, Wyo. 12
Clemens, Mo. 8
•Clinton, Ia. 🚗 7A, 73
Clyde, Ill. 23
Coburg, Ia. 41A
•Cochrane, Wis. 2
•Cody, Wyo. 🚗 12, 16, 17
•Coin, Ia. 46
•Colchester, Ill. 3
•Colmar, Ill. 3
Colona, Ill. 7
•Colorado Springs, Colo. 🚗 D, E, 1, 78, 78A
Columbia, Mo. 3A
•Columbus, Neb. 41
•Colusa, Ill. 75A
♁•Compton, Ill. 74
Comstock, Neb. 53
Concord, Ill. 7, 75B
•Concordia, Kan. 60
•Congress Park, Ill. 23
Conway, Ia. 28
Cora, Mo. 39
•Corning, Ia. 1
Corning, Mo. 9, 46
Corsicana, Tex. 78, 79
•Corydon, Ia. 38
Cosby, Mo. 38
Cottonwood, Ia. 34
•Council Bluffs, Ia., 1, 9, 12
•Council Bluffs Transfer, Ia. 1, 9
♁Cowles, Neb. 76
•Cowley, Wyo. 16
•Craig, Mo. 9
Crawford, Mo. 27
•Crawford, Neb. 12
•Crawfordsville, Ia. 49
•Creston, Ia. 1, 28, 31, 46A
•Crete, Neb. 1, 11
Cromwell, Ia. 1
•Crow Agency, Mont. 12
•Cuba, Ill. 44B
•Cuba, Kan. 60
•Culbertson, Neb. 1, 44A
Cullom, Neb. 55
•Cumberland, Ia. 46A
•Curtis, Neb. 52
Cushing, Neb. 54
•Custer, S. D. 37

Dalley, Colo. 52
Dakota City, Neb. 56
•Dalhart, Tex. 78
•Dallas, Tex., 🚗 78, 79
♁Dallas City, Ill. 75A
•Dalton, Neb. 14
Dalzell, Ill. 75
•Danbury, Neb. 70
•Danville, Ia. 1
Darlington, Mo. 38
•Davenport, Ia. 🚗 7A
•David City, Neb. 41
Davis City, Ia. 38
•Davis Jct., Ill. 20
•Dawson, Neb. 11
•Daykin, Neb. 65
•Deadwood, S. D. 37
Dean, Ia. 27
Deaver, Wyo. 16, 17
Decatur, Tex. 78
♁•Denrock, Ill. 73, 74
Denton, Neb. 11
•Denver, Colo. 🚗 1, 14, 16, 16A, 77, 78, 78A, 79
Derby, Colo. 1
Derby, Ia. 38
•Des Moines, Ia., 🚗 35, 36
•Des Moines, N. Mex. 78
•DeSoto, Wis. 2
Deweese, Neb. 69
Dewey, S. D. 12
•De Witt, Neb. 11, 69
Diamond Bluff, Wis. 2
Dickens, Neb. 52
•Diller, Neb. 61
♁•Dimmitt, Tex. 82
Dixon, Neb. 57
Dobbin, Tex. 79
Donie, Tex. 79
Donnelley, Ia. 35
•Donnellson, Ia. 33
•Dorchester, Neb. 1
Douglas, Ill. 18
•Douglas, Wyo. 13, 16
•Downers Grove, Ill., 23
•Downing, Mo. 27
•Dubuque, Ia. 🚗 2, 7A
Dumont, S. D. 37
Dunbar, Neb. 64
Duncan, Ill. 44C
♁•Dundee, Tex. 81
•Dunning, Neb. 12
Durham, Mo. 45
Dwyer, Wyo. 16

•**E**arlville, Ill. 1, 74
•E. Alton, Ill. 7
E. Bridger, Mont. 16
E. Des Moines, Ia. 35
•E. Dubuque, Ill. 2
E. Leavenworth, Mo. 9
•E. Moline, Ill. 7, 7A
•E. St. Louis, Ill. ♁
•E. Winona, Wis. 2
Easton, Mo. 3A
Eckley, Colo. 1
•Edgar, Mont. 15
•Edgar, Neb. 68, 69
•Edgemont, S. D., 12, 14, 37
♁Edgin, Tex. 82
•Edina, Mo. 45
•Edison, Neb. 1
♁Edmonson, Tex. 82
Edwards, Ill. 18
•Electra, Tex. 78
•Elk Creek, Neb. 12
Elko, Nev. (WP) C
•Elliott, Ia. 44
Ellsworth, Neb. 12
•Elmwood, Ill. 18, 44C
•Elsberry, Mo. 8
•Elsie, Neb. 52
•Elwood, Neb. 52
Ely, Mo. 3
Elyria, Neb. 54
•Emerson, Ia. 1
Emhouse, Tex. 79
•Endicott, Neb. 61
Englewood, S. D. 37
Eola, Ill. 23
♁•Erie, Ill. 74
•Essex, Ia. 41A
•Estelline, Tex. 78, 82
Estes Park, Colo. 16
♁Ethlyn, Mo. 75C
•Eustis, Neb. 52
•Everett, Wash. (GN) A
•Ewing, Mo. 45
•Exeter, Neb. 1

•**F**airfax, Mo. 46
•Fairfield, Ia. 1
•Fairmont, Neb., 1, 65, 66
•Fairview, Ill. 44B
Fairview Ave., Ill. 23
Fall Creek, Ill. 25
•Falls City, Neb. 11, 12
•Fargo, N. D. (GN) A
•Fargo, N. D. (NP) B
•Farley, Mo. 9
•Farmington, Ill. 7
•Farmington, Ia. 33
•Farnam, Neb. 52
•Farragut, Ia. 41A
•Farthing, Wyo. 16
•Farwell, (Posen) Neb. 53
Federal, Wyo. 16
♁•Fenton, Ill. 73
♁•Ferris, Ill. 75A
Ferry, Neb. 56
•Ferryville, Wis. 2
•Fiatt, Ill. 44B
•Firth, Neb. 12
Flagler, Ia. 35
•Fleming, Colo. 52
Flynn, Tex. 79
Foley, Mo. 8
•Folsom, N. Mex. 78
•Fontanelle, Ia. 46A
Forbes, Mo. 9
Ford, Ia. 35
Ford City, Mo. 38
•Forest City, Mo. 9, 11
Forker, Mo. 39
•Ft. Collins, Colo. 16
Fortescue, Mo. 11
Ft. Laramie, Wyo. 13
•Ft. Madison, Ia., 1, 8, 33, 34
•Ft. Morgan, Colo. 1
•Ft. Worth, Tex., 🚗 78, 79
•Fountain City, Wis. 2
♁Francis, Mo. 75C
♁Francis St., Mo. (St. Joseph) 28
♁•Franklin, Ill. 75B
Franklin, Ia. 33
•Franklin, Neb. 61
•Frannie, Wyo. 16
Frederick, Ill. 7
Fremont (Niles), Calif. (WP) C
•Fremont, Neb. 56
•Friend, Neb. 1
•Fromberg, Mont. 16
♁Fulda, Tex. 81
•Fulton, Ill. 7A
Funk, Neb. 1

•**G**alena, Ill. 2
Galena Jct., Ill. 2
•Galesburg, Ill., 1, 3, 3A, 7, 12, 18
•Galva, Ill. 1, 3, 3A, 72A
Galveston, Tex. 🚗 79
Garden Grove, Ia. 38
•Garland, Neb. 41
Garland, Wyo. 17
Garrison, Neb. 41
•Geneva, Neb. 66
Genoa, Wis. 2
Gentry, Mo. 38
Gerlach, Nev. (WP) C
Gerlaw, Ill. 47
Gibson, Neb. 55
Giles (Togo), Ia. 38
•Gillette, Wyo. 12
Gilson, Ill. 18
•Giltner, Neb. 58
♁•Girard, Ill. 75B
♁Girard, Tex. 80
•Glacier Park, Mont. (GN) A
Gladstone, Ill. 1
•Glendo, Wyo. 13, 16
•Glen Haven, Wis. 2
•Glenrock, Wyo. 13, 16
•Glenwood, Ia. 1
•Glenwood Springs, Colo. (D&RGW) C
•Golden, Ill. 3
♁•Goree, Tex. 81
Grafton, Neb. 1
Grainton, Neb. 52
•Grand Forks, N. D. (GN) A
•Grand Island, Neb. 🚗 12
•Grand Junction, Colo. (D&RGW) C
♁•Grand Ridge, Ill. 72
Granger, Mo. 27
•Grant, Neb. 52
•Grant City, Mo. 38
•Great Falls, Mont. (GN) A
•Greeley Center, Neb. 54
•Green City, Mo. 39
•Greenfield, Ill. 7
•Greenfield, Ia. 46A
•Greenwood, Neb. 10
Gregory, Mo. 8
•Grenville, N. Mex. 78
•Gretna, Neb. 10
•Greybull, Wyo. 16
•Griswold, Ia. 44
•Grover, Colo. 52
•Guernsey, Wyo. 13
•Guide Rock, Neb. 61
Guinn, Mo. 27
•Gurley, Neb. 14

•**H**addam, Kan. 60
Hager, Wis. 2
•Haigler, Neb. 1
•Hale, Mo. 39
Halsey, Neb. 12
Halsted Street, Ill. 23
•Hamburg, Ia. 9, 41A
•Hamill, Ia. 34
Hamilton, Ia. 35
•Hamilton, Mo. 3A
Hamlet, Neb. 44A
•Hampton, Neb. 12
•Hannibal, Mo. 1, 3, 3A, 8
•Hanover, Kan. 60
•Hardin, Mont. 12
Hardy, Neb. 61
•Harlem Ave., Ill. 23
♁•Harmon, Ill. 74
♁•Hart, Tex. 82
•Hartley, Tex. 78
•Harvard, Neb. 1
Harvey, Ia. 35
♁•Haskell, Tex. 81
•Hastings, Ia. 1, 29, 30
Hastings, Minn. 2
•Hastings, Neb. 1, 58, 59, 76
•Havelock, Neb. 10
Havre, Ia. 49
•Havre, Mont. (GN) A
♁Hawk Point, Mo. 75C
♁•Hawley, Tex. 81
•Haxtun, Colo. 52
Hazard, Neb. 12
Hazelhurst, Ill. 2
Heartwell, Neb. 1
•Hebron, Neb. 66
Hecla, Neb. 12
Hedley, Tex. 78
Helena, Mo. 38
•Helena, Mont. (NP) B
Helper, Utah (D&RGW) C
Helvey, Neb. 65
•Hemingford, Neb. 12
Hemple, Mo. 3A
•Henderson, Ill. 7
•Henderson, Ia. 30
•Hendley, Neb. 70
•Henrietta, Tex. 78
•Henry, Neb. 13
Hepburn, Ia. 46
Hereford, Colo. 52
Herlong, Calif. (WP) C
•Herndon, Kan. 70
•♁Herrin, Ill. 🚗 75B
♁Herrin Jct., Ill. 75B
•Hickman, Neb. 12
Highlands, Ill. 23
•Hildreth, Neb. 69
•Hill City, S. D. 37
Hillrose, Colo. 14
Hillsboro, Ia. 34
♁•Hillsdale, Ill. 74
•Hinckley, Ill. 2
•Hinsdale, Ill. 23
Hoag, Neb. 69
Holbrook, Neb. 1
•Holcomb, Ill. 20
•Holdrege, Neb. 1, 52
♁•Holliday, Tex. 81
Hollinger, Neb. 70
Hollis, Kan. 60
•Hollywood, Ill. 23
•Holstein, Neb. 59
Holt, Mo. 51
•Holyoke, Colo. 52
Homer, Neb. 56
•Hopkins, Mo. 28
•Horse Creek, Wyo. 16
•Hot Springs, S. D. 37
•Houghton, Ia. 34
•Houston, Tex. 🚗 78, 79
•Hubbell, Neb. 61
•Hudson, Colo. 1
•Hulls, Ill. 25
•Humboldt, Neb. 11, 12
•Humeston, Ia. 38
Hunnewell, Mo. 3
•Huntley, Mont. 12
Huntley, Neb. 59
Hurdland, Mo. 45
•Hyannis, Neb. 12
♁Hygiene, Colo. 77

Iatan, Mo. 9
•Imperial, Neb. 44A
Inavale, Neb. 61
•Indianola, Ia. 42
•Indianola, Neb. 1
Ingleside, Neb. 1
Inland, Neb. 1
Iola, Tex. 79
•Iowa Park, Tex. 78
•Ipava, Ill. 7, 44B
Ithaca, Neb. 55

♁•**J**acksonville, Ill. 75B
•Jamestown, N. Dak. (NP) B
♁•Jayton, Tex. 80
Jefferson City, Mo. 3A
♁Johnfarris, Tex. 82
•Johnson, Neb. 67A

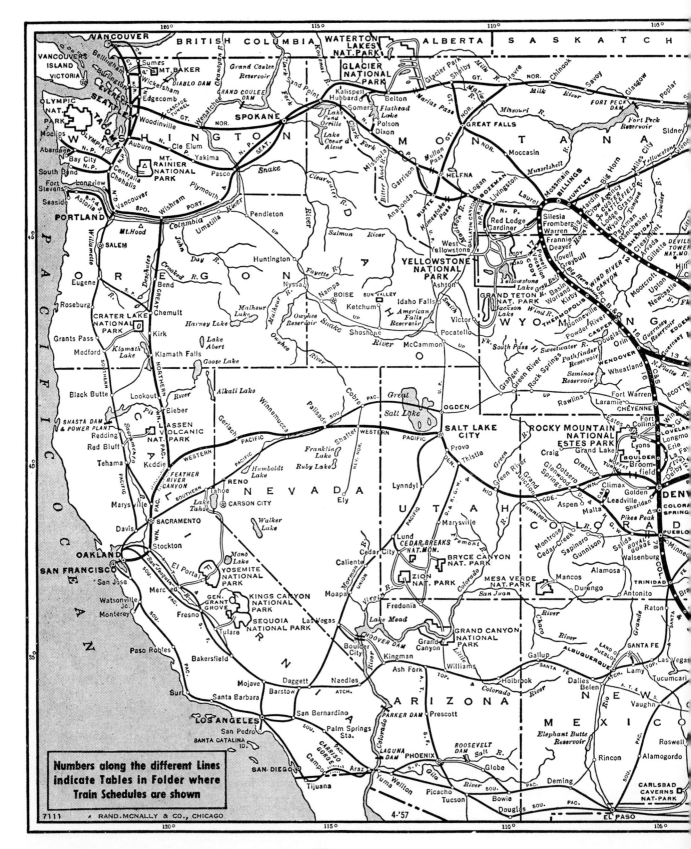

Numbers along the different Lines
indicate Tables in Folder where
Train Schedules are shown

7111   RAND McNALLY & CO., CHICAGO   4-'57

170

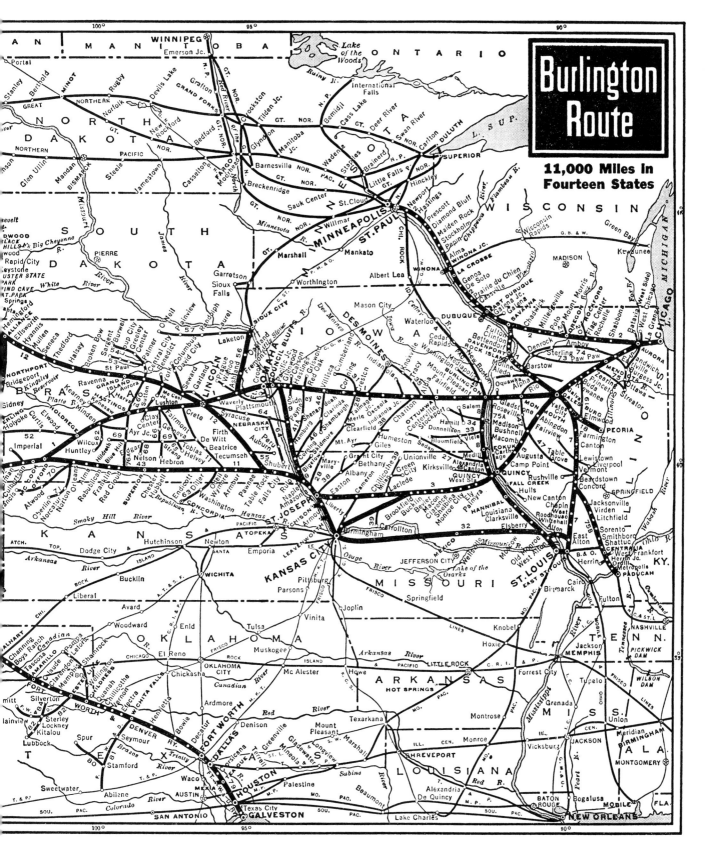

Burlington Route

11,000 Miles In Fourteen States

171

Index

Burlington Route